THE
DYSFUNCTIONAL
CHURCH

THE
DYSFUNCTIONAL
CHURCH

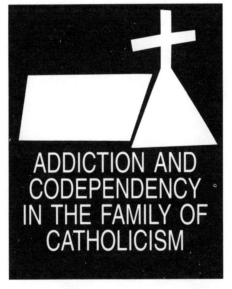

ADDICTION AND
CODEPENDENCY
IN THE FAMILY OF
CATHOLICISM

MICHAEL H. CROSBY

AVE MARIA PRESS Notre Dame, Indiana 46556

© 1991 by Ave Maria Press, Notre Dame, IN 46556

International Standard Book Number: 0-87793-455-X (pbk.)
0-87793-465-7

Library of Congress Catalog Card Number: 91-71250

Cover and text design by Katherine Robinson Coleman

Printed and bound in the United States of America.

CONTENTS

PART I

LAYING THE FOUNDATION

The original inspiration behind the Franciscan movement came from words addressed to Francis from the cross at San Damiano in Assisi: "Francis, go rebuild my house which is falling into ruins." Francis' first biographer, Thomas of Celano, notes that, at this time, "a deadly disease had grown up everywhere to such an extent and had taken ahold of all the limbs of so many," including those "who take refuge under the mere name of Christianity" (that is, religion/the church), that drastic action was necessary.

As a twentieth-century disciple of Francis, I attempt in this book to name the disease found in the institutional expression of today's Catholic church. It is my contention that the "deadly disease" undermining the church in our day is the addiction of the papacy and its extension in the hierarchy to the preservation of the male, celibate, clerical model of the church. This has happened in a way that has "taken ahold of all the limbs" of many of us in such a manner that our codependency has become diagnosable as well. I will try to show that this disease in the papacy and hierarchy, as well as in people like myself, has been observable and progressive, is manifest in repeated symptoms, and that, unless drastic action is taken, will prove deadly at least in the First World, where it seems to be affecting more people than elsewhere.

Chapter one provides the framework that later chapters will flesh out. It shows how addiction dynamics, especially those grounded in honor and shame, can be found in Matthew's gospel, our culture, the church, and many of our lives. Chapter two describes the addictive process manifest in addiction itself and in codependency, and how we have discovered in organizations the addictive processes that have been predicated to individuals. It will end by articulating the dynamics of the addictive process that can be uncovered in Matthew 6:19–34.

CHAPTER ONE

Introduction

To many people *addiction* and *authority* seem to be contradictory terms. How can addiction—which leads to death—be identified with authority which, in its root (*auctoritas*), means life? When contradictory terms are brought together (the nation is a home) they are called metaphors. Metaphors create meanings that are greater than the sum of their parts because of the interaction of those parts. Metaphors also define and establish social relationships.

This book will define patriarchal clericalism metaphorically as the specific addiction to authority that can be found in contemporary institutional Catholicism. Furthermore it examines addiction and authority in the Catholic church from a Matthean perspective. Since part of addiction is to make its patterns of thinking, feeling, and acting normative, some outside norm for right order must be found. Since the addiction to authority in the form of patriarchal clericalism has become normative, I have found in Matthew's gospel a corrective to the dysfunctional behavior that seems to pervade much of the institutional church.

The final words of Matthew's Jesus conclude the first gospel and summarize its most important teachings—including his understanding of authority and its purpose in the community of disciples throughout the world:

> Now the eleven disciples went to Galilee, to the mountain to which Jesus had directed them. When they saw him, they worshipped him; but some doubted. And Jesus came and said to them, "All authority in heaven and on earth has been given to me. Go therefore and make disciples of all nations, baptizing them in the name of the Father and the Son and the Holy Spirit, and teaching them to obey

everything that I have commanded you. And remember, I
am with you always, to the end of the age" (28:16–20).[1]

Besides the centrality of Jesus' authority in his final commission-
ing statement—"all authority in heaven and on earth has been given
to me"—a closer examination of other ideas in the passage[2] suggests
four implied stories: first there is *the story*, handed-down teachings of
Jesus; then comes "the culture's story," which involves "all nations;"
then there is "the church's story" insofar as the church is composed of
those baptized into the trinitarian Godhead who observe Jesus' teachings all days; finally, there is each person's story that must be the final
translation of the story in history.

Interrelating Four Stories in Matthew 28:16–20

Since the gospel must have relevance "always, to the end of the
age," we must find a way to weave together *the story*, our culture's
story, the church's story, and our story. To attempt to interpret the
gospel free of the anthropological and sociological data we know about
the culture and the church of the first century, or the character of
Matthew the storyteller, would do a disservice to the historical-critical
method as well as the narrative-critical method of interpreting the
gospel. At the same time, to isolate *the story*, thinking that a first-
century document has no relevance to our culture, our church, and
our lives, would be to relegate the story of Jesus to a time warp
unable to be opened ever again. As all four "stories" came together
in the first gospel, I believe we must find ways to bring them together
rather than to isolate them today. Consequently we must beware of
absolutizing any one story to the detriment of the other three.

When *the story* gets absolutized to the exclusion of the culture,
the church, or the individual stories to which it is addressed, fundamentalism and/or reductionism follows. When this happens we hear
people saying, "It's in the Bible and that's enough for me." Others
reduce the whole story to one or other of its parts. When this occurs
we hear many sentences beginning with "unless": Unless we have a
"personal relationship with Jesus Christ," or unless we are "baptized
in the Spirit," or unless we "submit to the keys of Peter," our salvation
is jeopardized.

A parallel tendency (often unconscious) exists to absolutize the
culture's story in a way that makes the scriptures, the church, and
our lives serve society's prevailing ideology. This results in cultural

imperialism. An example is society's rejection of a prophetic critique of the disparity between rich and poor people. I know of one Catholic parish in a wealthy suburb of New York where some parents insisted that certain scriptures not be interpreted to their children—such as the Beatitudes—"lest our children get funny ideas."

Another tendency to absolutize one of the stories can be found in the way the church's story often gets interpreted in legalism and dogmatism. In dogmatism, church teachings (even about scripture) can go beyond good scriptural exegesis itself. When the leaders define themselves as the only teachers and truth as their teaching, the hierarchy's interpretation becomes the absolute legal norm. Despite lip service to the scriptures as the first font of revelation, the second font, tradition, de facto takes precedence.

Finally, when my story becomes the absolute norm, I interpret the scriptures selectively and relatively, live in the culture isolated and individualistically, and make my own thoughts my ultimate magisterium. When applied to Catholicism, I become my own pope and/or a "shopping cart" Catholic, picking and choosing what seems to fit me best.

Just as Matthew's gospel reveals a horizon under the absolute authority of the risen Jesus which united the four stories into what we know today as *the story*, today, under that same authority, we are invited to find a way in which that story might have something to say to our culture, our church, and our lives. But how can the horizon represented in Matthew's first-century interpretation of the Jesus-story speak to our own third-millennium horizon or way of viewing culture, church, and our lives? If Matthew's story reveals a first-century horizon and ours another horizon separated by two thousand years, how can we find some connection, some fusion of horizons?

Images of Honor and Shame

Creating images and language to help fuse the horizons of the first and twenty-first centuries is no easy task. In researching the dynamics in Matthew's households of the first century, in which culture and cult were embedded, and our third-millennium culture and church, which have been separated, I have found a possible fusion or point of connection in the notion of justice viewed as the right order of relationships among persons and resources.[3] More specifically, when applied to functional or dysfunctional relationships, I have found a possible unifying notion in the images of honor and shame.

In his seminal work, *The New Testament World: Insights from Cultural Anthropology*, Bruce J. Malina notes that honor and shame were "pivotal values of the first-century Mediterranean world."[4] At the heart of honor and shame relationships were boundaries between self and others, nature, space, and time, as well as God (or the gods). Two millenniums later, in his pioneering work *Authority*, humanities scholar Richard Sennet has noted that "shame about being dependent is the legacy of the nineteenth-century industrial society to our own."[5] More specifically, speaking to the subject at the heart of this book, Sennet speaks of the issue of dependency and notes: "What we need to understand about the larger social dimensions of this bond is the strengths which have come to be seen in the dominant figures of authority, the paternalistic and autonomous figures. What kind of shame has their strength elicited among those who are dependent on them?"[6] Thus notions of honor and shame seem to underlie interpersonal dynamics in both epochs.

Malina notes that three sets of relationships around honor and shame dominated first-century interaction: power, sexual status or roles, and religion. Honor in these three areas represented "socially proper attitudes and behavior in the area where the three lines of power, sexual status, and religion intersect."[7] Honor involved two main components: 1) a person's or a group's feeling of positive self-worth, combined with 2) the public, social acknowledgment of that worth. Shame entailed two corresponding factors as well: 1) a person's or a group's feeling of negative self-worth, and 2) the public, social acknowledgment of that worth as negative.

Although Malina does not believe this first-century notion is dominant in our era, I find more parallels, given Sennet's notion of negation that gives rise to shame, which he finds endemic to our times. This "fusion" approach seems all the more significant when we consider that Malina's basic definition for shame for the first-century Mediterranean world contains the same elements as shame in our addicted culture, church, and lives today. Then, as today, shame reveals an individual's basic sense of being identified or separated from community. Consequently it can be healthy or unhealthy, life-giving or death-dealing, non-toxic or toxic.

Sennet connects shame and dependency, and so does addiction analyst John Bradshaw. However, Bradshaw distinguishes between healthy and unhealthy forms of shame. Healthy shame makes us aware of our limitations; toxic shame makes us feel *we* are limited. Bradshaw insists that "without the healthy signal of shame, we would not be in touch with our core dependency needs."[8] According to Bradshaw, healthy shame grounds all spirituality (see 2 Cor 12:7–10). It signals human limitations and reminds us that we are "not God," while also pointing us to that higher power or authority beyond ourselves that we call God. Unhealthy or toxic shame represents a rejection of one's self as flawed, limited, and alienated from others. In this sense shame constitutes the core of all addictive processes, since both addiction and codependency reveal self-alienation.

Even a brief survey of the various faces of honor/shame in relationships today convinces me that each of the four stories we will consider in this book involve dynamics that get triggered by a common "shame button." Only the expressions differ. In Matthew's story-world the shame button labelled people as "out" or "in" (see 10:5–6; 15:21–28 vs. 28:18–20). In our culture's story, the shame button revolves around patriotism, work, and consumerism. Institutional Catholicism has its shame button as well: loyalty or disloyalty to the Holy Father and the Holy See. When the shame button dominates in each of our personal stories, belonging or not belonging, independence or codependence manifest its expressions. Depending on the story, pushing these shame buttons can make healthy relationships dysfunctional. How these relationships can become dysfunctional and contribute to the addictive processes revealed in *the story*, the culture's story, the church's story, and my story will be the focus of this book. In a special way I will highlight how the shame button gets expressed in the manifestation of power, roles, and religion in Roman Catholicism.

Why This Book?

Pope Paul VI indicated eloquently in his encyclical *Ecclesiam Suam* (*His Church*) that the church is essentially dialogical.[9] Dialogue presumes a willingness in all parties to listen to each other's point of view; it assumes that one does not have all the answers. This book is my attempt to promote dialogue on a matter that has too often been kept quiet, silenced, or repressed.

A central tenet of addiction theory is that the addict is usually the last to admit and accept his or her addiction. Denial and refusal to talk about the problem become the norm. Thus I am not sanguine that dialogue will result from what I share here about addiction and authority in the church. When others before me have questioned some of the dynamics of the papal and curial leaders in Catholicism, secretive, one-sided, authoritarian, inquisitorial investigations have tended to be the pattern. With this book I have decided that I will no longer give the power to define the reality of the church to any human if that definition undermines either human dignity or a more equitable sharing of roles, or results in an insular religion.

While the nondialogical, judgmental approach seems to be a characteristic of the papacy and curia toward critics of the patterns of thinking and behaving of the institutional church leaders, it is not limited to the pope or Roman Curia. A recent experience I had with a bishop illustrates how normative it has become in many dioceses as well.

I was a keynote speaker at a three-day clergy convocation in the Midwest. In addition, I offered a twice-repeated workshop based on my research for this book entitled "Addiction, Authority, and the Crisis of Meaning in the Church." When the clergy days ended, I happened to meet the bishop of the diocese in the hallway. Although he had heard neither my keynote address nor the workshops, he challenged, "Mike, what's the matter with you?" Without hearing my arguments, he had concluded automatically that something was wrong—not with the object of my discussion or even my analysis of it—but with *me*. Later on I heard from others that he said, "Mike Crosby really needs help."

There *is* something wrong, and I *do* need help. My life in the institutional church has become increasingly unmanageable. I am admitting this and am trying to address what's wrong and am seeking help for myself. I am in need of recovery; I need to convert from my codependent obsession with controlling others and outcomes. I am admitting my powerlessness over my relationships with others (and myself) and am seeking to reorder my life in relationship with my highest power. In this effort I have found much help in the Twelve-Step program, therapy and spiritual direction, caring friends, and fellow Capuchins. As I seek recovery and the freedom that comes with this conversion, I seek to take this same good news to others who suffer in the same church family as mine. This constitutes a kind of "twelfth step" and is represented in this book: "Having had a spiritual awakening as the result of these steps, we tried to carry these messages to others, and to practice these principles in all our affairs."

That I have used Matthew's gospel as a critique of existing authority patterns in the church might itself be criticized, especially by scripture scholars who have been unable to find any relational dynamics that would bring about a fusion of first- and twenty-first-century horizons, and by people in the addiction field as well. Matthew, like John and Paul and prophetic voices before them, sculpts his story in dualistic imagery; dualistic thinking constitutes the heart of addictive ideology. Despite this external referencing and either-or approach there is something about the moral dualism of the scriptures that has relevance to the abuses that have taken place in our Catholic tradition. It also serves as a way of considering life that invites us to abandon one moral path and begin travelling another. At this basic level the word of God invites us today to a fundamental choice: addiction or wholeness.

I also realize these reflections and initial attempts to begin a serious dialogue on the abuse of authority in the church reflect the limitations that are part of my horizon. I am a white, male, First-World, United States born and bred Roman Catholic. My world view might not reflect the experience of others who share my background or those elsewhere, especially Catholics in other parts of the church. Indeed addiction terminology itself, although rapidly expanding, is quite unique in North America and often limited to its individual expressions.

The fact that I present material to reinforce my reflections on the addictive part of the institutional church and its body of leaders and the codependent support the rest of us give, does not constitute a rejection of it, them, or us. Nor does it imply that many good things are not being done or can't be done by any of us suffering from this disease. Rather, it merely recognizes that all of us—whom God has made good—share different manifestations of that part of the sin of the world I will define as the addictive process.

If this book can help initiate true dialogue within a setting that has often been monological, and if it aids recovery or conversion from less obvious forms of addiction and/or codependency in the Catholic church, much good will have been accomplished. I know that this paradigm already has done much to help me and others deal with our anger as we consider our part in the church. Meanwhile we all can be nourished by that prayer which has become a hallmark of so many Twelve-Step programs and meetings: "God grant us the serenity to accept the things we cannot change, the courage to change the things we can, and the wisdom to know the difference."

Thanksgiving

This book has taken years to develop. However, its underlying thoughts were structured during workshops I gave in 1989 at Innspire in Cottonwood, Idaho, and the renewal program at Sangre de Cristo, New Mexico. Writing this book—and keeping somewhat sane in the process—has been facilitated by a community of helpful people. Being a good codependent, I sought out others for verification of the ideas I've presented here. While they were not always verified, they were certainly made clearer by their comments.

I am deeply grateful to Frank Cunningham for his persistent efforts in having me write for Ave Maria and for his graciousness and guidance through this book's many stages. Others offered helpful reflections for various sections of this book; they cannot be mentioned here, except for my Capuchin confrere John Celichowski, who edited the first chapters in their very early stages. Those who thoroughly read and critiqued the entire book have my abiding gratitude. These include Francis Dombrowski, Diane Fassel, Joe Juknialis, Mary Ellen Merrick, Edward van Merrienboer, Mary Ann Niesen, and Eileen Sanchez.

I have often been asked: "What reaction do you get from your Order?" I can say I am most pleased with the support I have received. This has come from the brothers at the Capuchin House of Studies in Berkeley with whom I lived while writing this book, and the brothers of Solanus Community in Milwaukee who have been so supportive as I've edited it. In a special way I want to thank the Provincial Council of our Midwest Capuchins for encouraging the publication of this book and our Provincial Minister, Kenneth Reinhart, for his support. To these brother Capuchins and to our leadership in Rome who have struggled mightily to challenge Rome on the issue of clericalism, I dedicate this book.

CHAPTER TWO

The Dynamics of Addiction and Discovering Them in Matthew

In 1930 Sigmund Freud wrote *Civilization and Its Discontents*, in which he noted that the superego of a culture originates similarly to that of an individual. He suggested that "we may expect that one day someone will venture to embark upon a pathology of cultural communities."[1] What Freud envisioned, using pathology terminology, began occurring in the 1980s, using addiction terms. In 1981 I called our society "culturally addictive" and suggested Twelve-Step groups as a way of recovery from its addictive "isms."[2] In the second half of the decade others began identifying pathology in organizations using addiction terminology. Before determining how this has occurred, it might be best to begin by describing the etiology or origin of terms related to the addictive process.

Understanding Addiction and Codependency

Almost as many definitions for addiction exist as writers on the subject. This proliferation of approaches used to diagnose and treat addictions causes confusion and debate. The present debate has its origins in the nature of alcoholism. Once treated as a moral weakness, alcoholism was not called a disease by the American Medical Association until the mid–1950s. The diagnostic manual of the American Psychiatric Association avoids the term entirely. In time the notion of addiction moved from being identified with alcohol to any chemical substance. The World Health Organization defined addiction as "a state of periodic or chronic intoxication produced by the repeated consumption of a natural or synthetic drug for which one has an overpowering desire or need (i.e., compulsion). . . with the presence of a tendency to increase the dose and evidence of phenomena of tolerance, abstinence and withdrawal, in which there is always psychic and physical dependence on the effects of the drug."[3]

Generally when people speak of *addictive diseases* they imply a medical problem. When they speak of *addictive behaviors* they suggest a social learning or environmental problem. When using the term *addictive pathologies* they imply a psychological model. Most experts agree that any serious theory of addiction must account for all these variables but disagree about how they are combined. Because addictions represent a complex phenomenon, complete data on them are not as yet available. Thus writers have divergent meanings.

Dr. Robert Lefever views addiction as a "family disease" involving self-denial and caretaking, domination, and submission. He views it as an inner compulsion, an alien parasite, driving the afflicted to do things that are against their own better nature with destructive consequences.[4] The British doctor believes something in the *person* triggers addiction, not just something in the drug or substance or society. He has developed questionnaires to help determine if a person may be an addict. His data show that the addictive process remains basically the same for a caffeine addict and a compulsive shopper—only the specific substance or behavior of choice changes.

Anne Wilson Schaef defines addiction as "any process over which we are powerless. It takes control of us, causing us to do and think things that are inconsistent with our personal values; and leading us to become progressively more compulsive and obsessive."[5] She divides addictions into two broad categories: substance addictions (alcohol, drugs, nicotine, food) and process addictions (money-accumulation, gambling, sex, work, religion, worry).

The most exhaustive list of addictions I have seen is Gerald May's. For May, addiction is a "*state* of compulsion, obsession, or preoccupation that enslaves a person's will and desire."[6] Given such a definition, one can understand why May finds addictive behavior and addicts everywhere. For him, "To be alive is to be addicted, and to be alive and addicted is to stand in need of grace."[7] While May's categories include substance and process addictions, he centers these around 106 "attraction addictions" (covering everything from approval and golf to neatness and punctuality) and seventy-seven "aversion addictions" (ranging from airplanes and anchovies to public speaking and the rich/poor).

Stanton Peele and Archie Brodsky define addiction as "an unstable state of being, marked by a compulsion to deny all that you are or have been in favor of some new and ecstatic experience."[8] For Peele, who rejects a disease model for addiction,[9] addicts are people who have never learned to come to grips with their world and who thus seek stability and reassurance through some repeated, ritualized activity. The resulting addictive process is reinforced by a comforting sensation for the object of the addiction and by a gradual atrophy of other ways of behaving, feeling, and thinking.

If controversy around addiction exists, even greater debate dominates discussion about codependency. Some treatment centers, such as Hazelden, refuse to use the term. Others find everyone to be codependent. Such sweeping generalizations have generated strong criticism, especially since no empirical data (only clinical observation) exist regarding the extent of codependency in the wider population.[10] In the early days codependents were identified as "enablers" whose identity and dynamics revolved around an addict. While elements of this notion still exist in "adult children" groups, codependency now is viewed as living according to others' norms, or in reaction to others' thinking, feeling, and acting in a way that denies one's own thoughts and emotions.

Melody Beattie defines a codependent person as "one who has let another person's behavior affect him or her, and who is obsessed with controlling that person's behavior."[11] She counts among the major characteristics of codependent people caretaking, repression, obsession, control, denial, dependency, poor communication, weak boundaries, lack of trust, anger, and low self-worth.

Timmen Cermak, a medical doctor, has done much to develop diagnostic criteria for codependency. Cermak believes anxiety and depression constitute the common characteristics of both codependent persons and those classified as having a dependent personality disorder. However, he distinguishes between the two insofar as dependency/autonomy are the central issues in dependent personality disorders while issues of control constitute the heart of codependency:

> People who exhibit codependent personality disorders share
> an overwhelming devotion to will power as the preferable

avenue to achieving self-worth. Control of self and others, feelings, and things is blindly pursued as an antidote to free-floating anxiety. As in alcoholism, the means (i.e., will power) becomes more highly valued than effective attainment of the end (i.e., sobriety). For the codependent, loss of control is phobically avoided.[12]

In *Facing Codependence*, Pia Mellody and Andrea Wells Miller and J. Keith Miller organize the discussion of codependency around five symptoms. For them, codependents have difficulty: "1. Experiencing appropriate levels of self-esteem; 2. Setting functional boundaries; 3. Owning and expressing their own reality; 4. Taking care of their adult needs and wants; and 5. Experiencing and expressing their reality *moderately*."[13] Each of these core symptoms can get expressed in opposite ways as well. For instance, while one person can manifest low esteem, another may react in thoughts, feelings, and behavior that appear grandiose.

According to Robert Subby and John Friel, codependent patterns reflect a condition which emerges from any family system where certain unwritten, even unspoken, rules exist. For them, codependency represents "a dysfunctional pattern of living and problem solving which is nurtured by a set of rules within the family system."[14] Their approach, we will see, approximates my own.

The Dynamics of Addiction

Addiction and codependency involve anxiety and behavioral changes in our body and life itself. When we ingest certain chemicals our bodily processes develop certain patterns; addictive behavior easily evolves. The addictive cycle begins when one senses the need to act out for pleasure or to alleviate pain. In the process leading to the acting out, a mood change takes place. Fearing the diminishment of pleasure or the even deeper awareness of discomfort or pain, one seeks resolution by repeating the cycle. As the cycle continues an attachment builds. If not stopped it leads to obsessive thinking, feelings of anxiety about getting more pleasure or relief, and compulsive behavior to ensure the supply. At some point in the addiction cycle, cellular and genetic changes take place; the body develops a craving or dependency. Getting a fix becomes the controlling force. In alcoholism, intoxication becomes normal. Indeed, people need their chemical of choice just to function.

This cycle does not occur only when chemical substances are ingested. Dr. George Mann of the Johnson Institute makes it clear that psychological addiction "precedes the physical addiction marked by the cellular and genetic changes."[15] Thus whether a person abuses substances, processes, or relationships, *psychological addiction precedes the physical addiction and launches the addictive cycle.* Three phases in the development of an addiction (or, I believe, in the development of codependency as well) occur: 1) an automatic learning process (in the addictive cycle above, stimulus-response), 2) cellular changes, and 3) genetic changes.

The first stage of addiction develops at the primitive level of the autonomic nervous system which surrounds the spinal cord. The many nerves running from the spine to various body parts affect their behavior. For instance, when we experience fear, a nerve impulse travels to our adrenal glands, which then pour out adrenalin and norepinephrine. These affect our blood pressure and breathing. These various bodily changes affect feelings of fear. If not checked, they can lead to anxiety.

In the second stage the body experiences stress and seeks equilibrium. The nervous system's cells seek restoration of that equilibrium in three ways: through feedback, habituation, and adaptation. In feedback, cells react to certain stimuli. Habituation is the neurological process by which nerve cells become less sensitive and responsive to repeated stimuli. When neither feedback nor habituation create equilibrium, a new balance must be created. This is adaptation or, in Gerald May's words, "attachment." We become attached to whatever makes things normal for us, and we don't let go of that "normality" without a crisis.[16] May's contention that the cellular dynamic applies not just to chemical substances but to nonsubstance addictions as well relates to this book's discussion of addictive processes in organizations and their members:

> If we had been talking about addiction to money, power, or relationships, even if we had been talking about addiction to images of ourselves or of God, we could have said much the same about what happens to our nerve cells. We would probably be speaking of different systems of cells, but the patterns of feedback, habituation, and adaptation would be essentially the same.[17]

The third and final stage is genetic.[18] When the first two stages increase, a genetic change takes place. That is why, even years after an addiction has been stopped, the smallest experience of a substance might be enough to stimulate old cellular patterns. Genetically a person has become addictive and/or codependent; thus one admits to being "an alcoholic," "addicted to relationships," or "an anorexic."

Moving From Individual to Organizational Addiction

In the mid–1980s a chemical dependency counsellor, William L. White, became alarmed at the high casualty rate among his peers in professional counselling. At first he could not understand how highly competent, committed, and compassionate professional helpers could fall victim to some of the same addictive patterns they found in their clients. White began to discover a pattern: the same addictive dynamics in individual victims' pasts were being revealed repeatedly in organizational processes. Helped by his background in family systems theory, White began constructing individual histories as well as organizational histories. For instance, he notes:

> When one of the women who was a casualty used the phrase, "It's just like I was back in my family, it's like organizational incest," what she was referring to was her own incest experiences being replicated within the organization. As a staff person, she had been involved in a very abusive sexual relationship with the Executive Director of this agency.[19]

The specific model of family systems theory White found helpful came in the contrast between open and closed systems, a parallel I will apply to the Catholic church in chapter six. Since incest is "the final stage in the closure of family systems," White came to a similar realization regarding organizations:

> The same kind of sexual dynamics in organizations represent the last stage of closure in the same way as they do in family systems. That became the beginning of the concept of organizational incest, of progressive closure, of progressive violation of personal and professional boundaries. The latest stages of this result in the violation of sexual boundaries inside the organization.[20]

Sadly, White's insights have been corroborated in the 1990 archdiocesan report that addressed the cases of pedophilia among priests in Newfoundland. Their pedophilia, the "Winter Commission Report" concluded, had to be considered within the wider church-system of patriarchy and power abuse.[21]

Like White, Anne Wilson Schaef's connection between individual and organizational addictions began with personal experiences and reflection. From a previously unrecognized understanding of addictiveness in her extended family, Schaef began making connections to a wider system. She called this the White Male System and wrote: "I found myself saying this so frequently that it turned into what I called my 'hand-in-glove' theory: the addictive system and the White Male System fit together like a hand in a glove. I started seeing how the two systems support each other and how the White Male System uses addictions to perpetuate itself."[22]

Although some critics charged her with making too-facile connections between individual addictions and institutional dysfunctioning, Schaef's analysis struck a chord, particularly with people working in religious structures. Unable to find an adequate model in family systems, Schaef proffered something found in physics and brain psychology to guide her connections. This was a mirror-image model, which she found in the notion of the hologram. She writes:

> The essential feature of a hologram is that each piece of the hologram contains the entire structure of the entire hologram; each piece is not just a part of the whole, it has the entire pattern and way of functioning of the whole embedded in it. This is a useful way to look at the Addictive System. The system is like the individual, and the individual is like the system. In other words, the Addictive System has all the characteristics of the individual alcoholic/addict. And because we live in this system, every one of us, unless recovering by means of a system shift, exhibits many of these same characteristics.[23]

In 1988 Diane Fassel joined Schaef in writing *The Addictive Organization*. It connected individual addictive behavior, organizational addictions, and addictive systems. The model of the hologram connected all: "Individuals function the same way as the organization they inhabit. Organizations function the same way as the system they inhabit, and the system is made up of the individuals in the organizations. We do indeed have our hologram."[24] Fassel and Schaef concluded that the micro was in the macro (the "infrastructure"), and the macro reflected all its micro parts.

When I first read Fassel and Schaef, their "infrastructure" seemed adaptable to the model of social analysis that I had developed and used since the mid–1970s. In my model the world is composed of four levels: the individual, the interpersonal, the infrastructural (with its network of institutions, "isms," and ideology), and the environmental. It seemed quite easy to find the patterns of addictive self-centeredness, which reflects unhealthy narcissism at the individual level, reflected in and mirroring the self-centeredness of groups and institutions reinforcing the "isms" at the infrastructural level. Some of these "isms" relate to persons, others to resource-allocation, and others to processes. All are reinforced in the institutions by an ideology which justifies their expression. Some "isms" alienating persons in institutions are sexism, racism, classism, ageism, elitism, clericalism, ethnocentrism, and cultural imperialism. Those related to resources are consumerism, materialism, technologism, and nationalism. Process "isms" include perfectionism and workaholism.

Despite my initial sense that the hologram approach fit my social analysis, as I moved into the addiction paradigm and tried to understand how individual patterns can be found in organizational dynamics, the less it seemed to be helpful. I returned to family systems theories. At the same time I began developing a more adequate understanding of addictive social organizations through the discipline of social psychology called symbolic interactionism.

Symbolic Interactionism and Addictive Processes

Symbolic interactionists believe that the nature of the human organism can be understood only in the context of evolution. For them the origin of human understanding is grounded in human interaction. The "we" exists before the "I." One's identity is discovered through interaction. The main instrument for this communication involves symbols, which become language. When the one using the symbols connected to language is able to respond in like kind to others, these become "significant symbols." Sharing these significant symbols enables people to establish meanings and to control their own responses as well as those of others. For instance, if I notice a fire in a crowded theater, I might decide to use a subdued warning for better crowd control rather than shouting "Fire!" In communicating in this way, I not only control my own but others' behavior as well.

For symbolic interactionists, people act on shared meanings. Their actions in a particular situation depend on the way they perceive that situation. Their understanding of themselves in relation to their social group underlies their capacity to be aware of responses, to control the response, and to formulate hypotheses about the expectations and responses of others. As John Hewitt notes:

> Individuals act only because they acquire the capacity to do so as members of a society, which *is* the source of their knowledge, language, skills, orientations, motives, and many of the other capacities or dispositions they have. Society is temporally prior to any individual; it owes its continuity as well as its existence to individual conduct and it is only visible in conduct; it will persist long after the individual is dead.[25]

Since the "we" exists before the "I," so society precedes the individual. This helps reveal the way individual addictive behavior can be produced by interpersonal and infrastructural addictive dynamics. A symbolic interactionist approach overturns the concept of addicted individuals creating addictive organizations and addictive systems. If society precedes the individual, individual addictive behavior follows socially and culturally addictive conditioning. Cultural factors thus largely affect innate controls over human conduct. Cultural addiction would precede individual addiction. Hewitt writes:

> Our responses to this cultural environment are learned rather than inherited. Culture, which is grounded in our symbolic capacity and our use of language, is the source of what we know about the world, what we value, and how we think we should act. . . . It is the source of our ideas about what is worth striving for, whether it be material well-being or individual happiness; and it provides us with definitions of what is normal and right and what is deviant and wrong in our everyday conduct and in our relations with one another. Culture, to put it simply, is both our environment and the source of our responses to it.[26]

If culture helps define what is right and normal or wrong and deviant, this enables even dysfunctional behaviors like elitism and consumerism to become normative in the culture's story, or patriarchy and clericalism to become normative in the church's story, or workaholism and perfectionism to become the acceptable norm in our own stories. Since we are born into such a culture that reinforces its patterns with a certain language to designate normative meanings, for recovery to take place the familiar words and language must be changed to allow the creation of new meanings and new relationships among old objects. In religion this is the role of the prophets.

Family Systems and Addictive Systems

A primary unit studied by symbolic interactionists is the family. Families are small, medium, or large social systems composed of individuals relating to each other with normative language around strong, emotional dynamics that include honor and shame. They consist of intergenerational households, clusters of households, or in the case of the church, a "household of faith" which persists generation to generation. Family systems theory studies interaction among individuals within these groups and the effect of the groups on individuals and each other.

While concentrating on emotions, a family systems approach to addictive behavior (as that of symbolic interactionism) deemphasizes the notion that one's obsessions, anxieties, and addictions primarily involve something physiological or personal. While neither deny these dynamics, family systems theory suggests that individual patterns have more to do with our relationships—an individual's patterns reveal something about the family itself. Thus according to people like Edwin H. Friedman, family systems theory "can be extended to any relational system from a business partnership to a religious institution, where a problem in the 'flock' can show up in the burnout of its 'shepherd.' "[27]

Irrespective of faith, most clergy members are simultaneously involved in at least four distinct families, whose ways of thinking, emotions, and behavior interlock: one's own family, families within the organization, the organizational family itself, and this organization's participation in the wider family of organization, the temple or church infrastructure. These four areas represent my notions of the individual, interpersonal, institutional, and infrastructural levels. Because they interlock, what happens at the individual level of the family affects the interpersonal grouping of families; in turn, these influence the organizational family, and vice versa. Infrastructural family dynamics sustain them all.

A traditional approach to addiction is based on linear thinking, that is, cause and effect where A causes B, B causes C, C causes

D, and D causes E. The systems approach, however, sees *interdependent* relationships among A, B, C, D, and E. Family systems theory focuses on the systemic forces of intellectual, emotional, and behavioral processes rather than the specific symptoms, whether the "family problem" surfaces in a pattern such as bad school habits or addictive patterns such as anorexia, alcoholism, or drug dependency.

Just as individuals experience life cycles and stages of development, so do families and organizations. Furthermore, in family systems theory, as in addiction theory, most therapists recognize the need to distinguish between religion and spirituality. Religion, used ideologically, can reinforce dysfunctional patterns in a family and/or addictive processes; indeed it can be the source and rationalizer of both. On the other hand, spirituality enables a family to function freely and its members to be free of addictive patterns.

Given these understandings, we can now suggest tentative definitions for the notions that will be discussed throughout this book.

Definitions for the Addictive Process, Addiction and Codependency

Since I will define my terms related to addiction and codependency around notions of thinking, feeling, and acting it will be literally impossible to make a simple identification of individual and organizational addictive patterns. While individuals think, feel, and act, institutions do not think and feel, but they act. They do, however, manifest, especially through their leaders, thinking, feeling, and acting, and it is in this sense that I will say that individual addictive patterns can be found analogously in institutions and infrastructures.

No matter how we define addiction or codependency, each represents part of what I call the *addictive process*. The addictive process is any unhealthy and abnormal disease, at any level of life, that reveals a way of thinking (perceptions, assumptions, beliefs), feelings (emotions, passions, affections), and behavior (functioning, acting, deeds) related to control of someone or something (again at any level) that becomes progressively death-oriented.[28] It will be shown that the addictive process has both active (and recovering) addicts as well as reactive (and recovering) codependents. Conversely, the *process of wholeness* (or perfection in the scriptural sense [5:48; 19:21]) is any healthy or integrated holism, on any of the levels, which reveals a way of thinking, feeling, and behaving related to something or someone free of control that leads to a way of living that increasingly becomes transformative.

The addictive structure is part of the addictive process; it is what I call the infrastructure (in its unhealthy form). It contains addictive institutions, "isms" (which organize people and resources dysfunctionally), and ensures the perpetuity of those institutions through ideology. Rather than being an aggregate of its various parts, an infrastructure has a synergy insofar as it is larger than the sum of its parts. When an infrastructure is addictive its social ordering generates, promotes, and sustains institutional, interpersonal, and individual addictive behavior, anxiety, and obsessive patterns of thinking. Consequently, within it, thoughts will be obsessive and disordered, and characterized by denial and dishonesty. Feelings will be frozen or fear-filled and anxious; passion will be undermined and numbed. Behavior will be angry or rage-filled, erratic, and controlling.

Thus addiction can be considered any object or dynamic that controls, at any level, behavior, emotions, and thinking in such an obsessive-compulsive way that it leads to increasing powerlessness and unmanageability (at that level), and ultimately, death. Codependency represents any obsessive thinking, feeling, and/or acting related to rules or norms around control. It involves an intellectual, emotional, and behavioral condition that results from an individual, interpersonal, or institutional interaction with relationships and rules (overt or covert) that are ordered to control. These prevent the open expression of thinking, feeling, and activity in oneself and others, especially others who may be under the influence of the addictive process. Codependency is a progressive and potentially fatal disease. Because it is more subtle than addiction and because denial is often stronger in codependent people, it can be more life-threatening than addiction itself. Indeed, I tend to find codependency to be the ground for addictions.

The addictive system as well as addictive persons, groups, and organizations view codependency as normative for members and a sign of loyalty; independence can become the basis for shame. Honor and shame thus revolve around the issue of conformity and nonconformity to group or organizational rules and ways of relating. Since both addiction and codependency are part of the addictive process, the codependent expression supports the addictive dimension at all levels and, in turn, codependents are rewarded by the addictive system for their loyal support.

Given this understanding of the addictive process, addiction, and codependency, we now turn to Matthew's gospel to discover underlying dynamics that, in today's language, reveal their functioning.

Discovering the Dynamics of the
Addictive Process in Matthew 6:19–34

One of the best-known passages of Matthew's gospel is 6:19–34. The center of the text reminds us that human acquisitions cannot compare to the gifts of God—Solomon's glory cannot be compared to the "lilies of the field":

> Do not store up for yourselves treasures on earth, where moth and rust consume and where thieves break in and steal, but store up for yourselves treasures in heaven, where neither moth nor rust consumes and where thieves do not break in and steal. For where your treasure is, there your heart will be also. . . .
>
> No one can serve two masters; for a slave will either hate the one and love the other, or be devoted to the one and despise the other. You cannot serve God and wealth (6:19–24).

a6:25 Therefore I tell you, do not worry about your life, what you will eat or what you will drink, or about your body, what you will wear. Is not life more than food, and the body more than clothing?

b6:26 Look at the birds of the air; they neither sow nor reap nor gather into barns, and yet your heavenly Father feeds them. Are you not of more value than they?

c6:27 And can any of you by worrying add a single hour to your span of life?

d6:28 And why do you worry about clothing? Consider the lilies of the field, how they grow; they neither toil nor spin;

e6:29 yet I tell you, even Solomon in all his glory was not clothed like one of these.

d6:30 But if God so clothes the grass of the field, which is alive today and tomorrow is thrown into the oven, will he not much more clothe you—you of little faith?

c6:31 Therefore do not worry, saying: "What will we eat?" or "What will we drink?" or "What will we wear?" For it is the Gentiles who strive for all these things;

b6:32 and indeed your heavenly Father knows that you need all these things.

6:33 But strive first for the kingdom of God and his righteousness, and all these things will be given to you as well.

a6:34 So do not worry about tomorrow, for tomorrow will bring worries of its own. Today's trouble is enough for today.[29]

In this address, the one "label" the disciples receive deals with shame: "You of little faith." The passage also reveals notions of power, (sexual) roles, and religion. The disciples' little faith is evident in the underlying conflict about who/what will have power over them: wealth or God's reign. What has power over them involves religious overtones as well: "No one can serve two masters; for a slave will either hate the one and love the other, or be devoted to the one and despise the other. You cannot serve God and wealth." The anxiety over issues of power and religion has also been the case for the issue of sexual roles. The images used by Matthew's Jesus compares birds with "men's" work of sowing, reaping, and gathering into barns, while the lilies of the field are compared to "women's" work of toiling and spinning.[30]

I believe a closer examination of this passage reveals processes that we, using twentieth-century terminology, might call the addictive process. The passage also offers a way of recovery (conversion) from addiction: the spirituality involved in giving oneself over to the higher power of God's reign.

Building on the definitions above we can say that "where your treasure is, there your heart will be also" indicates whether one will be oriented to the addictive process or to authentic spirituality. Since the "treasure" indicates the *object* of one's thinking, feeling, and behaving, which are processes of the heart in the scriptures, we can tell to what degree one is oriented to the reign of God by the way one considers (orderly and faith-filled), desires (freely and courageously), and serves God (through detachment and dedication); we also can tell to what degree one has come under the influence of the reign of mammon in its various forms by the way one considers (disordered and obsessive), feels (fearfully and anxiously), and behaves (attached or addicted).

Using material shared with Luke (Lk 12:33–36; 16:13; 12:22–32), Matthew contrasts two possible scenarios related to one's treasure and one's heart. The beginning verses (6:19–20) set the theme around two conflicting objects or reigns. The one serves as the object of addiction—earthbound treasures; the other serves as the object of dedication—treasures in heaven. Writing for a more prosperous audience,[31] Matthew's Jesus shows that unless one's treasure is found in heaven, everything else can become earthbound. Only by first valuing heavenly treasures will people have the assurance that their treasures will not be consumed by moths, won't rust, or be stolen.

Moving from the literal use of the word for treasure, which usually involved a treasure-house (see 13:44, 52), Matthew now connects treasure with the figurative meaning of the inner store in the heart of every human (see 12:35): "For where your treasure is, there your heart will be also" (6:21). In the first gospel's anthropology, the heart represents the seat of physical, intellectual, and spiritual life. It constitutes the source of thinking, feeling, and acting. Thus, if the treasure represents some object, then an ordered or disordered heart represents the way we think, feel, and behave toward that object. With these two poles Matthew establishes for us the contrast between the addictive process and the process of wholeness. Within these poles, the next sentences concentrate on behavior, feelings, and thinking directed toward one object or another.[32]

1. Two Masters and Opposing Enslavements

Matthew begins with behavior that can be addictive or wholesome, depending on the object of the behavior: "No one can *serve* two masters; for a slave will either hate the one and love the other, or be devoted to the one and despise the other. You cannot *serve* God and wealth [*mamonas*]" (6:24). The object of our lives will be one *reign* or another; our acting will indicate to what degree we might be "a slave of" one of those reigns. Our feeling will indicate where our desire is directed; our thinking will reveal what kind of relationship lies at the core of our heart. Our thinking, emotions, and behavior reflect a fundamental ordering of life, and even our body (6:25), toward the reign of God or mammon.

Matthew's notion of the kingdom revolves around power.[33] Power comprises the essence of images dealing with relational notions around

"reign." God's reign is revealed on earth in the power of the person
and authority of Jesus Christ (13:41; 16:28; 28:18). However, on earth
another can have power over people. This is wealth. Although the
derivation from the original Aramaic word is uncertain, a generic understanding of *mammon* means "that in which one trusts."[34] It refers to
resources like property and "earthbound treasure." Mammon opposes
God's reign in that it is materialistic, anti-godly, and sinful. Friedrich
Hauck desribes well the contrast between the two powers or reigns:

> In the earthly property which man gathers (Mt 6:19ff), in
> which he erroneously seeks security (Lk 12:15ff.), to which
> he gives his heart (Mt 6:21), and because of which he ceases
> to love, Jesus finds the very opposite of God (Mt 6:24 par.).
> Because of the demonic power immanent in possessions,
> surrender to them brings practical enslavement (Mt 6:19ff).
> The righteous must resolutely break free from this entangle-
> ment and stand in exclusive religious dependence on God
> (Mt 6:24 par.).[35]

Matthew's use of "to serve" (*douleuein*) involves relationships
and actions identified with being a slave: submission, obedience, and
service. In Matthew's time situations existed wherein slaves had more
than one owner. It was very hard for a slave in such a situation to honor
equally their varying wishes and interests. Thus Matthew's Jesus says
the slave would love the one and be less attached to the other. From
the Greek scriptures available to Matthew, when *serve* referred to God
it did not characterize an isolated act but rather total commitment to
this highest power called God. Matthew kept this notion of exclusive
commitment and obligation[36] in declaring that one could not be a slave
of mammon and God. When God would be the object of the heart's
thinking and desire, *commitment* would reflect the behavior. When
Matthew specifies the mammon-objects of *service*, eating, drinking,
and clothing are its behavioral manifestations (6:25, 31).

In today's addiction terminology, when one is enslaved to eating,
it is called gluttony, an obsession with abstaining from food is called
anorexia, and gorging on food and then attempting to purge it is named
bulimia. When people become "given over" to drinking alcohol they
become alcoholics. When others are "born to shop," they can manifest
obsessiveness related to what they will wear. All these reveal some
form of what I previously described as addiction, that is, any behavior

that reveals a loss of freedom resulting from the control of another person, substance, or process over one's thinking, desires, or behavior.

Addictions arise from disordered attachments to eating, drinking, or other objects, relationships, and/or processes. Since attachment opens the door to addiction, detachment closes it. Therefore, the way of spirituality demands that we become increasingly *detached* from whatever would deter God's *reign* or power in our life. Detachment becomes freedom from desire. When detachment moves to this form of "letting go," the behavior is called commitment or dedication.

2. Anxiety versus Courage

The main emotional obstacle to dedication, Matthew makes clear, is worry (6:25, 27, 28, 31, 34). Excessive worry or anxiety reveals the feeling or desire that leads a person to act addictively. In the addictive anxiety lies disordered desire. The first manifestation of this disordered desire is fear. According to May:

> Addiction exists wherever persons are internally compelled to give energy to things that are not their true desires. To define it directly, addiction is a *state* of compulsion, obsession, or preoccupation that enslaves a person's will and desire. Addiction sidetracks and eclipses the energy of our deepest, truest desire for love and goodness. We succumb because the energy of our desire becomes attached, nailed, to specific behaviors, objects, or people.[37]

When my desires become disordered and geared to mammon, fears of "not enough" begin and, if no reordering of the desire takes place, anxiety can result: I begin to become obsessed with the idea that I'll never get enough. Fear represents the apprehension engendered by some specific object, person, or situation perceived as a threat to one's sense of being secure with "enough." If I am on an airplane and one of the engines falls off, I probably will experience fear. However, if every time I get on a plane I become obsessed about a possible crash, its emotional expression will be anxiety. Anxiety is the apprehension that arises when some unspecified object, person, or situation is perceived as a threat to my very existence or self-understanding. Shame is such a threat.

In Matthew, feelings of fear and anxiety have their opposites in freedom and courage. Although Matthew uses fear and anxiety or "loss of heart" somewhat interchangeably, in contrast to the psychological description above, he contrasts them with courage in 14:27 and "taking heart." Thus, when the disciples saw Jesus "walking on the sea, they were terrified, saying, 'It is a ghost!' And they cried out for fear. But immediately he spoke to them and said, 'Take heart, it is I; do not fear' " (14:26–27).

If disordered desires toward mammon reveal a diseased heart of fear and, ultimately, anxiety and addiction, then ordered desires enable liberation from their control. Such liberation constitutes biblical freedom. When freedom is experienced emotionally, and when that freedom is geared to being given over to the reign of God, one has the courage, with Peter, to make a commitment to Jesus as one's higher power (14:33).

Traditionally the reality of desire or longing has been interpreted as a need. This represents the empty dimension of the heart, the "hole" in the "whole" heart (see 22:37). This assumes that fullness precedes emptiness; original grace grounds any original sin; spirituality predates addiction. In other words, a definite kind of spirituality of wholeness and integrity precedes the addictive process of emptiness and want even though both originate in desire.

We interact with people and things because we notice them. As we think about them we experience another dynamic: we desire them. At first glance this desire or wanting might seem like an emptiness; however, as Sebastian Moore shows so well, it actually represents a form of wholeness:

> "Just wanting" is a feeling good that wants to go on feeling good and looks for things to feel good about. This is very clear in the child. The child—like the dolphin—is a bundle of pleasureableness. Freud describes our original condition, moving in the amniotic fluid, as the "oceanic" condition.
>
> Thus as we move . . . from the definite, specific wants, back to the undifferentiated "just wanting," we are moving towards *not emptiness but fullness*.[38]

When desire is geared to mammon, fear and anxiety will be its emotional expressions while attachment and addiction will be its behavioral forms. When desire is grounded in the reign of God, freedom and courage reflect its affective dimensions while increasing detachment and commitment reflect its deeds. When a hole exists in the heart, it is accompanied by a desire for mammon-objects, which easily leads to addictive behavior. When wholeness of heart persists, holiness accompanies it.

If, as Augustine asserted, our hearts are made for God, then our heart's desire is ordered to God. Disorder exists when something else begins reigning over us. If my heart desires God it implies that I sense myself desired by God; if my heart desires mammon, it most likely is because I think I am undesirable and need one of its addictive forms to cover my shame.

3. "Considering" as Obsessive or Faith-filled

In urging his anxious audience to change its addictive behavior of being given over to its mammon-forms, Matthew's Jesus realized the need for a change in their thinking. To change their thought and perception processes, he used an image from nature to give them confidence: "*Consider* the lilies of the field."

In extra-biblical sources, "to consider" meant "to examine closely," "to learn," "to grasp," or "to note." In the First Testament[39] one's behavior or moral conduct was to be closely examined (Gn 34:1ff; Lv 14:36). Matthew offered his readers a moral examination of their conduct—was it ordered to God or mammon? His Jesus invites the disciples to "consider"—examine closely—their inner fears and insecurity. At the same time he invites them to the freedom and courage that result from a sense of being whole as God's children (6:30–32).

Addiction can have its cause in confused and obsessive thinking that leads to fear and anxiety and attachment toward mammon forms; on the other hand mammon forms can affect behavior, feelings, and thinking. Parallel dynamics occur in spirituality. The grace of God's reign can be so powerful that one's behavior, emotions, and thought processes are deeply affected. Usually, since God's grace grounds itself in human dynamics, thinking, passions, and deeds affect how we respond to God. For Matthew's Jesus, the key is faith.

After inviting the disciples to consider the lilies of the field and the grass, he asks them to consider how the fulfillment of their needs is the concern of God. If God would so take care of the lilies and grass, "will he not much more clothe you—you of little faith?"

Every human has faith in someone or something. As a human activity, faith involves relationships. It generates emotions of courage, trust, and loyalty. When human activity generates courage, it does so around values. I have faith in you because _____. The "because" reflects values. Relationships of trust and loyalty revolve around issues of honor and shame; these help or hinder one's sense of belonging to a group whose members share certain values.

If we would unite all the centers of value, the overarching center of value becomes the most dominant object of our faith. In secular terms, James Fowler calls this supraordinate center of value an "ultimate environment" and concludes that in "Jewish and Christian terms, the ultimate environment [of our faith] is expressed with the symbol 'Kingdom of God.' In this way of seeing, *God* is the center of power and value which unifies and gives character to the ultimate environment."[40] Where I have my ultimate environment reveals my faith.

When we lose faith, we lose meaning and become depressed, aggressive, suicidal, or addictive. In the latter case, mammon and its various forms become our ultimate environment. Our whole bodies and lives, Matthew's Jesus notes, are centered in the object of our anxiety and addiction. Their power now reigns over us. It focuses our obsession and anxiety. However, when our faith—even if it is "little faith" (6:30)—is geared to God's reign, the resulting freedom and confidence empower us to become detached from false centers of value and become committed to God's true reign. From this perspective we might better understand why Matthew's Jesus would say: "Therefore do not worry, saying, 'What will we eat?' or 'What will we drink?' or 'What will we wear?' For it is the Gentiles who strive for all these things; and indeed your heavenly Father knows that you need all these things. But strive first for the kingdom of God and his righteousness, and all these things will be given to you as well" (6:32). Unbelievers, with disordered faith, "seek all these [addictive] things;" those with faith "seek first his kingdom and his righteousness."

The first two steps in recovery from living on the side of the addictive process are stopping and striving. In addiction language, conversion is recovery. Before conversion begins, we must let go of disordered thoughts, feelings, and behavior related to what will be eaten, drunk, worn, or experienced. Just as we cannot serve two masters, we cannot remain in an addiction and also seek God's reign over us. We must stop the addictive behavior itself; then we can strive for another reign over us. Seeking first God's reign does not imply a both/and approach. Neither do most people dealing with addictions. In alcoholic recovery, most say, being half sober is akin to being "kinda pregnant." In this sense Matthew's use of *first* is unique here among all the gospels and is so exclusive that it carries the implication of "only."[41] An alcoholic must seek first sobriety; one drink can compromise it all.

What must be sought above all is God's reign and moral order of justice. *The* treasure, ultimately, is the reign of God. One shows evidence that the reign of God has become one's higher power through good deeds of justice.[42] Storing up heavenly treasure involves the promotion of justice. Thus Friedrich Hauck notes: "Jesus takes up the Jewish image and teaching that man should not assemble earthly and material things, but that he should do good actions by which the righteous lay up treasure in heaven (Mt 6:19–21; Mk 10:21 and par.; Lk 12:33f)."[43]

Matthew ends his presentation of the conflict between what I have interpreted as the addictive process and the process of wholeness with wisdom that has become a keystone in contemporary programs addressing addictions and codependency—*one day at a time*. "So do not worry about tomorrow, for tomorrow will bring worries of its own. Today's trouble is enough for today" (6:34).

Rather than living in the present, addicts and codependents obsessively worry about the future; they are preoccupied with controlling access to the objects of their addictive thinking, feeling, and acting. When our anxiety centers on insuring earthbound treasures as the objects of our addiction, control of those objects dominates our hearts. To keep his disciples from seeking control in this way, Matthew's Jesus urges them not to care for the next day, but to deepen their faith in the providential care of their heavenly Father, their higher power, who will give them their daily bread (6:11, 32).

The translation of Jesus' admonition, "Today's trouble is enough for today," does not adequately reveal how it addresses the basic problem of addiction—the lack of confidence in God to meet our desires. The opposite of this is found in freedom from want, which results when our life is oriented to having "enough" in God. Thus "enough," assuming the justice of 6:32, implies that people can be content with the goods allotted them by God's providence. God's daily provision suffices to meet our real needs.

PART II

INTERVENTION

At one time people in the helping professions believed addicts would not change unless a "bottoming out" took place in their lives. However, in time, they discovered that by intervening in the addict's life change was possible before the bottoming out took place.

When an intervention takes place, the addict is confronted with one piece of data after another pointing to the addiction. The cumulative effect reveals an addictive pattern which, hopefully, will lead the person to change.

In the following sections I have accumulated data that point to addictive thinking, feeling, and behaving in each of the four stories, especially in the church's story. My hope is that the presentation of data about present behavior will lead to an admission that the behavior is addictive.

CHAPTER THREE

The Story

Does the First Gospel Address the Addiction to Authority?

The previous chapter showed that, for symbolic interactionists, people act on shared meanings. Shared meanings create a "world of meaning" that constitutes the language of group life and organizations. This meaning-world is communicated to its members through a set of codes that determine human interaction. However, in living together humans experience problems of coordinating life and relationships. According to Barrington Moore, these problems of "social coordination" involve issues of authority, the way roles are defined (especially for women and men), and how resources are distributed.[1]

Moore's threefold issues for social order have their parallels in the first two of Malina's characteristics for first-century social interaction: power (authority), sexual status and/or roles, and religion. For Malina's first-century world as well as Moore's world (of any epoch), the principal problem for social coordination involves authority. Where will it lie? Who will exercise it? Over whom will it be expressed? Will others obey it or resist it? Why?

According to Moore, authority refers to the coordination and control of "the activities of a large number of people. It reaches into all spheres of social life and exists to some degree in all known societies, even in those primitive ones that lack regular chiefs."[2] Authority involves the recognized power and right to command, to enforce a code of living, to exact obedience, to decide and declare, to influence, and to judge.

41

Since all relationships among humans imply forms of authority—coercion, persuasion, education, control—it should be evident that Matthew's story, as well as all four "stories," had their own structures of authority. It affected the lives of individuals and households at all levels. Consequently, to grasp Matthew's approach to authority, first we need to consider the authority of Jesus in the context of his interaction with the authorities of his day.

The Authority of Jesus in Conflict With the Authorities

In Matthew's gospel, authority—from the Greek word *exousia*—is considered the source of Jesus' power and the basis of power in the church. As such, it represents the source of God's life (21:24, 27) and activity in Christ (7:29; 9:6; 21:23ff [4x]), the apostles (10:1), and the church (9:9; 28:18). In Matthew, authority also has an organizational nuance, referring to the recognized influence of someone over another or others (8:9). The former represents the source of grace; the latter the source of conflict and, we will try to show, the object of what appears to be addictive dynamics. A brief examination of their differences in Matthew is in order.

Exousia is used ten times in Matthew. It is part of the "all things" Jesus received from God (see 11:27), including the *exousia* to preach, to heal (9:6), and to teach (7:29), which Jesus shared with the apostles (10:1) and the church (9:9; 28:18). As the kind of human power over others (8:9), *exousia* serves four times as a basis of conflict between Jesus and "the chief priests and the elders of the people." In one particularly sharp exchange, they questioned Jesus in the Temple area regarding the source of his authority: "Jesus said to them, 'I will also ask you one question; if you tell me the answer, then I will also tell you by what *authority* I do these things. Did the baptism of John come from heaven, or was it from human origin?'...they answered Jesus, 'We do not know.' And he said to them, 'Neither will I tell you by what authority I am doing these things'" (21:24–27).

This conflict is a microcosm of the conflict over authority that Matthew threads throughout the first gospel. It is many-sided, involving Jesus and political leaders, Jesus and religious leaders, the religious leaders among themselves, Jesus and the leaders among his own disciples, those disciples among themselves, the Jews, and others. After Jesus' central role in situations of conflict, the Jewish leaders influence the plot of Matthew's story most.

In all fairness, not all the Jewish leaders were antagonistic toward Jesus.[3] Among the leaders of the Pharisees some would not have agreed with his condemnation.[4] After the fall of Jerusalem the Pharisees kept together a divided and conquered Jewish people. They gathered remnants of various groups and invoked the Jewish Law to unify them. As often happens, however, this positive development had a negative side: the Law became an end in itself for many. Those who interpreted the Law wielded—and sometimes abused—tremendous power. Tensions around that abuse seem revealed in Matthew.

At the time of Jesus the tentativeness of Rome's political authority mandated that Rome buttress its power through religion and the religious leaders. In the case of the Jews, religious-political-economic-cultural authority resided in various leaders in the community. Key among these were the chief priests, the Sadducees, the Pharisees, the scribes, and the elders. Because, in varying ways, all benefitted from Roman rule, each of these groups legitimated its dominant role. This was especially true of the Sanhedrin, the highest native governing body of the Jewish family. The Sanhedrin contained representatives of all the above-mentioned groups.

After the first Jewish rebellion (66–70 C.E.), the Sanhedrin ceased to exist. With its aristocratic members generally discredited, the authority-basis of the Jewish leadership was thrown into turmoil. The only group with some credibility was the Pharisees, who had been less identified with the upper classes and the Roman accomodationists than the other groups. The Pharisees gradually came to envision the Law as the unifier of a divided people; the households or families of Judaism would serve as loci for the most effective practice and transmission of Judaism. The mentors with the authority to interpret the Law would be the Pharisees.

It was not long before concentration of the power of interpretation in the hands of a few corrupted the Pharisee-controlled house-synagogues. Jamnian Pharisaism—itself a reaction against clerical corruption and founded on the highest ideals of establishing unity within the community—itself became institutionalized. The "seat of Moses" on which the scribes and Pharisees sat (23:2) referred to their authoritative position in the house-based synagogues. Instead of expounding on principles of justice, their self-serving casuistry obscured the message of the Law and the prophets (5:17–20; 12:7; 23:3). As he observed the dynamics in the house-synagogues "down the street," Matthew found parallels in his own house-churches.

Matthew wove the tensions between the early Christian house-churches and the synagogue households into his interpretation (written in the 80s or 90s) of the Jesus event, particularly Jesus' conflicts with the Jewish leaders. These conflicts may have been magnified to address Matthew's concerns about the abuse of authority he was finding repeated in the house-churches that were his audience. In fact, he may have projected onto the tradition of Jesus elements of his own house-churches' conflicts with Jewish leadership and/or internal leadership. Because some of the Pharisees had converted and joined Matthew's house-churches, and because leadership within these communities seemed to be taking on negative pharisaic attitudes, Matthew narrated the Jesus event to highlight Jesus' challenges to the abuse of authority.

According to Matthew's story, Jesus' authority at his birth challenged the existing political authority, which threatened Herod and all Jerusalem (2:1–12). It continued to his death, which was decided, in part, because of his alleged kingship over the Jews (27:11), a regency that would have made him Caesar's rival. Even the events surrounding his resurrection forced the authorities to develop an explanation to maintain their power positions (28:11–15).

According to Moore, systems of authority generally specify why persons holding authority have that status and how they obtain it or are maintained in it.[5] The Jewish leaders—the scribes, the Pharisees, the Sadducees, the elders, and the chief priests—held authority and had status.[6] They obtained their authority and status over a period of time. They maintained their authority because of the people's willingness to submit to them and Rome's political reasons to reinforce their form of social coordination.

Into the world of their authority Jesus came as a charismatic leader,[7] teaching with authority in a way that left the crowds spellbound (7:29). He healed bodies and forgave sins with authority (9:6), which drew more crowds. Matthew presents Jesus as someone seen as undermining the pattern of authority present in the existing social coordination (controlled by the Jewish leaders) with at least four challenges. Each of these put him in conflict with the leaders as he called for a reordering of 1) existing forms of table fellowship, 2) Torah and Temple; 3) the Sabbath to meet human needs; and 4) a new kind of more-collegial form of human interaction in the community.[8] These challenges show Jesus' form of authority (21:23–27) in direct conflict with the authority of the Jewish leaders (9:3, 11, 34; 12:2, 10, 15, 24–37, 38–45; 13:10–15; 16:1–4; 19:3; 21:12; 23:39; 26:27). As Kingsbury notes: "They rightly perceive that he stands as a moral threat to their authority and therefore to the religion and society based on that authority" (15:13; 21:43).[9]

Chapter 23 stands as Matthew's unique narration of Jesus' confrontation with the Jewish leaders in a litany of abuses unparalleled in any of the gospels. It ends with Jesus' lament that "Jerusalem" (the leaders) would not convert (23:37). With that he predicts its Temple's abandonment (the source of their power), leaves it, and becomes more specific about its destruction and the aftermath (23:38–28:1ff). However, having had conflicts building and peaking throughout the gospel, from the third prediction of his passion, death, and resurrection, Matthew shows how the conflict between Jesus and the leaders intensified to the point where he would "be handed over to the chief priests and scribes, and they will condemn him to death" in Jerusalem (20:18). Thus, every pericope from the beginning of the pilgrimage to Jerusalem, the center of authority, until the final diatribe against the leaders in Jerusalem's Temple, shows how this conflict around authority builds until Jesus finally silenced his opponents (22:46).

This section (with its parallels in Mark 10:32–34 and Luke 18:31–34) begins with Jesus going to Jerusalem. He predicts he will be delivered to the Jewish leaders for condemnation and to the Gentile leaders who will mock, scourge, and crucify him (20:17–19). Then, Matthew writes (with Mark 10:35–45), the mother of the sons of Zebedee came asking for positions of power in his kingdom. This generated conflict among his followers and Jesus' response about correct use of power (20:20–28):

> You know that the rulers of the Gentiles lord it over them, and their great ones are tyrants over them. It will not be so among you; but whoever wishes to be great among you must be your servant, and whoever wishes to be first among you must be your slave; just as the Son of man came not to be served but to serve, and to give his life as a ransom for many (20:25–28).

At this point all three synoptics tell the story of the healing of the blind. In Matthew 20:29–34 and Mark 10:46–52 there are two blind men; in Luke 18:35–43 there is one. One might wonder why this story would be included in stories related to conflict between Jesus and the leaders. In my mind it can only be understood when we recall that the leaders had eyes to see, but would not convert and follow Jesus (13:13–15), unlike the disciples who had eyes to see and would follow him (13:16–17). Asking that their eyes might be open, the "two blind men" had their eyes touched by Jesus. "Immediately they regained their sight and followed him" (20:29–34).

Following this passage Matthew adapted his material from Mark in chapter 21:1–46 to highlight the tension over the conflict about the notion of authority in 21:23–27. The chapter begins with Jesus ordering his disciples to go into a village to get an ass and a colt for the subsequent entry (in recognized authority) into Jerusalem (21:1–11). In the following pericope (21:12–16) Matthew rearranged the Markan material to have Jesus' "cleansing of the temple"—the center of the nation and cosmos—take place the same day as his authoritative entrance into Jerusalem. The city was the center of Jewish political, economic, religious, and cultural life. He leaves the city (21:17) and upon his return he sees a fig tree and curses it for not bearing fruit (21:18–19). Matthew's unique placement of this story at this point is parabolic. The leaders have not borne fruit and thus are to be rejected (21:18–22); they have questioned his authority in their blindness (21:23–27).

Building on these four pericopes (21:1–27), Matthew continues his conflict with authority theme with two parables. The first is the story of the man whose second son obeyed his command (21:28–32); the second tells about the householder (21:33–43 [44]) who leased his property (authority) to others who abused it and tried to appropriate it for themselves. The passage ends with Jesus declaring: "Therefore I tell you, the kingdom of God will be taken away from you and given to a people that produces the fruits of the kingdom" (21:43). The juxtaposition of these passages makes it clear that Matthew portrays the chief priests and the Pharisees directly challenged about their authority abuses. Personally confronted, the leaders tried to kill him: "When the chief priests and the Pharisees heard his parables, they realized that he was speaking about them. They wanted to arrest him, but they feared the crowds, because they regarded him as a prophet" (21:45–46).

Chapter 22 begins with the story of the wedding banquet, which again indicates a rejection of those originally invited (22:1–10) as well as a rejection of the new members of the table who abuse their position (22:11–14), quite possibly applied to Matthew's present situation in his house-churches. "Then," he concludes again, "the Pharisees went and plotted to entrap him in what he said" (22:15). The rest of the chapter has a triad of challenges by three different groups of leaders, all challenging his teaching authority by beginning with a term of honor ("teacher") which, in fact, is used by Matthew as a sign of insincerity. First the Pharisees "sent their disciples to him, along with the Herodians" (22:16–22). Then, that "same day, Sadducees came to him" with their challenge (22:23–32). Jesus' response about marriage left the crowd "astounded at his teaching" (22:33), but when "the Pharisees heard that he had silenced the Sadducees, they gathered together" to challenge Jesus about the greatest commandment in the Law (22:35–36). Responding to them with his twofold command of love (22:37–40), Jesus responded to their questions with his own challenge about "David by the Spirit [who] calls him Lord" (22:41–44). The example revealed David's true approach to authority in contrast to their own abusive ways. With David, a human authority was willing to submit to a higher power; the leaders were not. "No one was able to give him an answer, nor from that day did any one dare to ask him any more questions" (22:46). Having silenced his opponents, Matthew now has Jesus enter into the diatribe against the leaders for one abuse of authority after another, ending with his leaving the Temple, the seat of their authority (23:1–24:2).[10]

From the beginning to the end of Matthew's gospel, but especially with this section (20:17–24:2), it becomes clear that the underlying reason for the death of Jesus is the unwillingness of the leaders to submit to his authority. All conflicts with him are predicated on the basis that the leaders were obsessed with maintaining their position, were threatened by Jesus' authority, and, finally, had to destroy him in order to maintain their supply of authority.

Conflict over authority constitutes the underlying issues related to social coordination throughout Matthew's gospel. I have shown that this underlying conflict revolved around different authority codes. With the assistance of the social sciences, Bruce Malina and Jerome Neyrey have shown that "*conflict* is the stuff of this gospel." They add:

> From start to finish, the whole gospel is one extended ac-
> count of Jesus' conflicts, from the genealogy in chapter 1
> that legitimates Jesus' familial standing as one of honor,
> to Herod's quest for the life of the child in chapter 2, to
> the battle between Jesus and Satan in chapter 4, to Jesus'
> fight with the Pharisees in chapter 12, eventually to his
> confrontation with the chief priests in chapters 21–27.[11]

Having had this all-too-brief excursus into Matthew's gospel to
discover that its underlying dynamics revolve around authority conflicts, we can now ask whether or not, using twentieth-century imagery,
this obsession of the leaders with keeping control of their authority
can be called addictive.

Does Matthew's Story Reveal Patterns of Authority Addiction in the Leaders?

Returning to our definition of addiction and its dynamics in Matthew, we can ask if Matthew's gospel reveals that the leaders of the
Jews (and, by projection, the leaders of Matthew's house-churches)
evidence addiction and, if so, was their addiction to authority? To
determine this a quick review of our terminology is in order.

Addiction represents any obsessive thinking, feeling, and acting
around maintaining control of the object of the addiction. Matthew's
portrayal of the leaders reveals a progressive pattern of conflict with
Jesus and his authority, which the authorities, in their obsession with
keeping control over him (and all others), saw as a threat to their position (their "supply"). Unwilling to admit their problem, they denied
it and sought to protect their supply. They developed an increasingly
secretive and obsessive pattern of behavior geared to ensure the preservation of that which had come to control their lives. Although they
had eyes to see and ears to hear, they were not able to convert because of the depth of their disease. When the final challenge came
they were so threatened by a possible loss of their authority that they
killed in order to keep their position. In the process, Matthew shows,
they destroyed themselves and their institution.

Furthermore, this chapter has shown that Jesus' teaching and healing, as manifestations of God's *exousia*, threatened the authority of
the leaders. While Jesus' teaching with *exousia* drew more and more
crowds and increasingly made them distinguish between Jesus' authority and that of "their scribes" (7:29), it was the symbolic way

Matthew portrays Jesus' healing with *exousia* that truly reveals Jesus as the one intervening to reorder a disordered social system.

Anthropologists have shown that sicknesses we call "diseases" today, with our concerns for causes and symptoms, the first century considered "illnesses" that reflected more deeply some social dysfunctioning that needed reordering. For instance, leprosy—the first illness that Matthew's Jesus "cleansed" (8:1–4)—culturally represented a condition that threatened communal integrity and holiness; it thus demanded separation from the community. According to John Pilch, this social meaning of sickness in the First Testament must be understood if we are to grasp the fuller significance of Jesus as a healer.[12] Jesus approached such disorder with the goal of healing an illness rooted in disordered familial and social relationships more than curing people physically afflicted.

Today, while addiction etiologists argue whether or not it is a disease, none disagree that addiction is an illness that affects social relationships. From this perspective, Matthew's Jesus' intervention of healing stands against the social illness that pervaded the leaders of the system around him. In a special way the disease of blindness that controlled the leadership group was contrasted with the recovery that resulted in discipleship for those who were willing to acknowledge the higher power of Jesus' mercy (8:27–34; 20:29–34).

If addiction represents a repeated and progressive pattern of compulsive behavior that cannot be stopped and which leads to one's own destruction, the way authority came to dominate the thinking, passions, and decisions of the leaders indicates that, indeed, Matthew's story does reveal an underlying addiction to authority among the Jewish leaders. Jesus' effort at an intervention failed (23:37); he thus established an alternative group grounded in *his* authority (28:18), which would share in his authority and try to walk converted to his teachings. Within this new group his authority would be shared in two ways that would definitely bind people or loose them. However, we will now see how the seeds of conflict were sown for the new community by these two different manifestations of authority in the church.

Two Approaches to Authority in the Church: 16:19 and 18:18

Without elaborating further on the many passages that reveal the escalation of tensions between Jesus and the leaders, I want to highlight three critical passages around power and authority, which

Matthew places in his fourth book.[13] The first passage begins by
saying:

> Pharisees and scribes came to Jesus from Jerusalem [the
> seat of authority] and said, "Why do your disciples break
> the tradition of the elders? For they do not wash their hands
> before they eat." He answered them, "And why do you
> break the commandment of God for the sake of your tradi-
> tion?" (15:1–3).

He immediately rebukes the leaders' abuse of authority by their
sanctioning the transfer of money, originally intended for the care
of parents, to support the Temple—and the leaders as well (15:4–5).
Rejecting such an interpretation of the Law, Matthew's Jesus declares,
"So, for the sake of your tradition, you make void the word of God"
(15:6). This misinterpretation, which reinforced their own position but
misled the people, made the leaders "hypocrites" (15:7) and "blind
guides" (15:14) with corrupt hearts (see 15:18).

These shaming images indicate the first gospel's central insight
about the leaders: They seemed to support traditions that perpetuated
dysfunctional relationships and kept people from the resources they
needed. In the process God's word could be nullified to ensure the
leaders' positions of power. The conflict Matthew's Jesus had with
such abuse of power is good to keep in mind when considering the
other two passages I want to highlight from the fourth book: 16:19
and 18:18. Both address the power of binding and loosing. In the first
it is given to Peter; in the second it is promised to the members of the
church themselves. Considered in light of 15:1–20, these two passages
involve the core issue addressed in this book: *When, for the sake of
tradition, Peter's power to bind and loose is absolutized in a way that
subordinates the power of the other members of the church, the word of
God itself can be nullified in order to preserve abusive power patterns
in the institutional church.*

The passage on Peter's confession of faith (16:12–20) is preceded
by a warning about the leaven (the false teaching) of the Pharisees
and Sadducees (16:5–11). Adapting Mark, Matthew has Jesus ask,
"Who do people say that the Son of Man is?" (16:13). After various
replies he asks the disciples, "But who do you say that I am?" (16:15).
When Simon replies, "You are the Messiah, the Son of the living God"
(16:16), Matthew alone has Jesus respond:

Blessed are you, Simon son of Jonah! For flesh and blood has not revealed this to you, but my Father in heaven. And I tell you, you are Peter, and on this rock I will build my church, and the gates of Hades will not prevail against it. I will give you [*singular*] the keys of the kingdom of heaven, and whatever you [*singular*] bind on earth shall be bound in heaven, and whatever you [*singular*] loose on earth shall be loosed in heaven (16:17–19).

This passage represents the theoretical context for what I call the *church of Matthew 16*, a model of authority expressed in the contemporary hierarchical church, a model becoming increasingly absolutized in Latin Rite Catholicism.

The parallel passage describing what will be called the *church of Matthew 18* is found in the discourse addressing disorder in the church (17:34–19:1) and the need for an alternative model of community based on affirmation (18:12–14) and correction (18:15–19). Where the power to bind and loose is given to Peter in 16:19, the exact same magisterial and jurisdictional power to bind and loose is given by Jesus to the church itself in 18:18: "Truly I tell you [*plural*], whatever you [*plural*] bind on earth will be bound in heaven, and whatever you [*plural*] loose on earth will be loosed in heaven."

Matthew 16:19 reinforces a hierarchical principle of authority in the church, while 18:18 grounds authoritative binding and loosing in a collegial principle. Taking Matthew's fourth book as a whole, you cannot have the exercise of authority in 16:19 apart from its expression in the church of 18:18. Conversely, you cannot have authority in Matthew 18:18 divorced from that in Matthew 16:19. These passages are equal parts of the story and have been part of the church's story since the beginning.

The next chapter will show how it evolved that the institutional leaders of the church tended to stress Matthew 16 to the diluting, if not outright negation of the other. The former text has been reinforced ideologically to justify a unilateral expression of authority that might not be grounded in the scriptures but has become ensured by years of tradition. Thus, for the sake of tradition, some weightier things are being left undone (23:23)—especially right judgment in the church on the issue of authority itself.

The normalization of hierarchical authority to the detriment of greater collegiality became clearer to me when I addressed a gathering of diocesan personnel with their bishop on the issue of addiction and authority in the Catholic church. When I asked for comments, the bishop asked me to clarify what I meant by "church." I indicated that "the church of Matthew 16" represented the hierarchical church, especially the papacy and its curial support system, then the bishops *as a body*, including, to a lesser but no less real degree, the local clergy. He objected, saying that not all bishops agree with the pope and Curia on such issues as women priests, married priests, and remarried divorcees.

I responded that my experience verified his comments. However, I added that, while individual bishops may differ privately on such positions, they perpetuate an addictive system by publicly presenting (like the body of Jewish leaders at Jesus' time) a united front supporting the Roman opinion. Despite individual differences (as with various leaders at Jesus' time) the bishops as a body may disagree significantly but keep silent for various reasons from fear of higher authorities to peer pressure. Exceptions exist among bishops such as Raymond Hunthausen, Remi DeRoo, Rembert Weakland, and Kenneth Untener.

To further specify what I meant, I compared data about the churches of Matthew 16 and 18 as I described them. As of 1985 sixty-eight percent of Matthew 18 favored birth control, one hundred percent of Matthew 16 opposed it; fifty-two percent of Matthew 18 supported women priests, one hundred percent of Matthew 16 rejected the notion; sixty-three percent of Matthew 18 favored married priests, one-hundred percent of Matthew 16 opposed the idea; seventy-three percent of Matthew 18 supported remarriage after divorce, while one hundred percent of Matthew 16 opposed it.[14]

While morality cannot be based on opinion polls, neither can it be non-representative of those in whose name some define it. I noted that such a united front by the body of bishops indicated a behavior among the hierarchy not that different from the leaders in Jesus' day. It seemed that while my questioner may have been one of those bishops who disagreed—privately—he became part of the body of the one hundred percent by his public silence. Although he didn't disagree with my explanation, a day or so after I left the diocese, the bishop told a diocesan meeting that I had done "the church a great disservice" by not defining more clearly what I meant by church. In case there may still be misunderstanding, chapter five will trace how the church of Matthew 16 came to dominate.

CHAPTER FOUR

The Culture's Story
Examining Mammon Addiction in the United States

The All-Pervasiveness of Addictive Processes

This chapter will examine more deeply the "culture's story" from the perspective of addiction. Just as an individual's unhealthy narcissism may get expressed in individualism in an addictive way, so "isms"—consumerism, militarism, sexism, racism, perfectionism, workaholism—in our society reveal addictive patterns, which shape our mind-sets, the ethos of our political and economic institutions, and the national ideology.

Examples showing that addiction and codependency are becoming increasingly identified as cultural characteristics abound. Such addictions are even being exploited by advertisers.

> A 1990 advertisement for Konica copiers and fax machines brags, "Workaholism Runs in Our Family."

> A full-page ad in the Minneapolis Star Tribune (1989) for Gaviidae Common ("If you love shopping you've got a complex") showed the doors of forty-two stores under the headline, "We have outlets for compulsive behavior."[1]

An addiction that increasingly characterizes our culture's story is the addiction to mammon itself. This addiction is attributable not just to individuals but to the society itself. One commentator describes the 1980s in the following way:

> Systems flawed by greed. Bankrupt morality. Skewed values.

It was a time of fast bucks and decency be damned;
a time when political appointees peddled their influence
like street vendors and the stock market was rigged like a
bad wrestling match. It was a time when men and women
boasted of their perjury and sneered at the rules, waved the
flag and thumped the Bible with one hand and stole from
the national treasury with the other.

From the stock exchanges of New York to the futures
pits of Chicago; from college campuses to Indian reserva-
tions; from the White House and the federal bureaucracy to
the defense industry assembly lines, ethics in America in
the 1980s took a bigger beating than Grenada, OPEC and
the Berlin Wall combined.

Avarice and corruption and sleaze surrounded the decade like swamp gas and the experts who try to fathom such
human oddities are uncertain if the worst has passed.[2]

Two years before the crash of 1987 a *Business Week* cover feature
stated that the United States had evolved into "a nation obsessively
devoted to high-stakes financial maneuvering as a shortcut to wealth."
It went on to warn, "Only when fear overcomes greed will the casino
society rein itself in. The question nagging all concerned is how big a
jolt is needed to alter the seductive calculus of speculation."[3] When the
crash took place two years later, calls for conversion echoed across the
land, but because the obsession with "more" continued to echo more
strongly, the addiction continued. The same calls about changing "the
system" were generated when the stock market plunged 191 points
two years later. But the pattern continued.

When the Iraqis invaded Kuwait, threatening to control the nation's oil supply, it was once again "our way of life" that was threatened. As social critic Russell Baker wrote,

We are all hostages now, and by our own consent. It is our
addiction to imported oil that has undone us. "Just say no,"
Nancy Reagan used to advise the young tempted by drugs.
Neither her husband nor anyone else of public consequence
dared issue the same good advice to a vast public of all ages
that was hopelessly hooked on oil.[4]

Greed and "being given over to mammon" reached new highs—or
lows—when Procter & Gamble was accused of trying to manipulate

and control the "Just Say No" campaign itself in order to enhance corporate profits. After the corporation contributed $150,000 to the "Just Say No" foundation, it claimed an exclusive right among packaged goods firms to send ads and coupons for its products to children along with anti-drug pledge cards.[5]

The tendency to judge people by what they own gets dictated by social norms and (un)written rules from infancy, gets reinforced in childhood, and dominates the adolescent processes. If one doesn't wear certain clothes, drive certain cars, or go to certain malls, one gets shamed. On the other hand, having money ensures honor. Anxiety—fear of being "without"—has become a component of materialism.

Anxiety is the emotional fuel that energizes addiction whether in individuals, groups, institutions, or society itself. Such anxiety drives our system. What is there about the system that creates and sustains such emotions? Since the "business of America is business," somehow we must not look to business managers only, but to the system itself, to find the source of our anxiety.

Today, United States business defines itself almost exclusively in terms of market share, short-term profits, and stock prices. Consequently human values such as workers' rights, adequate health care, and environmental health take second place to economic, money-based values. From the cradle children learn that the way to "be better" is to "do better"—and "doing better" means earning more money. These attitudes are now pandemic. In 1967 forty-four percent of college-age youth believed it "essential or very important to be very well-off financially"; in 1985 the percentage had jumped to seventy-one percent.[6] When young people are raised believing that getting ahead means adaptation to the money society they become its addicts. As Norman Lear writes:

> The notion that life has anything to do with succeeding at the level of doing one's best, or that some of life's richest rewards are not monetary, is lost to our kids in this short-term, bottom-line climate.[7]

When any one of the four "stories" we discussed earlier becomes absolutized, the other three become its servants. Thus, when money as part of the culture's story dominates, my story, the church's story, and even *the story*, become enslaved to it. For example, the church both here and elsewhere diminishes in influence as family income increases. Alan Riding writes of Spain:

> In a country that was long considered one of Europe's most Catholic nations, the prosperity that has followed the return of democracy here barely a decade ago has fed an extraordinary process of secularization that is rapidly eroding the church's traditional influence over society.
>
> Having lost its role as moral guardian and political arbiter of the nation's affairs, the Spanish church is experiencing a deep internal crisis as it struggles to find a new place for itself in a contemporary Spain seemingly more interested in mammon than God.[8]

Mammon-addiction has affected my story as well—more than I care admitting. Since 1973 I have subscribed to *The Wall Street Journal*. In the mid-1980s I decided to invest a few thousand "secure" dollars from twenty-five Midwest groups for whom I act as consultant in one-hundred shares of a certain stock. Within a month a tender offer was made and the stock showed a twenty percent increase. Instead of returning the monies to the money market they had come from, I bought other stocks. Each day I anxiously awaited the *Journal*. I started reading the market report first, actually feeling a kind of "high" as I turned to "my stocks." My "rush" was repeated each afternoon when the *San Francisco Examiner* came with the market reports as of 2:00 EST. When I realized that I had become addicted to my morning and afternoon stock market data, I decided to quit investing in stocks entirely.

The addictive dimension of money is well-articulated by Lewis H. Lapham, editor of *Harper's*:

> Unhappily for all concerned, the pathologies of wealth afflict the whole society, inhibiting the conduct of government as well as the expressions of art and literature. The rituals of worship produce deformations of character in institutions as well as individuals, in the making of third marriages as well as in the making of laws and Broadway musicals. It isn't money itself that causes the trouble, but the use of money as votive offering and pagan ornament.[9]

Lapham's comments about the cultural addiction or "pathology of wealth" inhibiting the conduct of government are reinforced daily in the media. In 1989 and 1990 revelations were made of multi-billion dollar waste, mismanagement, and fraud in the Federal Housing Administration which helped the rich at the expense of the poor. At the same time United States taxpayers were told it would cost every one of them at least two thousand dollars to make up for the looting of the country's savings and loan industry.

When money and avarice dominate economic and political decisions, corruption is not far behind. Felix G. Rohatyn states that

> greed and corruption are the cancer of a free society. They are a cancer because they erode our value system. They create contempt for many of our institutions as a result of the corrupt actions of individuals. The continuity of institutions is too important to be sacrificed to the unfettered greed of individuals. I have been in business for almost 40 years and I cannot recall a period in which greed and corruption appeared as prevalent as they are today.[10]

In spite of the outcries of business people, congressional legislation for ethics, and consumers' and citizens' mistrust of business people and elected officials and demands for change, the same addictive dynamics continue. Not only have they continued, as in any addictive process, they seem to have gotten worse. Harry Schwartz, a member of *The New York Times* editorial board, concludes that conditions in the system "that permit such problems to persist are fundamentally more corrupt" than anything individuals do. Thus "an institutional problem can only be solved by institutional change."[11]

Classism, Racism, and Sexism

A *Business Week* article published in 1989 noted that the pursuit of economic well-being has conferred enormous wealth on America and many of its citizens, yet left a great many behind:

> The family income statistics for the U.S. in the 1980s tell a disturbing tale. In 1987, the last year for which data are available, the richest 5% of American families captured fully 16.9% of the aggregate income in the U.S. That's a bigger pot than in 1979, when that group earned 15.8%, or in 1969, when they took a 15.6% share of aggregate income. By contrast, the poorest fifth of American families—a group

four times the size of the richest group just described—
earned 4.6% of national income in 1987, down from 5.2%
in 1979 and 5.6% in 1969.[12]

Within the increasing division between classes, the income of
black people as a whole has also decreased relative to whites. In
addition, even when blacks "play by the rules," the system is stacked
against them. In the twenty years ending in 1989 their real income
fell by one third and their chances of getting into or staying in the
middle class fell by half. At a time when the nation's economy was at
its peak and unemployment rates were dropping, blacks in the United
States at all levels lost economic ground at a precipitous rate.

The situation for women is not that dissimilar. Though women
are closing the gap somewhat, a 1987 Census Bureau study showed
that women in comparable jobs still earn only sixty-eight percent of
men's salaries. In the service sector, where many women work, there
seems to be little incentive to invest in new technology or labor-
saving work methods that boost productivity. The reason? Instead of
substituting capital for labor, as many European employers have done,
more women are hired. Furthermore, there is an "invisible barrier that
blocks [women] from the top jobs."[13] At the same time women at the
other end of the spectrum, living in poverty, face the "feminization of
poverty." In 1988 over one-third of the poor lived in female-headed
families.[14]

One can only conclude that within the classist system of the United
States, racism and sexism dominate. The addictive system is a classist
system, and the classist system has race and sex demarcations as its
characteristics. Thus Anne Wilson Schaef concludes that "the Addictive System and the White Male System are one and the same." She
writes,

The power and influence in it [the Addictive System] are
held by white males, and it is perpetuated by white males
—with the help of all of us. As the prevailing system
within our culture, it runs our government, our courts, our
churches, our schools, our economy, and our society. I want
to emphasize here that I am not talking about individuals.
I am talking about a system that all of us have learned and
in which we all participate. There are as many White-Male
System women as there are men operating in our culture
today. I am talking about a system, a worldview.[15]

Cultural Imperialism and Militarism

Besides affecting "isms" related to class, sex, and race, the culture's story needs to be promoted and protected. This is where our society's addiction to cultural imperialism and militarism becomes quite evident. Society's "shame button," which we call patriotism, demands our silence in face of actions that we condemn with justification when performed by other nations. For example, Iraq's invasion of Kuwait (ruled by an undemocratic authority) was oppression, but the United States invasion of Panama (ruled by an undemocratic authority) was liberation.

For the first ninety years of the twentieth century the military-industrial-governmental complex was justified because of the threat of various foreign nations. Then the bomb became the deterrent to ensure the supply we needed to maintain our addictive way of life. Company after company lobbied Congress in the name of patriotism and made contributions to the Political Action Committees in the name of promoting democracy. Yet they profited through fraud, cost overruns, and inflated prices; the nation's addiction to armaments continued as the companies' addiction to profits was insured. As alcoholics are dependent on their booze to ensure their security, so the nation became dependent on the bomb. To defend its addiction, the ideology-makers created a new rationale for maintaining a supply, even when the Cold War ended. According to Richard Barnet:

> There appears to be *no* conditions, not even the disappearance of the USSR, under which it would be safe to give up our dependence on the Bomb. It used to be said that it was the "closed society" in the Soviet Union that made it necessary to clutch the Bomb. Or it was the nature of the Soviet system. The fact that society, ideology, and policy in nations long proclaimed as enemies are rapidly changing appears to have no perceptible effect on nuclear policy, except to encourage the search for new enemies. Now it is suggested that "instability" and "revolution" in the Third World make appropriate targets for the "discriminate" use of nuclear weapons. Having taught India, Pakistan, Israel, South Africa and others that no nation can be truly safe without the Bomb, the nuclear powers are beginning to use nuclear proliferation as the prime argument against disarmament.[16]

Possibly the present economic system in the United States needs more and more weapons as much as any other addict needs a fix.

Workaholism

A couple of years ago I was lecturing in a city where a confrere was in a recovery program for compulsive gamblers. I called him and asked how his program was going. After talking about it he asked me, "And how's your workaholism going, Mike?" Immediately I responded, "Oh, I'm not a workaholic; I've taken those tests in the newspapers and I always pass." Since then I have realized that I was in denial about my work-addiction.

Workaholism affects thinking, feeling, and behaving because it reflects the addictive process—with work as the addiction. The workaholic's mind rarely leaves the job, feelings (especially anxiety) revolve around issues of stability and success related to the work, and behavior indicates the consuming influence of work over other values. The roots of work-addiction stem not only from the desire for more money; they lie deep within the individual's psyche as well. It may be a flight from anxiety or a form of escapism from domestic problems. Adult children of addicts may have a high need for control and be obsessive about making sure all details are right; they also must remain in control of others. Those with low self-esteem (possibly because of shame-based childhood experiences) might be motivated to work more and harder if they think it will give them feelings of self-esteem. In the process of workaholism bodies break down more rapidly—another example of how addictions lead to death. Yet honor comes to those who overwork, while shame befalls those who choose other values. A person who chooses to attend a child's high school performance rather than spending more time at a work-related function for the company is not likely to receive "honor" for the choice. One is honored and rewarded, rather, for making business work the most important object of one's affections.

Because work, for many, has become a god, workaholism becomes their worship. The result, like any addiction, is loss of spiritual values. The greater the workaholism, the less one's spirituality. According to Schaef and Fassel, workaholism not only has become the norm in people's lives, but addictive organizations—from the corporation to the church—promote workaholism as a value.[17] Workaholism as a value has supplanted spirituality.

For the addictive organization under the control of mammon, work becomes but one more commodity; people become "given over to" work as a means to the end of making more money or having more power. In the process they themselves become commodities in the addictive organization. First, they become commodities in the wheel of production and then, as market shares, they approach work intending to buy more commodities and/or symbols to manifest to others their significance.

Given the way work is promoted ideologically to make workaholism normative and given its religious overtones ("Idleness is the devil's workshop"), perhaps it would be wiser to change the term workaholism (which does not have a pejorative meaning like alcoholism or drug addiction) to work addiction. The change in terminology might lead to an admission of the deleterious effects of work addiction on persons and their relationships.

If the culture's story raises workaholism to a form of heroic virtue, the church's story often canonizes it—especially if the work is freely given to the institutional church. Fassel and Schaef report that the church actually promotes work addiction. They note: "Theologically and in practice, the church puts before us the picture of the good Christian as one who works hard. The good martyr is the typical codependent who works selflessly for others and never attends to his or her own needs. We have heard of 'designer drugs'; workaholism may be the designer drug for the church as well as for the corporation."[18]

Given the decreasing numbers of priests, the need to generate more output from those available results in even faster burnout and low morale. The number one cause of the problem of morale among priests in the United States, according to the Bishops' Committee on Priestly Life and Ministry, is the role expectation, which leaves "many feeling trapped, overworked, frustrated and with the sense of little or no time for themselves." Further, "the continuing shortage of clergy casts its shadow on both present ministry and future hope. Official directives which focus on duties 'only the priest can do' tend to increase the workload and make for less effective ministry."[19]

When Mammon Becomes Normative

In the culture's story, where workaholism has become normative and a badge of honor, one can see how shamed people feel when they cannot find a job. This is one of the most negative aspects of our political economy. To work is an honor; to be out of work is shameful. It isn't surprising, then, that violence increases in unemployed families as do suicides among those out of work. If work is the entryway into the culture of mammon, workaholism becomes as addictive as consumerism itself. The two are, by definition, cross-addictions in mammon-based societies. When addiction becomes normal, healthy behavior gets criticized. When the addictive process dominates a system, the body-politic begins to corrupt.

If the United States of America will be destroyed it seems it need not come from any outside enemy. As Pogo says, "We have met the enemy, and they is us." We have entered the corruption; its death surrounds us. Even the classic restraint of religion seems to have lost its effect. A major reason for this is that, in the United States, by and large, the church's story has become the servant of the culture's story. Consequently the story about serving the least of the brothers and sisters becomes irrelevant as Catholics increase their wealth and work hours, getting more deeply caught in the nation's addictive disease. When the nation's Catholic hierarchy reminds the laity of their biblical heritage and republican values through pastoral letters—such as the ones on race, war and peace, and the economy—they remain unread and unenacted. A major reason why is explained in a cartoon showing a lonely bishop in a field saying to the pope, "The American flock was right behind me, but then we passed a shopping mall."[20]

The story of our past exploitation can often be forgotten as we enter more deeply into the political economy and reap its rewards. Unmindful of our past, we find it hard if not impossible to be in solidarity with those who are now where our ancestors once were. As part of a family that has become addictive, we, the children and grandchildren of immigrants, allow sexism and racism against the poor and new immigrants to go their addictive ways. Participation in such an addictive process numbs our memories. Yet the bishops remind us that, "as descendants of immigrants who came often as aliens to a strange land," we share similar stories: "The stories of our past remind us of the times when our church was a defender of the defenseless and a voice for the voiceless. Today as many Catholics achieve greater economic prosperity, we are tempted like the people of the Exodus to forget the powerless and the stranger in our midst."[21]

I consider the statement above the most pastorally significant insight of the first draft of the bishops' letter on the United States economy. It directly addresses the reality of a prosperity that becomes addictive so that eyes get blinded, ears go deaf, and hearts refuse to understand lest recovery take place. Yet in the final draft—the official version addressed to Catholics and public policymakers—that section no longer appears. What happened? Possibly the bishops lost their courage, fearing the loss of the flock, as both passed the shopping mall!

Addiction and the Environment

Despite protestations of concern about the greenhouse effect, global warming, and toxic wastes, the average United States citizen generates over three pounds of trash a day—a national total of roughly 158 million tons a year. Neither corporations nor consumers have indicated a willingness to accept increased prices for environmentally safe products or more taxes to address pollution.

Despite air, water, and land pollution, the addictive process of mammon's control dominates the whole environment, the global household family. As with all addictions, perhaps it will stop only when we realize our own lifestyle has made us "reach bottom." In the words of Pope John Paul II:

> Modern society will find no solution to the ecological problem unless it takes a serious look at its life style. In many parts of the world society is given to instant gratification and consumerism while remaining indifferent to the damage which these cause.... The seriousness of the ecological issue lays bare the depth of man's moral crisis.[22]

Given the addictive culture of procurement, it just may happen that our addictive lifestyle will destroy the earth and, in the process, destroy us. As we continue to debate acid rain and cleaning up oil spills, as we close freeways because of smog and move people from toxic waste dumped by corporations, our culture's story becomes the autobiography of an addict that, if not stopped, will destroy both self and others. There will remain only the lament from the story told long ago: "Therefore the land mourns and all who live in it languish, together with the wild animals and the birds of the air, even the fish of the sea are perishing" (Hos 4:3).

CHAPTER FIVE

The Church's Story 1
Examining Addiction in the Institutional Church

The church's story will cover three chapters. This chapter examines the historical processes that have led the institutional church to its current addiction to authority. It then specifies how this power addiction gets expressed in the addictive process geared to the preservation of the male, celibate, clerically controlling model of the church. Finally a family systems approach shows this addiction's presence not only at the systemic, institutional level among the church's hierarchy, but also in dioceses and at the congregational/parochial level. Consequently, many ministers in the church family incorporate addictive and/or codependent processes in their own thinking, feeling, and acting.

The next chapter applies Malina's model of closed systems based on honor and shame to the church and shows how power, sexual roles, and religion are organized within it. The chapter builds on the notion of church power as an obsession with the preservation of the male, celibate, clerically controlled model. It shows how individuals identify themselves with their roles and perceive any threat to their position as a threat to their person. It then outlines how this authoritarian model gets extended not only to the key areas in the church affecting thinking and behavior, but to areas that should have nothing to do with such an approach. The experience of the Roman Curia's effort to make my Capuchin Franciscan Order "clerical" will be used as a case study. Then, dealing with sexual roles, I will show how patriarchal clericalism not only increasingly alienates informed women in the church, but is attracting a much higher percentage of homosexual people and dependent personalities into the clerical caste. Finally, I will show how the "religion" of the Latin Rite of Roman Catholicism, which has resulted from this addiction, has become an insular, white, Western European phenomenon, which identifies its unspiritual behavior as religion.

These reflections lead to the final chapter dealing with the church's story. I will return to chapter 23 of Matthew, which can be read as a scathing critique of the present clericalization of the Catholic church by its institutional leaders. I will show how the scribes and Pharisees addressed by Matthew's Jesus in the gospel become, for us who must make the gospel come alive in the church, the church leaders who abuse their power by misinterpreting *the story*. From this foundation I will apply the "woes" addressed in chapter 23 to contemporary practices within the institutional church.

Centralizing Power in the Institutional Church

In chapter two I broadly sketched the tension related to authority in the church between the church of Matthew 16 and the church of Matthew 18—the more hierarchical model opposed to the more collegial approach to power and authority in the church. This chapter discusses the historical events that resulted in the domination of the former over the latter.

Once the "church" evolved after the dispersion from Jerusalem (Acts 8:1), its actual governance was not limited to "the Twelve." At the Council of Jerusalem (about 49 C.E.), different interpretations about governance are clearly evident. In the Acts of the Apostles it appears that opposing viewpoints about disciplinary matters and the Law were presented. While these were resolved by Peter and James, their decision resulted only after conferring with the others (Acts 15:1–29). Paul's version contrasts with the version in Acts. No mention is made of the hierarchical approach of Acts. Rather, the Letter to the Galatians details an impassioned debate among the council's members. The letter makes it clear that the council's conclusions were not handed down by Peter and James. Rather, after a full hearing of the various positions, the participants reached a kind of consensus (Gal 2:1–10).

While any tensions between the hierarchical church of Matthew 16 and the collegial church of Matthew 18 seem to have been balanced at the council, toward the end of the first century the seeds of clericalism were already being sown. Writing around the year 110, Ignatius of Antioch divided the clergy into grades: the bishop, the council of the presbyters, and the deacons. Members of the congregation were to agree with their bishop; however, the bishops were elected by the local churches. Despite the stratification, then, hierarchy in the community flowed from and was controlled by the collegial dimension.

With the rise of gnosticism a certain way of ecclesiastical thinking evolved which predicated a unique power to certain teachers who possessed esoteric knowledge of hidden mysteries, which they alone could interpret. At the same time, desiring to maintain orthodoxy, church structures became more institutionalized, evidencing a more clearly defined hierarchical organization. Yet, even though this increasingly hierarchical dimension is clear, the hierarchy itself remained controlled by the collegial dimension. Around 215 Hippolytus wrote that all elections of the hierarchy were to be within the context of the people.[1]

In 254 Cyprian of Carthage wrote that the people had the power to reject bishops they considered unworthy.[2] While grounding ultimate authority in the people, Cyprian also stressed the hierarchical dimension. From the argument he had with Stephan I in 255, his views about the bishop of Rome not having jurisdictional power or not possessing any infallible source of doctrine are clear; yet he acknowledged a primacy of place of the bishop of Rome in reference to local churches wherein local bishops presided. Cyprian insisted on the collectivity of bishops, within which a unique position of honor was accorded the bishop of Rome, an honor due to historical connections, not juridical power.

No evidence exists that Rome exploited the Matthew 16 text before the middle of the third century. The Roman church did try to exert its authority over other churches; however, its rationale for doing so had more to do with its political position in the empire. Furthermore, the whole church was too busy reacting to persecution to spend much time on internal, jurisdictional debates.

Persecutions in the first centuries resulted in mushrooming numbers of converts. As the church's population became overwhelming, issues of governance arose; the church needed some kind of structure to help it organize itself. From its inception its whole existence had been within an empire where hierarchy and patriarchy were normative for institutions. It is little wonder, then, that the model of patriarchy and hierarchy soon became the church's norm. The framework for the church's accommodation to the patterns of authority was established.

Increasingly the institutional church's structures mirrored the Roman legislative hierarchical mode. With the Edict of Milan under Constantine in 313, Christianity became legally secure. The emperor transferred various privileges to the Christian clergy (the first use of the term in this sense), exempting its members from the onerous and expensive task of compulsory public office in the towns, and in non-urban areas from paying district taxes. Thus began officially sanctioned class status between the state and church, with the secular underwriting the spiritual. With this, the power of the clergy over the laity received a legal foundation if not a theological base.

The justification for this undermining of the lay basis of the church involved a return to *the story* with a unique twist. Fourth-century writings show Matthew 16 being translated as Peter and the bishops with *their* local churches instead of the local churches with *their* bishops and Peter. The first three hundred years witnessed the church constituted more collegially as a Catholic assembly of local churches, who determined their leaders. The fourth century marked the beginning of a clerically controlled institutionalization of the church. The church was to be hierarchically centered around the papacy as the empire was centered around the emperor. However, the emperor and the empire had precedence.

When Constantine moved the seat of the empire to Constantinople, the emperors continued functioning very much like priest-kings. However, in the West this unloosed another dynamic. With that move the already existing tensions between the Eastern-based and the Western-based local churches increased. By 410, with the sack of Rome by Alaric, the Roman Empire in the West effectively lost its emperor and clerics stepped in to fill the authority lacuna. The cohesion needed for governance came through laws that further concentrated power and privileges around the priests. At the apex of this priestly class stood the bishop of Rome.

Eastern Emperor Justinian asserted Roman power in the West again, but the effort lasted briefly. With the civil authorities in disarray again, the clerical leaders once more filled the void. More and more bishops and popes assumed the functions of civil authorities, and clerics became the custodians of Roman law.

Because the state bestowed money and privilege on the clergy, many became quite wealthy. Responding to the resulting abuses, "evangelical" movements with the goal of a more communal life had taken reformers into the desert. There they reverted to collegial models of governance that reflected those in the early church; the college of members held the power and leaders were chosen from the college. Despite such efforts, the church of Matthew 16—the institutional church with its clericalization—was definitely on the ascendant. By the time of Pope Gelasius (492–496) the notion of papal primacy as a dominant civil force had developed into a full theoretical justification for clerical dominance. He insisted that civil and religious powers should be distinguished but added that, in various aspects, religious power dominated civil power. Naturally he claimed supreme religious power for himself and his office. With Gelasius, the term *pope* for the bishops of Rome became normative.

To maintain its position of dominance, clerical power needed secular reinforcement. In the year Gelasius died, church leaders sought to ensure this through another important link with the civil rulers. In Rheims the Frankish chief Chlodwech (Clovis) accepted baptism, along with thousands of his troops. With each of his successive conquests, his new faith was imposed on the defeated population by the clerics. Because of clerical control and dominance, the newly baptized began to view "church" with a locus of power more in Matthew 16 than Matthew 18.

The end of the sixth century and beginning of the seventh was dominated by Pope Gregory the Great (590–604). As de facto ruler of the lands of the former western Empire, especially central and northern Italy—which were dominated by various Germanic tribes—he tried to win over the "barbarians" to Christianity. He was successful in converting the Lombards. At the same time he worked to reform and educate the clergy, who were but a few degrees removed from illiteracy, including scriptural understanding.

At this time the addictive force of money and power had infiltrated the thinking, emotions, and behavior of a significant number of the clergy. This elicited many calls for clerical reform. While ecumenical councils tried to reform corruption in the clergy and the absolutizing tendencies of the papacy, their efforts seemed feeble. Clerics continued to create ways to maintain their positions and Roman popes played politics to ensure their increasing power.

By now the popes controlled much of the center and south of Italy, due in great part to the largesse of the Frankish king Pippin. Around 770 the Lombards made a move on that area. Adrian I (772–795) appealed to the son of Pippin, who had become king of the Franks in 768. Karl defeated them decisively in 774. By Christmas Day of 800, when Karl (known in England since Norman times as Charlemagne) was crowned emperor by Pope Leo III, a new era had begun. Christian control of society in the West was theoretically accomplished. The Christian kingdom-on-earth had arrived—but at a price. From this time until the latter part of the eleventh century the ultimate control of the kingdom would be with the secular arm, not the religious arm. Now "lay investiture" began in earnest. Many monarchs appointed bishops, giving enormous control over church affairs to secular rulers.

From 850–950 the Frankish empire went into rapid decline, with the clergy declining intellectually and morally with equal speed. The increasingly ignorant and incompetent clergy received part of their support from fees charged for the administration of the sacraments. This opened the way to multiple abuses and clerical corruption. But if the clergy was corrupt it was because, like a fish, the head had corrupted first. According to John Dwyer:

> Higher offices in the church often had huge benefices attached to them and this led to the practice of *simony*—the buying and selling of church offices. The initial investment might be high, but then one was assured of a regular income for life. Needless to say, this practice inflicted a number of bishops on the church who had no interest in preaching the gospel and whose lives were indistinguishable from those of other members of the nobility. Most of the Popes of the period were members of noble Roman families, for whom the papacy was a prize sought only for the prestige and wealth attached to it. These men lacked all concern for the universal church and they had no understanding of the role of the Bishop of Rome in promoting the unity of this church and in striving to spread and to deepen the faith.[3]

A classic case of papal politics, which made sure the chair of Peter stayed in the same family, was the way Alberic II (936–954) maneuvered so that his illegitimate son would follow Alberic's brother Sergius (John XI) on the papal throne. With John XI's death, the see of

Rome was occupied by Alberic's son, who took the name Pope John XII (d. 964). In 962 John XII crowned Otto I emperor in exchange for temporal control over most of Italy. In turn, John recognized imperial suzerainty over the papal states and agreed that future popes could not be consecrated unless they made an oath of fealty to the emperor as their overlord.

With the restoration of the Holy Roman Empire under Otto I and his successors, a better class of men tended to be appointed as bishops of Rome. These popes, in turn, made genuine efforts at reform; however, their individual efforts were stymied because clerical corruption had become endemic to the system. Indeed, clerical corruption would remain normative until the 1070s with Pope Gregory VII (1075–1083). With him and his successor Leo IX came the first serious, church-wide reform. Although codifying canon law to be centered "on the primacy of the Roman church,"[4] the reformers primarily directed their concerns to a small number of clerical abuses such as clerical marriage, lay investiture, and especially, simony.

The Gregorian reforms seemed to parallel and, indeed, might have been a partial response to another phenomenon taking place in the eleventh and twelfth centuries: the rise of money as a form of wealth. With the increase in social mobility and exchange among different sectors of society, a more fluid medium of exchange was needed. Money became the concrete way wealth could be transferred, and wealth ensured the authority of the class possessing it.

While social liquidity and the abstraction of power in institutions existed in some measure before the eleventh century, they came to constitute the "double leitmotif" of social history as well as what Alexander Murray calls the "psychological history" of the Middle Ages, especially the twelfth and thirteenth centuries. Among the various "mental habits," according to Murray, two were especially fundamental: "One was the habit of desiring more and more money, a habit which medieval theologians usually called avarice. The other was the habit of desiring that power and dignity which society concentrates in its institutions. Despite some confusion, this usually went under the name of ambition."[5]

As wealth and avarice increasingly dominated the secular sphere of society, power and ambition became pandemic in the religious sphere. In the last chapter we saw how wealth and greed characterize the addictive processes in the culture's story; now we can examine more closely how the addictive processes connected to power in the church's story came to be all-pervasive.

Increasing Papal Control and the Imposition of Clerical Celibacy

In the Middle Ages three abuses came to adversely dominate relationships in the church: clerical marriages, lay investiture, and simony. In some ways they were interrelated. Clerical marriage dissipated power into other families besides the papal family, diluting the latter's power. This erosion of papal power called for decisive action, which would have long-term results.

As with many religious reforms buttressed by invoking values to gain popular support for the imposition of the values of those in power, the effort to end lay investiture was argued in the name of collegiality. However, with clerics controlling the church, any collegial re-ordering proved short-lived. For all intents and purposes, the collegial character would be all but abolished with Gratian's *Decrees* (1140).

Gratian's *Decrees*, the forerunner to modern canon law, was an effort to achieve some degree of uniformity in the church. At the same time—probably unconsciously—its attitudes, laws, and practices also represented an even greater concentration of clerical control in the church. In one of the decrees dealing with the election of bishops Gratian wrote: "It is commanded that the people be summoned not to perform the election, but rather to give consent to the election. For election . . . belongs to priests, and the duty of the faithful people is to consent humbly."[6]

Another way of gaining papal control over church governance involved wresting control of church offices from clerics themselves. These were often passed within families; now they would be controlled hierarchically, ultimately resting in the pope himself. The imposition of celibacy on the clergy would also stop decisively the passing of benefices from father to son. Instead, the power to pass on clerical power would be in the hands of another family, that controlled by the bishops and the papacy.

Although attempts to encourage celibacy took place quite early in various local churches, the Council of Toledo in 633 decreed that clerics could marry only with their bishop's permission. Gradually the legislation around celibacy moved from declaring clerical marriages illicit to invalid. The Second Lateran Council of 1139 nullified any marriage attempted by a cleric. At the Fourth Lateran Council in

1215 celibacy became mandatory throughout the Western church. This decision, according to Delhaye, "is the earliest example of general legislation based on the papal authority of decretals and the collaboration between Rome and the bishops acting collectively."[7] The legislation was based on discipline rather than dogma.

Besides the call for a crusade, one of the main results of the Fourth Lateran Council, called by Innocent III (1198–1216), was the solidification of episcopal power and the absolutizing of papal control. While a good part of the rationale for celibacy involved the elimination of simony, this conciliar decree hardly ended simonious thinking and feeling. A new form of simony resulted; now, clerical power became the medium of exchange and the addictive object in the church instead of money. The papacy received privileges and powers from local princes and governments, who in turn were given the right to name clerics to offices. In the following centuries Catholic rulers regained much influence in episcopal appointment through the right of patronage. In varying degrees the practice still has remnants in concordats; in exchange for powers and privileges, the Vatican makes various promises.

By the twelfth century not even priests were allowed to have a hand in the three essential stages in the making of a bishop—election, confirmation, and consecration. Episcopal elections were left to the metropolitans of the various regions. However, even here, the papacy viewed such power of metropolitans as potentially conflictual with papal power. Thus an attempt was begun to limit their power as well. This was accomplished canonically through an interpretation of the law that enhanced the papal position and claims in episcopal confirmation. Again, the rationale was articulated around another value: the need to maintain church order and discipline. Canonists promoted a pyramidal model of the church with each lower rank humbly obeying the higher rank and the pope reigning at the pinnacle. The canonists held, "Just as the consent of the archbishop is necessary in the confirmation of the bishop . . . in the same way the consent of the supreme pontiff is needed in the confirmation of the archbishop."[8]

Despite Rome's increasing efforts to control the election of bishops, as late as 1829 popes appointed only a limited number of bishops outside the papal states. Two principal methods of choosing candidates for the episcopacy were election by cathedral chapters and royal or imperial patronage.[9]

With the loss of the papal states, however, and the Catholic expansion into non-European lands, Rome was finally able to get control of the nomination and selection of bishops throughout the world. When the Code of Canon Law appeared in 1917, it declared that the bishop of Rome "freely appoints" other bishops and that any right of others to appoint was but a concession.[10] At that time just about half the world's bishops were appointed by Rome. Today, Roman control of episcopal appointments in the Latin Rite is almost complete, and where local churches previously controlled elections, that power has been effectively undermined by the papacy of John Paul II.

Clerical Persecution of Deviation

Clerical control centered in papal domination resulted in the institution's clericalization in another way besides breaking lay investiture, simony, and clerical marriages. During the late tenth century the institutional church began to counter those ideas and behaviors it considered deviant. According to R. I. Moore, the eleventh and twelfth centuries witnessed what became a permanent change in Western society: the habituation of persecution. This notion of "deliberate and socially sanctioned violence began to be directed, *through established governmental, judicial and social institutions,* against groups of people defined by general characteristics such as race, religion or way of life; and that membership of such groups in itself became to be regarded as justifying these attacks."[11] In the name of uniformity of thinking, persecuting behaviors differing from the norm was now rationalized. The church dominated the persecution.

The four main groups to bear the brunt of the persecution were heretics, Jews, lepers, and any people perceived to be against civil and ecclesiastical interests. To a minor degree homosexuals and prostitutes were targets for persecution as well. Persecution of these groups was "justified" to such an extent that it became "normal" among the people.

The increase in persecution paralleled the papacy's effort to achieve hegemonic uniformity. The papal reforms of Gregory and his successors in the eleventh century reveal a struggle to impose Roman authority over local tradition. Among people used to local control, this papal imposition was considered heretical and radical; however, papal reformers considered them necessary to achieve uniformity. This uniformity would be aided by an ideology that would make the reforms "normal" and deviations from the norms "heresy." According to R. I. Moore:

> While the heretic was always accused of innovation, the greatest source of religious novelty in this period was the church itself, or to be precise the reforming church. Those who denied the necessity of infant baptism, of the sanctification of matrimony, or intercession for souls in purgatory, of regular attendance at Mass and confession to priests, were not rebelling against ancestral patterns of faith and practice. Whatever the theology of the matter, these were innovations in the daily life of the faithful that throughout the period under discussion and beyond were gradually being pressed upon the priesthood and its flocks by the episcopate, which was itself dragged slowly and painfully into line by a papacy captured for reform in the revolution of the eleventh century.[12]

Moore shows convincingly how, in the early Middle Ages as well as in the subsequent centuries, persecution—which began as a weapon in the competition for political influence—gradually was turned by the victors into an instrument for consolidating their power over society at large. Rather than arising from the people's concerns about correct interpretation, persecution at this time invariably revolved around an obsession with ensuring and maintaining clerical control. Not only did it become a "device to secure power in the hands of an emerging and corrupt clerical class,"[13] it also revealed an attempt to undermine any power the community itself would have in defining where deviation might lay. For instance, in noting four cases of heretics being burned because of popular action in the twelfth century—at Soissons in 1114, Liège in 1135, Cologne in 1143, and Liège again in 1145—a common factor can be found. All of them involved a conflict between popular jurisdiction, which had condemned the accused by traditional methods, and bishops or abbots, who wanted to ignore these verdicts and reserve the trials to ecclesiastical tribunals. According to Moore, "What was at stake on these occasions was not the question of heresy *per se*, but that of how and by whom it was to be dealt with."[14]

The persecution of deviation in the Catholic church was enshrined in the codes of the Council of Trent (1563), which conceived of hierarchical authority as domination and control. These notions continued to be written into subsequent canonical texts, including the 1917 Code

of Canon Law. Canon 335 of the 1917 Code envisioned the governing power of residential bishops as legislative, judicial, and *coercive*.
Canon 2214.2 of the Code quoted directly from the code of the Council of Trent, which noted that if a serious transgression gave rise to
the "need for the flogging cane, then is rigor to be tempered with
gentleness." While the new Code of Canon Law has eliminated the
flogging cane, it continues to include the coercive dimension as an
exercise of hierarchical control.

The term *clericalism* first appeared in reference to the institutional church in the nineteenth century. Before the French Revolution the clerical structure of the church depended on secular powers.
However, after the revolution a movement of Catholics known as
ultramontanist—that is, those "loyal" to Rome and its centralizing
tendencies—tried to secure church independence from the state in a
way that would increase papal authority and promote a clergy "loyal"
to Rome. The main instrument for this clericalization was education—
ensuring that the clergy would be more educated than the laity. If
clerical power could no longer be grounded in secular control, it might
be maintained through the force of ideas. Those fearing that this effort
at institutionalizing clerical power represented an effort to restore the
monarchy called it clericalism; in turn, these "deviants" were called
anticlerical.

With clericalism came increasingly a demand for obedience to the
defining powers of the pope. Loyalty to the hierarchically controlled
church, especially the "Holy See," was elevated to become normative
for Catholics. Disloyalty became the shame button branding any who
deviated in thinking, feeling, or behaving from that norm. Public shaming around the notion of disloyalty was used as a vehicle to ensure
orthodoxy and orthopraxy. In the United States creative bishops such
as John Carroll, who supported bishops elected by local clergy, and
John England, who developed a "general convention" of clergy and
laity, soon learned that such deviance was not acceptable to Rome.
They received little support from their brother bishops, who were
becoming increasingly tolerant of Roman intervention in the United
States church.

In 1863 two events took place that challenged the increasing ef-
forts at absolutizing papal prerogatives that characterized the reign of
Pope Pius IX (1846–78). A speech in Belgium defended the liberal
Catholicism of Lamennais, and another in Munich demanded Roman

respect for the right of Catholic theological faculties in the German universities to free research and discussion. A year later Pius IX issued a response in *Quanta Cura* or *The Syllabus of Errors*. This encyclical listed eighty of what Pius considered the most dangerous and serious errors of the day. It ended with another form of persecution—it condemned those who supported absolute freedom of religion and freedom of the press, as well as those who defended the notion that the pope should adapt to contemporary conditions. Despite an initial outcry, opposition soon became muted.

Next Pius IX called the First Vatican Council. On July 18, 1870, the *Constitution on the Infallible Teaching Authority of the Roman Pontiff* was approved by an overwhelming majority of the assembled bishops. Now, instead of physical persecution being the apparatus for clerical control, condemnations and efforts to ostracize would become the norm. Twenty-five United States bishops supported the definition. Archbishop Kenrick and Bishops Verot and Domenec were among fifty-five bishops who addressed a letter of opposition to Pius IX. They left Rome the night before the vote so as not to be shamed themselves or to embarrass the pope by casting negative votes. Only two bishops, including Edward Fitzgerald of Little Rock, voted no in the final tally. The outcome was a triumph for the ultramontanists.

While the key statement in *Pastor Aeternus* explains that a pope teaches infallibly when speaking *ex cathedra* ("from the chair") in a matter of faith or morals, there has been a tendency by the popes to extend their power beyond the chair to the entire body of church teaching. In 1987 Pope John Paul II declared that assent to the magisterium "constitutes the basic attitude of the believer and is an act of the will as well as of the mind" and that, in the area of church teaching, dissent is "unacceptable."[15] Dissent, according to such a view, represents deviation from the acceptable norm and, as such, becomes a sign of disloyalty. Instead of turning our minds and wills over to the power of God, they must be turned over to the magisterium. Such unquestioning assent now constitutes faith.

With Pope John Paul II, the obsession about the prerogatives of the church of Matthew 16—to the actual exclusion of *any* authority in the church of Matthew 18—has turned 180 degrees from the theology and practice of the early church. In February 1990 he told Brazilian bishops that the "people of God is not the holder of the authority inherent in apostolic succession, as if the episcopal ministry constitutes a form of popular delegation or is tied to this people in terms of duration or ways of acting." The ministry exercised by the bishops "is of divine origins," he added. "It does not need, therefore, to be ratified by anyone." Inverting this authority "runs the risk of subordinating, in a certain sense, the episcopal ministry, the faith and Christian life, into options made to the measure of humans."[16] For Pope John Paul II and the Curia, laity have options and opinions, theologians have conclusions and considered opinions, and the magisterium has divine assistance and truth.

Institutional Maintenance vs. Evangelical Mission

When sociologists study organizations they distinguish between the logic of mission and the logic of maintenance. The logic of mission considers an organization's goals and the way it functions to realize those goals. The logic of maintenance studies the way the organization seeks to perpetuate its interests. While both logics are essential for organizational survival, they often conflict. When this happens there exists a tendency, social scientists have discovered, to place more weight on the logic of maintenance than the logic of mission.

When an institution's self-interests begin to outweigh its goals, sociologists see such behavior as dysfunctional and, in the long run, undermining the well-being of the institution. The orientation of the organizational leaders becomes geared toward the institution's own reinforcement and perpetuation, even though this may disregard the goals and purposes for which it was founded. In other words, preservation of the institution precedes proclamation of the message.

Gregory Baum has investigated what happens when this insight of sociologists is applied to the Catholic church. He notes that, while its official teaching tends to be formulated in accordance with the logic of mission, "defensive, narrow and sometimes paranoid institutional concerns make church leaders speak out and act against principles that in fact belong to the church's official teaching." Baum finds that this is particularly obvious in *four* areas:

> The logic of maintenance, which demands that the church protect its international unity, often prompts the Vatican to disregard the principle of subsidiarity, a constitutive element of Catholic social teaching. Second, the logic of

maintenance, which demands that the church protect its internal cohesion, often prompts the Vatican and regional bishops to condemn class struggle in terms at odds with the new teaching on solidarity of and with the poor. Third, the logic of maintenance, which demands that the church protect the authority of the ecclesiastical government, often prompts the Vatican and regional bishops to speak out and act in a manner that contradicts the new teaching on human beings as subjects. And finally the logic of maintenance, which demands that the church protect its economic base, often prompts popes and bishops to manifest their solidarity with the powerful and affluent sector of society, at odds with the newly defined preferential option for the poor.[17]

Possibly the most blatant example of this "maintenance over mission" or "preservation preceding proclamation" approach can be found in the general tendency toward silence on the part of the papacy, Curia, and German bishops in the face of the Holocaust. Only when the latter realized that Hitler's regime was intent upon destroying the church as an institution did they begin to speak out, yet even these protests were accompanied by declarations of loyalty to the state. At this point, according to Guenter Lewy: "The Church's opposition was carefully circumscribed; it was rooted in her concern for her institutional interests rather than in a belief in freedom and justice for all men. In this the German episcopate followed a policy very much in keeping with the church's traditional mode of operation and thought."[18] Lewy's analysis seems to bear out, at least in this case, sociologist Sidney Hook's contention that "in any crucial situation, the behavior of the Catholic church may be more reliably predicted by reference to its concrete interests as a political organization than by reference to its timeless dogmas."[19] When one must maintain the supply, other values can be sacrificed; maintenance undermines mission.

Patriarchal Clericalism: The Core Addiction in the Institutional Church

According to another sociologist, F. X. Kaufmann, many of the organizational principles that guided the church as a movement have been rigidified and sacralized the more bureaucratic the institutional church has become. In the process of this "normalization," the church has become institutionally blind to the addictive side of its organizational life.[20]

An organizational "blind," in addiction terms, refers to the denial that keeps addictive processes at work in the addict. In Matthean terms, organizational blind refers to those who have eyes to see, ears to hear, and hearts to understand, who refuse to deal with reality lest conversion take place (13:14–15). Sociologically, it keeps an organization from facing the shadow side of its behavior.

John Coleman, S.J., has noted that political scientists often refer to actions of governments under the rubric of *raison d'etat*, the intractable self-interest of states in conducting a foreign policy, the action consequences of protecting state sovereignty, and the bottom-line organizational imperatives of the state. As a sociologist of religion, Coleman has asked if the same notion might not be used to discover the "*raison d'eglise*, the organizational imperatives of a church, its bottom-line, non-negotiable interests and institutional purposes."[21] According to Coleman, "the hierarchical principle in world Catholicism is the first and strongest nonnegotiable institutional interest of the church. The Vatican will risk polarizing and splitting national churches, gutting their momentum and innovation, rather than yield power over episcopal appointments."[22]

Building on the historical development treated thus far as well as the sociological material above, it is clear that the hierarchical principle is fundamental to the maintenance of the Catholic church and, indeed, the preservation of its very mission and proclamation. This institutional preoccupation revolves around the obsessive thinking, passionate feelings, and addictive behaviors of key leaders in the Catholic church with the insurance of a certain addictive process: *the preservation of the male, celibate, clerically controlled model of the church.* Clerical control dominates Catholicism's hierarchical and organizational operations; maleness and celibacy are clericalism's secondary manifestations.

At this point I want to be clear about who is involved in the disease I call addictive patriarchal clerical control that is debilitating the body of Christ in its Catholic, institutional form. Primarily I include the key actors and activities affecting the whole church's life that emanate from Rome. More specifically, I refer to the papacy with its curial extensions, which affect the institutional church's external dealings (Secretariat of State), and its internal affairs, which affect the way people think (Congregation for the Doctrine of Faith) and worship (Congregation for Divine Worship and Sacraments), how clerical power is maintained (Congregations for Bishops, Clergy, and Seminaries and Institutes of Study), and how that clerical power tries to seep into other key entities in the church (such as the Congregation for Institutes of Consecrated Life and Societies of Apostolic Life [CICLSAL]). In a lesser but no less significant role (especially since it comes closer to the actual experience of church), I refer to the bishops as a body, and clerics (like myself) in our local situations. While some curial congregations possibly may be free of the addiction to clericalism itself, and while there may be some exceptionally collegial and pastoral bishops, and many, many priests who are deeply holy as well as deeply committed to a more collegial model of church, all of us, as clerics, are part of the system because of our sworn obedience and loyalty to the key actors.

While supported by the hierarchical body as well as other codependent Catholics, the heart of the addiction and the "identified patient" resides in the papacy and the Curia. My hypothesis that these are obsessed with the preservation of the male, celibate, clerically controlled model, must be tested. One must look at the consistent ways of thinking and operating by the papacy and the Curia. This can be done by reflecting on their interventions (for and against) as well as their statements.

The Vatican has acted decisively and consistently against any local church, bishop, or theologian whom it perceives as undermining its authority (from Holland to Hunthausen and Cathedral Chapters to Curran). It has actively supported and rewarded those groups and bishops who promote papal interests and issues (from CELAM [under the dominance of the Columbian hierarchy] and Opus Dei to Cardinal Lopes Trujillo and Bishop Donald Wuerl). Finally, the statements to national hierarchies and groups of bishops on their *ad limina* visits to the Vatican consistently show the papal obsession with obedience to the hierarchy and the priority of papal prerogatives. The maintenance of patriarchal clericalism in Catholicism has supplanted the message and mission of Jesus Christ.

This is a good point at which to discuss further what I mean by *clericalism*. In simplified terms it represents the concentration and practice of power and control in the priestly group or caste. According to the task force dealing with clericalism commissioned by the Conference of Major Superiors of Men, an extended meaning of clericalism involves

> the conscious or unconscious concern to promote the particular interests of the clergy and to protect the privileges and power that have traditionally been conceded to those in the clerical state. There are attitudinal, behavioral and institutional dimensions to the phenomenon of clericalism. Clericalism arises from both personal and social dynamics, is expressed in various cultural forms, and often is reinforced by institutional structures. Among its chief manifestations are an authoritarian style of ministerial leadership, a rigidly hierarchical world view, and a virtual identification of the holiness and grace of the church with the clerical state and, thereby, with the cleric himself. As such clericalism is particularly evident in the ordained clergy, though it does not pertain exclusively to it. Persons other than clerics can exhibit the traits of clericalism. Lay people, religious men and women are all liable to the pitfalls of clericalism in certain situations. Generally speaking, exclusive, elitist or dominating behavior can be engaged in by any person or group within the church. Such behavior is properly termed clericalism when it rests on a claim to special religious expertise or ecclesial authority, based on role or status in the church.[23]

The organizational blind of the Catholic church dictates that its clericalizing tendencies be justified in the name of preserving church unity. The organizational blind has created a religious or theological justification of its behavior based on an interpretation of *the story* that reinforces Matthew 16 to the exclusion of Matthew 18. This viewpoint is grounded in the ideology that, before Christ ascended into heaven, he left the church completely organized with a hierarchical structure, teachings that must be controlled by the members of that hierarchy, and sacraments and ministries that are also under their control. This ideology ensures the continuance of elitism and clericalism in the institutional religion called Roman Catholicism. According to Leonardo Boff, this rationalization of faith in the name of religion is part of the process of attributing to God what has been determined by humans:

> It is proper to ideology to present as natural what is histor-
> ical and to present as divine what is human. This is how
> the human gains an unquestionable value that is imposed
> on everyone and the historical takes on an element of dom-
> ination. Therefore, we can speak of the pathological aspect
> of Catholicism in its capacity for becoming an element for
> human oppression.[24]

Boff's "pathological aspect of Catholicism" is another image for
the addiction to the male, celibate, clerically controlled model of the
church in the name of church unity, the avoidance of sectarianism,
and the religion of Catholicism itself. This addiction process not only
affects the church as a family, but also becomes the only way the
institutional church can deal with other religious families within it,
especially religious orders.

The evolution of clericalism and papal control in the Catholic
church also reveals an evolution into the disease of clerical and papal addiction. Just as any addiction represents a *process*, the addiction to power in the Catholic church, whose "drug of choice" is the
preservation of the male, celibate, clerical model of church, evolved
historically.[25]

An adaptation of the Jellinek Chart for alcoholism (as a chemical addiction) to clericalism in Catholicism (as a relational addiction)
reveals the historical degeneration of the institutional church into its
disease:

A CHART OF CLERICALISM ADDICTION
IN THE CATHOLIC CHURCH

PRE-ADDICTION PHASE (symptoms not recognized by others)

- Collegial approach dominates, but with conflicts over authority (90)

- Increasing control of hierarchy over local churches (110+)

- Toleration of the hierarchical over the collegial (250+)

  EARLY PHASE (increasing "blackouts"—equivalent to "blinding")

- Start of local imposition of celibacy on clergy (c. 300+)

- Beginning preoccupation with maintaining control (313+)

- Effort to ensure clerical control of elections through law (325)

- Challenges from others, but pattern continues (450+)

MIDDLE PHASE (gradual normalization of the behavior)

● Rationalization: In the name of uniformity, papal control is legitimated by Gelasius; religious power over secular (492+)

● Gives up control to state in order to maintain other control (492+)

● Grandiose, aggressive behavior increases (590+)

● Calls for reform fail as clerical consciousness and behavior increase (600s–700s)

● Papal control of society theoretically accomplished (800)

● Decline of state, which supported clericalism, externally; internal decline of clergy through simony and marriage (850–950)

LATE PHASE (papal power and clericalization become habitual)

● Moral deterioration and impaired thinking; to break simony and clerical marriages, celibacy is imposed; persecution of those challenging mores becomes the norm (950–1250)

● Social deterioration; clerically controlled persecution increases (1250+)

● Fears of any perceived threats to universalized priesthood (Martin Luther, 1517+)

● Reformation fails to redirect clericalism and provides further reason for maintaining more control (1517+)

● Obsession about papal prerogatives, preservation of male, celibate, clerical model (1850+)

● Increasing numbers of priests leave clerical state; millions in the "family" denied sacraments (1965+)

● Ever-weaker appeal made to justify male form of clericalism (such as appeal to earthly Jesus, 1985)

● Alibis collapse

● Admits complete powerlessness

● HITS BOTTOM: Stops clericalism; seeks first the kingdom of God

After "hitting bottom," the Jellinek Chart has a recovery side that returns the addict to serenity and peace of mind. However, because the chart is based on *experiences* of this recovery, and since such conversion from clericalism has not yet become evident, the recovery of the institutional Catholic church from its controlling dynamics cannot yet be charted.

Because the church can be considered a family, family systems theory can be applied to it depending on the strong presence of two factors: the degree of emotional interdependency in relationships within the family, and the degree to which its way of operating becomes central to the members' thinking, feeling, and behaving. An increasing number of therapists are finding a striking similarity between family systems and church systems. In his studies Edwin H. Friedman parallels emotional processes in the minister's own family, the local church as a family (as well as a family of families), and the organization itself as a family. An examination of the three levels in the Catholic church shows that dysfunctional behavior around the preservation of the male, celibate, clerical model characterizes each level.[26]

If the papacy and hierarchy are addicted to power in the preservation of the male, celibate, clerical model of the church, it follows that clerics in the church invariably will be addicted in the same way or be codependent enablers of the addictive process in others. Objective data related to addictions such as alcohol among the clergy show no unique difference from that found in wider society. Data related to codependency among Catholic clergy and/or church ministers and involved members is scarce. However, from the limited data available, the underlying thesis about addiction and codependency among clerics in the church seems to be reinforced.

Building on the insights of Alfred Adler and Harry Stack Sullivan, David C. McClelland discovered that people drink to make themselves feel more powerful. He found that people with a personalized need for power (p-power), who can be characterized by strong wishes to exert direct influence over others, tend to drink heavily. People with a need for socialized power (s-power) possess indirect wishes to influence others; they tend to drink moderately. McClelland found that both light and heavy drinking increased the frequency of thoughts of power; light drinking increased thoughts of social power, and heavier drinking increased thoughts of personal power.[27]

Andrew A. Sorenson applied McClelland's conclusions to the clergy to see if and to what extent alcoholic priests might be motivated by power needs. He found that alcoholics among Roman Catholic

diocesan priests were five times as likely as nonalcoholics to manifest
p-power, while nonalcoholic priests were more than twice as likely
to manifest s-power. All religious priests studied demonstrated a need
for power. Nonalcoholics were twice as likely to express socialized
need for power, while alcoholics were three times as likely to express personalized need for power.[28] Sorenson's findings reveal that
male clerics in the Catholic church reveal an obsessive pattern related
to power either for personal ego needs (p-power) or for power over
others in the name of mission (s-power). Such a power need continually creates dysfunctionality insofar as the theoretical value promoted
among priests highlights humility as the stated virtue even as its *raison
d'eglise* demands power as the real virtue. If this study is accurate,
the average priest thrives on patriarchal clericalism despite his protestations to the contrary.

Catholic Codependency

Clericalism would not exist in the church and the hierarchical
principle would not have effective control if priests and laity did not
allow it to happen. Thus the disease of the former is reinforced by the
codependency of the latter. How this situation occurred and continues
needs more investigation, but a few comments are in order here.

The pontificates of Leo XIII, Pius X, and Pius XI articulated a vision that identified the Catholic church with the hierarchy, especially
the pope and Curia. Because this view could not last without reinforcement from the family members, another phenomenon occurred during
their reigns—the gradual control over the laity by the hierarchy and
papacy. Their internal lives were controlled through the sacraments
and piety and their external witness through hierarchical control of
Catholic Action and, later, lay ministry.

"Devotions and doctrine," especially as promoted in the mid-
nineteenth century, were essential to a maintenance of the hierarchical,
clerical church. At the center of all was the pope. For example, in
1860 Frederick Faber published a pamphlet entitled "Devotion to the
Pope," which connected devotion to the Blessed Sacrament and submission to clerical authority. "The Sovereign Pontiff," Faber wrote,
"is the third visible presence of Jesus among us . . . . The Pope is the
Vicar of Jesus on earth . . . . By divine right he is subject to none . . . .
He is a monarch . . . . He is the visible shadow cast by the Invisible
Head of the Church in the Blessed Sacrament."[29] While conformity

to God's will has been at the heart of Christian spirituality since the gospels, Faber's conflation of Jesus and the pope reflected a dynamic that reinforced codependency among the faithful.

In such a system the pastors teach and the people are taught; the shepherds lead and the flock follows. Such an approach to the interior life results in prayer that makes people not only submissive to God but obedient and dependent on human instrumentalities to have access to God. Thus people remain in the purgative way; the way of illumination and union is reserved to the "elite." Dependency is ensured through clerical control.

The hierarchy also ensured its control over the laity by controlling all forms of lay involvement in the apostolate. With the loss of the working classes in Europe, increasing anticlericalism, the effort to supplant former social hierarchies with the power of money, and the emergence of various lay movements in the late nineteenth century, the Vatican sensed a threat to its *raison d'église*. In Pius X's encyclical *Il Fermo Proposito* (1905), he equated "the church" with the hierarchy's "spiritual and pastoral ministry" and Catholic Action almost exclusively with clerical action:

> Voluntary associations which directly supplement the church's spiritual and pastoral ministry must be subordinate in every detail to the church's authority. But even associations of the other type, whose purpose was to restore in Christ a truly Christian civilization, and which constituted Catholic Action . . . can in no way conceive themselves as independent from the advice and superior direction of ecclesiastical authority.[30]

Whereas Pius X considered those involved in Catholic Action mere auxiliaries of the hierarchy, Pius XI viewed the laity so involved as participators in the apostolate of the hierarchy. Under strict obedience to the hierarchy, Catholics acting from the hierarchy's social teachings and under their orders would be able to re-catholicize society. According to Ana Maria Bidegain, Catholic Action can be characterized by two essential aspects, which were meant to reinforce the *raison d'église*. The first was strategic—the defense of ideological and practical church privileges. The second was organizational—"to create a powerful organization of the mass of the Catholic people, a real church party (but not a political party), whose aim was to give direction to the Catholic masses and to have a kind of army to be used in defence of church power or to gain other privileges according to the political, social and cultural struggle."[31]

Since that time Catholic Action is not considered "real" ministry by the papacy and Curia unless it is clerical. When women and non-ordained men serve in the church they are not sharers or participators. They cooperate and collaborate (*cooperari*) with the hierarchy in the mission of the church (that is, the mission of the hierarchy). I still feel the pain of the youth ministers who made a pilgrimage to Rome to attend a young people's congress. Although they identified themselves as "youth ministers," their title was changed unilaterally to something like "youth workers" when they were introduced to Pope John Paul II. The fact that lay ministry is not considered ministry unless it somehow receives clerical recognition reinforces the *raison d'église* wherein power resides not in the universal call of the baptized but in clerical ordination and delegation. To insist on such terminology and/or to submit quietly to its use without challenge further perpetuates a codependent organization. To challenge the notion and/or to refuse to equate ministry with clerical control invites being shamed as "disloyal" to the church.

In his 1980 speech at the Canon Law Society in Baltimore, Bertram F. Griffin referred to Anne Wilson Schaef's insights about people who work in "addict-like organizations and become addicts themselves, if not chemically dependent, then co-dependent."[32] A way to ensure this codependency in the church is through canon law.

Griffin noted that the Council of Trent's association of "ecclesiastical authority with control, power and status" is "deeply rooted in our canonical tradition and ways of thinking." Despite changes in the actual wording of canon law, he concluded that some in church government "cannot conceive of authority as service without control. Some would even maintain that control and coercion is a service to the church."[33] When the members of the church quietly and uncritically acquiesce to that canonical control, they reflect their codependency.

The fact of codependency among hierarchy, clergy, and laity cannot be isolated to its clerical origins and control, however. It is also maintained because people in church ministry bring their own codependency and other dysfunctional patterns into the church family itself. The dynamics of dysfunctional families can be repeated in congregations and parishes as well. These dynamics become especially evident in the various roles people play and in interpersonal relationships that subvert their stated goals.

First of all, dysfunctional family roles tend to get repeated when addicts and codependents enter the ministry. Depending on the dynamics in their family of origin, ministers often fill the traditional roles of the self-reliant and perfectionistic *hero*, the accomplished and successful *do-er*, the reclusive and self-effacing *lost child*, the ever-happy *mascot*, the nurturing and helpful *enabler*, the bumbling and scorned *scapegoat*, and the asexual and forever-giving *saint*.[34] These can be found in every parish and in every presbyterate.

Second, studies indicate that a tendency exists among clerics, who are members of the helping professions, to use power over people in a way that reinforces their own position. Adolf Guggenbühl-Craig has noted that people often enter the helping professions to control others. This can be especially true of clerics: "The power drive is given freest reign when it can appear under the guise of moral rectitude and good."[35] While such "helpers" evidence high motives and may even make decisions that can be helpful to others, the stronger their need for power the more it will betray them into making some very questionable decisions.

Third, because most people are unaware or in denial about the debilitating power for disruption that the clerical role represents, they can undermine any effort to bring a more collegial dimension into church life. Thus they maintain, by default, the hierarchical and patriarchal model of church. Such people need not be priests. They can be any who take on the patterns of clericalism prevalent in the system. While a lay person can "out-clericalize a cleric," priests who actually minister in the clerical church are particularly susceptible.

In her research into teamwork in Catholic campus ministry, Judith Rinek discovered that even groups that considered themselves quite functional often disintegrated due to power-related problems of a cleric. These problems became more aggravated the more hierarchical the cleric became. In one case study she showed how, despite the best intentions, collegiality was undermined precisely because the cleric on the team could not give up his years of clerical training and institutionally supported role of superiority. In particular three factors contributed to the subversion of the team being studied: 1) self-deception on the part of the cleric; 2) inadequate structures and processes in the college; and 3) an overall negative influence of the overall system itself, which fed into the clerical hierarchy. The "most devastating implication of clericalism" Rinek found, however, was that the ministry itself was identified with the work of the priest.[36]

Unfortunately, what Rinek terms "most devastating" is, in fact, normative for the *raison d'église*.

CHAPTER SIX

The Church's Story 2
Power, Roles, and Religion in the Institutional Church

Power, sexual status, and religion were the organizing concepts marking boundaries around issues of honor and shame in the Mediterranean society of the first century. Matthew's gospel was sculpted within this context and addressed to the church of this era. Almost two millenniums later these same dynamics reveal the key areas wherein the addictive patterns of the institutional Catholic church are expressed as well. In fact, power, sexual roles, and religion are intertwined in the Catholic church around honor and shame. This chapter will examine how these three organizing principles are expressed in a way that ensures the continuation of the church's patriarchal clericalism.

Power in the Institutional Church

The previous chapter showed how our church leaders' addiction to power in the form of their obsession with the preservation of the male, celibate, clerical model of the church dominates thinking, passions, and behavior in the institutional Catholic church. The toll on the people directly involved in the addictions is great; their identity gets equated with their role and their persons get hooked by power itself. To ask such people to critique patriarchal clericalism in the church is tantamount to asking them to self-destruct.

For instance, when a priest is named bishop, his nomination is made known only after a thorough examination of his thinking and activities (and probably his emotions as well) has been made; if he fits the norm and will support the established patterns of patriarchal clericalism, he is considered worthy to be so honored. Inevitably, given his position in the church family, the new bishop will consciously or un-consciously begin identifying himself—and become identified by the members—with his role as leader in the institutional church. For most, this identification develops in such a way that their personal identity gets subsumed in their role. Thus any criticism of the institution that has given them this identity will be considered as undermining their very persons. What might be said of bishops is equally applicable to other clerics and religious. Fearing the loss of their identity makes them unable to be free of their fear. If not checked, the fear can eas-ily move into anxiety and full-fledged addiction to preserve the role. David Lonsdale writes:

> For many, their personal identity is inextricably bound up with the status and authority that ordination or "being a reli-gious" has been seen to confer in the past. The fear of losing this status and the authority that goes with it undermines their personal identity itself, because they do not have an identity apart from that status. Fear of loss and change is provoking a profound spiritual crisis in individual people and as a consequence in the wider community.
>
> In these circumstances, then, certain abuses of author-ity evidently have their roots in fear. Increasing participa-tion by lay people in the church's life often seems like a creeping encroachment on authority that threatens to swell into a flood. The fear of loss of status and even identity that this provokes inspires in some people a sharp reaction which sometimes takes the form of increasing assertions of authority, dictatorial behaviour and repression of others' initiatives.[1]

Keeping in mind the confusion that results in people when their roles get equated with their persons, this chapter examines how clerical power dominates the present ecclesiastical patterns; how these patterns are forced onto other groups in the church, especially religious con-gregations; how sexual roles as well as racial roles get determined by Western, male-dominated clerical power; and finally, how all these deviations from the dream of Matthew articulated in *the story* continue in the church's story in the name of religion.

Insights From Family Systems Theory

According to Edwin Friedman, everything that pertains to the emo-tional processes in personal families is equally applicable to emotional processes in churches and hierarchies, which function as extended family systems. For those who would argue that in a situation like the institutional church, the family members change more frequently and are not related, Friedman notes how such a view misunderstands the nature of organic systems.[2]

Organic systems have their own organizing principles inherent in their structures. These principles go beyond being the sum of their parts. Indeed, we are becoming increasingly aware that addiction in organic systems now affects the third, fourth, and even fifth generation of family members.

When family theory is applied to the institutional Catholic church, various family concepts have particular relevance: the identified patient, homeostasis, differentiation of self, multi-generational patterns, emotional triangles, and control. These concepts get expressed in the institutional processes of thinking, passions, and behavior of the Catholic church in a way that feeds into and from the addiction, not only of the leaders but of the members of the church as well.

The *identified patient* in a family, according to family theory (and symbolic interactionism as well), is not the one who is perceived to be the sick member as much as the one in whom the family's sickness, pathology, or addictive patterns happen to surface. If the disease seems centered in the top leader or leaders, the family will certainly be dysfunctional. The overall health and functioning of any organization depend primarily on one or two people at the top; the more the leaders live out of a self-definition free of identification with roles, the more functional the family will be. This is true whether the relationship system is a personal family, an orchestra, a parish, a sports team, or a religious hierarchy. According to Friedman,

> the reason for that connection is not some mechanistic, trickle-down, domino effect. It is, rather, that leadership in families, like leadership in any flock, swarm, or herd, is essentially an organic, perhaps even biological, phenomenon. And an organism tends to function best when its "head" is well differentiated. The key to successful spiritual leadership, therefore, with success understood not only as moving people toward a goal, but also in terms of the survival of the family (and its leader), has more to do with the leader's capacity for self-definition than with the ability to motivate others.[3]

One need not probe here the families of origin or possible cross-addictions in the papacy or its top curial officers (such as normal chemical addictions like alcohol or food) to discover addictive patterns of behavior around power, sexual roles, and religion. The past and present leadership in Rome clearly shows an obsession with the preservation of power and certain sexual roles in the Catholic church, all justified in the name of religion.

This addictive process works its way into the heads of local churches and their curias as well. Often it takes its expression in ministerial burnout. When Archbishop Quinn of San Francisco took a sabbatical because of burnout, what was not said was more important than what was said. For years he had tried to give the Catholic church some credibility only to be undermined by Rome. Whether it was his sensitivity to homosexuals, his dialogical approach with women and men religious, his courageous speech at the 1985 Synod of Bishops on the Laity, where he called for a review of the official position of the church on birth control, or his efforts at collegiality, he continually met challenges from Rome and its codependents in the right wing of the church. His inability to address publicly these invasions of his boundaries likely contributed to his ultimate breakdown.

Friedman calls such burnout as that experienced by Archbishop Quinn *identified burnout*. The burnout of the individual points to a system that is itself burning out; the leader merely shows the symptoms more surely than the others in the organization. By focusing on the burned-out leader, the individual, we actually contribute to the problem, deny the institutional dysfunctioning, and ensure that more members who try to be faithful to all stories will burn out too.

A second dynamic treated in family theory involves *homeostasis*, the tendency of an entity to preserve its basic organizing principles through dynamics of self-correction in the face of any internal or external force. John Bradshaw has used a mobile to visualize the dynamics of homeostasis; no matter what pressures are exerted upon it, it will always return to balance. In a global church, no matter what kind of pressures are exerted to change clericalism in the family in some local churches—like the United States or Canada—offsetting balances will come from other local churches still "loyal" to Rome.

The deacon in *his* parish, the bishop in *his* diocese, or the Curia official in *his* office is able to function in a clerical fashion because those surrounding him in the parish, the diocese, or the office allow that behavior to continue. As Friedman makes clear, "Problems will recycle unless the balancing factors in the homeostasis of the system shift."[4] If the members don't start acting differently themselves and don't respond differently to the addictive behavior, no change is possible.

A third dynamic in family theory revolves around the notion of *self-differentiation*. When a person is identified with a role, self-differentiation is most difficult to achieve. I know of one priest who was named bishop without the Congregation for Bishops realizing that his stance on women's ordination did not echo that of the institutional church. Once they knew, he was called to Rome and told that he could never deviate publicly from the official position. He has been silent on the matter since his consecration.

According to Friedman, differentiation involves the ability "to maintain a (relatively) nonanxious presence in the midst of anxious systems."[5] This is difficult in the addictive church where anxiety related to clericalism and its rules and rituals seems built into the processes. In the Curia this anxiety gets expressed consistently when right-wing groups write letters challenging local bishops' pastoral decisions and/or liturgical practices. Bishops on their periodic visits to Rome are regularly challenged to give account for their alleged deviations. Rather than dialoguing with compassionate Curia officials as peers who understand the dilemma of serving people of many different mind-sets, they are accused of disloyalty or challenged on orthodoxy.

Multi-generational patterns are also examined by therapists treating pathology in families. Data shows that people are more likely to become alcoholic if an ancestor was alcoholic, or if they are part of ethnic groups that have a significant proportion of alcoholics. The same processes apply when considering the multi-generational patterns that reinforce male, celibate patterns for the clergy. According to C. Margaret Hall:

> The perpetual inclination of groups to reinforce past patterns of behavior in the present influences the resistance to change in organizations, such as changes in the position of women. . . . Strong resistance continues to occur, even when all members of an organization affirm that they are intellectually receptive to change. The organization has an automatic emotional tendency to try to maintain the old

system of comfortable established relationships and secure equilibrium.[6]

For a church evangelically grounded in change to have become constitutionally resistant to change reveals deep conflicts. These conflicts are not limited merely to the top levels of the church; they get manifested even in parish and ministerial teams. On one occasion I witnessed a priest on a team as he planned to fire a woman team-member because of her assertiveness and popularity. Knowing I was aware of his plans, he tried to explain his dilemma by saying, "But Mike, I can't change." Indeed, what other model of church had he learned? The disease of clericalism is multi-generational. What model of recovery can replace the addictive process?

A fifth way families become dysfunctional involves intellectual, emotional, and behavioral *triangulation*. The basic law of triangulation states that when any two parts of a system become anxious, they will focus upon a third party as a way of stabilizing their own relationship. Thus one parent identifies with a child in a conflict with his or her spouse. People or prelates who are "overfunctioners" are more likely to get caught in the sharp angles of triangles. In the church a form of triangulation takes place when right-wing groups, such as Catholics United for the Faith in local parishes and Opus Dei and Communione e Liberazione in dioceses hook into papal efforts to preserve clerical constructs and undermine approaches at collegiality and lay empowerment.

The final way families become dysfunctional involves *control*. Anne Wilson Schaef and Diane Fassel argue that, while dishonesty and denial may be the clearest characteristics of individual addicts, control is the prime trait of the addictive organization. They suggest that because organizations are so complex, perhaps organizations look to control as a method of reducing chaos.[7] However, because one of the ways this control is exercised in Catholicism is by proliferating structures and rules, this often leads to further degeneration and more efforts to control—a kind of control that feeds on control. Schaef and Fassel conclude: "Structurally, control is built into every level of the addictive organization. In an addictive organization, personnel practices are built on concepts of punishment."[8]

The unique form of punishment inflicted by some members of the Curia on many who need their assistance or who must give them accountability involves shame. The shaming approach used most frequently by Curia officials challenges the thinking or the behavior of the visitor who, figuratively, is "called on the carpet." Correction without care is control.

Extending Patriarchal Clericalism Throughout the Family

Besides their preoccupation with having the "right kind" of bishops and clergy, perhaps there is no greater obsession on the part of the papacy and the Curia than the control of religious orders. Even though many officials in the Congregation for Institutes of Consecrated Life and Societies of Apostolic Life (CICLSAL) are not members of religious congregations, they believe they have the power to define how the charism of religious life should be exercised in contemporary society.

Probably no major religious order exists, either of women or of men, that has not had extended, non-dialogical, authoritarian experiences with the top officials of CICLSAL. Invariably the concerns of the officials at CICLSAL with the various religious orders revolve around two main issues: ensuring a hierarchical model instead of collegial forms of government, and the demand for some visible sign of "witness" (even when groups are cloistered). From reports on the way these issues are handled, it would be safe to say that the Congregation's approach can be categorized easily as obsessive.

This obsessiveness was evident in the papal imposition of a superior for the Jesuits. It lay behind the effort of the Secretariat of State to impose a rule of life on the Carmels for women. More evidence of the obsession with control (even when it counters its own hierarchical model) can be found in the arbitrary imposition of the decision by CICLSAL to withdraw the German Province from the jurisdiction of the Generalate of the School Sisters of St. Francis (based in Milwaukee). Although this violated CICLSAL's concern about line-authority within religious congregations, it ensured that curial power could be imposed as long as groups of women as forward-thinking as the School Sisters would allow it to happen. This effort at control was shattered when the School Sisters' leaders broke the imposed silence and shared with their members what happened.

Conflicts between Rome and religious orders invariably revolve around preserving a hierarchical model within religious life and a clerical model within groups of men having priests. Since my own congregation, the Capuchin Franciscans, is one of those groups having priests, I will spend the next pages using its relations with the Congregation as a case at point.

Many religious orders of men were founded as communities of equality with some members ordained priests and others not ordained. Over the years, however, as is the case with most religious movements founded on equality, the clerics gained ascendancy and, ultimately, control. What began as a community of equality under Francis in 1209 became, under Bonaventure in 1260, a clerically controlled bureaucracy.

A key document of the Second Vatican Council and subsequent papal statements declared that the appropriate renewal of religious life involved a simultaneous interaction of three "stories": the gospel, the culture, and the founding charism of each congregation. Faithful to this agenda, congregations of men and women began reading the signs of the times by returning to the gospels according to the charism of their founders.[9] For the three Franciscan branches (Observant Franciscans [19,000 in the world], Capuchin Franciscans [12,000], and Conventual Franciscans [4,000]) this demanded a restructuring of thinking, feeling, and behaving from a clerical to a collegial approach. However, despite what the Holy Spirit led the Second Vatican Council to declare, the men at the Curia ruled otherwise. CICLSAL required that the male Franciscan Orders include in their constitutions the statement that they were clerical, that is, that only clerics could hold the position of major superior (as well as minister of canonically erected local houses).

When it came time to submit their constitutions, the Conventual Franciscans tendered a version that reflected the clerical-consciousness of the Curia. They inserted in their constitutions the words: "Our Order is numbered among the clerical institutes by the Church." However, the Observant and Capuchin branches decided to follow the lead of the Vatican Council and the papal decrees on the appropriate renewal of religious life. Both submitted constitutions in which all offices would be open to all perpetually professed in their respective orders.

The Observant Franciscans were challenged on the issue by the Congregation for Religious, which appealed to the part of existing Canon Law that said if a congregation had been clerical by reason of history, it was sufficient to make it clerical. In 1987 the General Minister of the Franciscans chose to submit to the Curia's demand for inclusion of the clerical control in the Order's constitutions. However, the Observants' wording made it clear that they considered themselves an Order of equals even though numbered among the clerical institutes by the institutional church.

The Capuchins began discussions with CICLSAL in generally the same way as the Observants; however, they added more material about their own reform of the Franciscans in 1523 and showed how the reform also reinstated the equality of all men in the Order with their subsequent availability for all offices in the Order. On January 23, 1986, at a plenary session of the Congregation for Religious, the Minister of the Capuchin Order stated unequivocally: "In my service as minister, if I had to promulgate a text of the Constitutions declaring our Order to be a clerical Order, I would have the feeling of going against my conscience."

After this, the Order was told by the Congregation to put the statement in the Constitutions. The Capuchins appealed to the Holy Father for a ruling. Not long after, the Order's curia received a reply from the Congregation that its request had been considered, but that it was the decision of the Holy See that the clerics-only clause be put in the legislation. However, since the Capuchins had a Polish councilmember who knew a Polish secretary of the pope, he asked if the pope actually had considered the Capuchins' request. When the secretary indicated the pope never handled the appeal, the Order made a formal appeal to the pope. As of this writing, there has been no response. The standoff remains.

A family systems approach speaks of the "identified patient." In this sense the one in the family who is identified as diseased is but part of a diseased family. With this in mind, it would be wrong to separate CICLSAL's effort to clericalize the Order from the clerical mentality and processes in the Capuchins themselves (ourselves). Clericalism is all-embracing throughout the Catholic church whether we think of its magisterial teachings or how we think, feel, and act from the impact of those teachings on us. Changing from clerical perceptions, passions, and practices does not come easily.

It is too simple to label CICLSAL, or leaders in it, as clerics trying to maintain the patriarchal clerical model and mentality. If we approach this issue as a family, such activity merely makes them the "identified" group with the disease when, in fact, the disease is family-based. We *all* suffer from clericalism and hook into each others' disease. As a former member of the Capuchin's General Definitory

in Rome (who was a prime architect in the Order's challenges to
CICLSAL on the clericalism issue) said:

> One point alleviates the Congregation's case: it has sanc-
> tioned what it saw! The Congregation's attitude has un-
> masked our own clericalization. For this, we must say
> "Thank you" to the Congregation. Never would the said
> Congregation designate as "teachers" the Little Sisters of
> Jesus or the Sisters of Mother Teresa. The image projected
> by these religious women corresponds exactly to what they
> really are! On the contrary, our image, at least throughout
> the last decades, was clearly clerical. I believe that our weak
> spot is there: Our image corresponds to what we really have
> become. (The Order of Brothers has become an Order of
> Clerics). This is so true, that we must now be vigilant and
> active on two fronts: Keep on making our point with the
> Congregation of course; but, most of all endeavor to really
> live like BROTHERS.[10]

To be a priest in a clerical congregation in a clerical church continually challenges us to conversion of thinking, feeling, and behaving.
I may have disposed of my clerical collar the day I realized I kept
it by my side when I drove so that I could quickly put it on if I
got caught speeding, but this was just a beginning. Disposing of my
clerical thinking and perceptions is a much more difficult matter.

Closed Family Systems

According to Fassel and Schaef, the addictive system is first of
all a closed system.

> It presents very few options to the individual in terms of
> roles and behaviors, or even the thinking and perceptions
> a person can recognize and pursue. Basically, an addictive
> system calls for addictive behaviors. It invites the person
> into the processes of addiction and addictive thinking pat-
> terns. Even if we ourselves are not addicted to a substance
> or a process (which is unusual in this society), since the
> addictive system exists as the norm for the society its pro-
> cesses are always available to be tapped into by anyone at
> any time.[11]

From what has been said thus far it should not be too difficult to conclude that the institutional church represents a dysfunctional family system in contrast to a functional one. It is closed rather than open; it functions to meet a few key members' personal needs rather than all members' basic needs; its rules operate to keep the system closed by reserving power to only a few in contrast to functional family rules that operate to maximize all the members' potential. In a dysfunctional family, roles become identified with persons, continually getting enacted in a rigid, anxious manner; functional family rules distinguish the role from the person, are invoked only when needed, and then in a relaxed, flexible way.

We can tell when power in the church is positive and when it is negative when we consider the kind of dynamics that reflect that power in the family system itself; that is, power in the church will be negative if the family system is closed, and positive if the church is open. Dysfunctional family systems lower self-worth; healthy family systems build self-worth. The former reflect a negative, addictive abuse of power, and the latter a positive, healthy expression. In the church the former reveal the consequences of an obsession with preserving the male, celibate, clerical model; the latter offer a dream of what a more collegial community might look like. Sharon Wegscheider-Cruse contrasts the two types, which might be considered two poles of a continuum between addictive systems and healthy options:

PAINFUL FAMILY SYSTEMS THAT LOWER SELF-WORTH	HEALTHY FAMILY SYSTEMS THAT BUILD SELF-WORTH
1. No-talk rule	1. Communication is open
2. Internalized feelings	2. Feelings expressed openly
3. Unspoken expectations	3. Explicit rules
4. Entangled relationships	4. Respect for individuation
5. Manipulation and control	5. Freedom highly valued
6. Chaotic value system	6. Consistent value system
7. Rigid attitudes	7. Open-mindedness
8. Reveres past traditions	8. Creates new traditions
9. Grim atmosphere	9. Pleasant atmosphere
10. Frequent chronic illness	10. Healthy people
11. Dependent relationships	11. Independence and growth
12. Jealousy and suspicion	12. Trust and love[12]

Even a cursory reading of the characteristics above places the institutional church among the family systems that lower self-worth. And while not all twelve points are equally applicable, the aggregate does give a general sense of a family system that reflects dysfunctionality, feeds on dysfunctioning members, and nourishes dysfunctional "identified patients." This contributes to the sustenance of an addictive process that affects the way the members think, feel, and act.

First of all, there is the no-talk rule. Silence and secrecy characterize curial transactions. In the dispute of the Vatican with the sisters who signed the so-called abortion ad in *The New York Times*, each congregational leader involved was told not to talk to the others. They violated the no-talk rule by keeping communication open so they would not be divided and conquered.

The Congregation of Education denied Archbishop Rembert Weakland an honorary doctorate at the Vatican-controlled School of Theology at the University of Fribourg because of his approach to abortion; it never discussed its concerns with him. "He [Weakland] says that if Rome is angry with him, it is because he broke the secrecy that is the Catholic Church's normal way of handling such matters."[13]

The no-talk rule gets extended into the decisions made among the body of bishops as well. Although a significant number of United States Catholic bishops privately disagree with the Vatican on the birth control issue, and while the vast majority of Catholics disagree, the 1990 National Council of Catholic Bishops' statement on "Human Sexuality" reinforced the traditional teaching. In the mind of one member of the NCCB, Bishop Kenneth Untener of Saginaw, the bishops' failure to discuss any modifications made the church like a "dysfunctional family unable to talk about a problem that everyone knows is there."[14]

Besides a no-talk rule, there is a don't-feel rule, especially in terms of sexuality. Priests are expected to keep their feelings to themselves or to sublimate them for the sake of the ministry, especially if those feelings are sexual and, even more, if those sexual feelings have a homosexual orientation. One of the most painful feelings facing people in ministry is the sense of loneliness, yet it rarely gets addressed. When people try to bring issues about intimacy into open discussion, or when they spend "too much" time with a specific individual, they are often identified as deviant from the celibate norm.

Entangled relationships in contrast to respect for individuation characterize closed family systems. While every family can deal with its eccentric characters, the institutional Catholic church cannot deal well with those who dare to question its structural dynamics. Institutional critics are silenced and their writings monitored. For example, in a letter dated April 6, 1983, from Joseph Cardinal Ratzinger of the Congregation of the Faith to the Minister of the Capuchin Order, he urged:

> I am anxious to take this opportunity to invite you, Father, in your capacity as minister general, to keep an eye on the doctrinal opinions of Fr. Bühlmann. . . . An opportunity to exercise the above-mentioned vigilance by applying the norms that define the granting of the imprimatur is offered to you, Father, in the book that Fr. Bühlmann is in the process of writing, in collaboration with K. Rahner and J. B. Metz. About this book he himself has said that "it is naturally unavoidable to criticize certain existing structures."[15]

That manipulation and control rather than freedom and collaboration characterize the institutional church has already been discussed. However, while there seems to be a consistent value system with which many hierarchical leaders expect lock-step compliance, history shows that, in many places, church teachings have made total about-faces. Yet church leaders seem obsessed with leaving the impression that papal teachings never change. A good case in point is the way papal social teachings adapt to changes in the culture. For instance, concerned about the rise of lay leadership in two social reform movements in Italy and in France, which he saw as threatening to clerical authority, Pope Pius X condemned a system of cooperatives that would enable every worker to become in some sense an owner-employer. In support of his condemnation he declared: "It is in accordance with the pattern established by God that human society should have rulers and subjects, employers and employees, rich and poor, wise and ignorant, nobles and common people."[16] Today cooperatives are praised.

Rigid attitudes dominate an investigation of the mind-set of the clerically oriented hierarchical leaders in the Catholic church. This is typical of any family where the no-talk rule dominates. At one particularly difficult meeting of our General curia with a major official of SCRIS (the old name for CICLSAL), one councillor after another presented theological, historical, textual, conciliar, and other reasons

why we should not put in our Constitutions the statement that we are a
clerical order. The only response from the official was "You're going
to be a tough group to convince."

In such a context past traditions are revered and there seems to be
an obsessive fear about creating new traditions lest people question
the notion of continuous infallibility. Probably the most striking case
of this phenomenon can be found in the celebrated scenario around the
decision by Pope Paul VI to maintain the teaching of the magisterium
on birth control.

In 1963 Pope John XXIII established a commission to study the
birth control question. After John XXIII's death, Paul VI enlarged the
group, instructing it to give priority to morals and doctrine. During
the Second Vatican Council, Cardinals Léger, Suenens, and Alfrink,
along with 87-year-old Patriarch Maximos IV Saigh of Antioch called
for change in the official teaching. By their applause the majority of
bishops signaled their approval. By the last meeting of the commission,
Paul VI had added still more cardinals and bishops. Yet just over
twenty percent of the members agreed with the traditional teaching.
Despite this overwhelming opposition to the "official teaching," on
July 29, 1968, *Humanae Vitae* reiterated the traditional stance on birth
control.

In *Why You Can Disagree and Remain a Faithful Catholic*, Philip
Kaufman asks: "Why was this teaching so rigidly maintained? Members of the birth control commission who insisted on the intrinsic evil
of contraception conceded that they could not prove their position. Ultimately the real reason had little or nothing to do with reproduction.
The decision was made to safeguard the magisterium, the teaching of
two popes as recent as Pius XI and Pius XII."[17]

Well-known moralist Bernard Häring, who was a member of the
commission, reports the following anecdote. One of the members who
was adamantly opposed to any changes, the Jesuit moralist Marcelino
Zalba, said: "What then with the millions we have up to now sent to
hell, if these things can be changed?" To this, Patty Crowley, one of
the lay members of the commission, responded gently, "Father Zalba,
are you so sure that God executed all of your orders?"[18] A gentle
reminder by a member of the laity that all authority in the church is
ultimately Jesus'.

Another manifestation of a closed family system can be found in
an overly serious attitude toward life, a lack of playfulness among its

key members, a grim atmosphere. Since Rome considers its role to be the source of church-salvation, it is small wonder there is so little self-differentiation, so much anxiety, and a dearth of joy in so many official church circles and Vatican offices.

In its obsession with orthodoxy (as in birth control issues, the role of women in church leadership, and the preservation of an exclusively hierarchical form of governance), church leaders from the Vatican to the chancery increasingly are determined to reserve to themselves authoritative church teaching. Despite statements of clear support for the necessity of theological speculation by the bishops as a body, an increasing number of bishops seem to hold theologians in suspicion. The theoretical support by the bishops of theologians seems to have eroded if one considers their reaction to the Vatican efforts to censure Charles Curran.

Writing on the "emergence of a party line" among the bishops as a way of rebutting Charles Curran's civil suit against the Catholic University of America, Richard McBrien commented on the logic of one of the bishops, Donald W. Wuerl of Pittsburgh. After presenting the bishop's rationale for Curran's censure, McBrien notes:

> But the most telling assertion in Bishop Wuerl's argument is the following: "The work of theological development is to push our understanding of the faith to new and more profound limits. It is the task of the bishops to note when the limits have been crossed." Bishop Wuerl begs these questions: *How* do the bishops know when "the limits have been crossed," and *by what process* do they know it? Why should theologians waste their time and energy trying to discern the meaning of revelation and the content of faith if the bishops somehow already know the answers—and without ever having had to crack a book, or learn an array of foreign languages, or engage in careful exegesis of a text, or sort out the complexities of history, or fashion sustained and compelling arguments that will survive the critical scrutiny of a wider community of scholars?[19]

Having examined the issue of power in the institutional Catholic church and considered it in light of a painful family system that lowers self-worth or a healthy family system that builds self-worth, I would like to conclude with a personal experience. At our 1987 chapter, David Schwab, a non-ordained, perpetually professed brother was elected by my whole Province to be Vicar Provincial. Since he was not a cleric, and therefore without powers of jurisdiction, we had to "postulate" him for the position with an appeal to CICLSAL. Despite all the arguments supporting our election of him that were addressed to the Congregation, its two-word response to the petition was that the arguments were "not valid." I consulted David Schwab about various details in the process. The thing that struck me most was his lack of rancor even as he said: "I thought I was ready for the rejection, but when it came it really hurt. I realized I am not equal in this Order." One more example of a member of the church being shamed by its officials! If a sign of a painful family system is the lowering of self-worth among its members, the fact that the Curia made David Schwab a second-class citizen, less than clerics, should be enough to invite recovery. Perhaps it might generate just enough grieving over such debilitating clericalism to indicate the viability of other ways to think, feel, and behave in institutional Catholicism. One way might be found in my province's response to CICLSAL's refusal to give Schwab canonical authority. We named the next-ranking cleric our technical Vicar Provincial. David Schwab was named Assistant Provincial and received our fraternal obedience. We gave him *our* authority; it really did not matter if CICLSAL did or not. Possibly more of such responses may indicate independence and growth rather than continued dependency in our relationships.

Sexual and Racial Roles in the Institutional Church

According to Malina, the second dynamic that characterized social life in *the story* revolved around sexual roles. The first victims of patriarchal clericalism are the clerics themselves. In the effort to maintain a male, celibate clergy, the institutional church in Western Europe, Canada, and the United States has been undermined by two main factors: a decline of existing clergy through leave from the priesthood and death, and a decline in new entrants into seminaries. At the same time another phenomenon—reinforced by the no-talk rule—involves the clergy and sexual issues, many of them quite public.

In one week, a host of separate items about sexuality involving clergy and potential clergy surfaced. New York's dailies alleged Bruce Ritter's misuse of Covenant House funds while having an affair with a former male prostitute; the *National Catholic Reporter* featured a major book review on homosexuality among the clergy as well as many letters responding to an earlier article by Andrew Greeley entitled "Bishops Paralyzed Over Heavily Gay Priesthood: One Result is Double Standard on Celibacy"; and I received a letter from a friend, a lay theologian and lay administrator of a large parish, who had recently begun the process of preparing for the priesthood. He wrote:

> As you know, I've been in a formation program this fall, considering the priesthood. But it's clear now that I won't be chosen after all. The problems have to do, believe it or not, with my being gay and also open. I've been open for so long that it's now impossible to be hidden again, both because of the sheer number of people who know and because psychologically I just can't live a hidden life again. My sponsoring bishop is nervous about all that so even though they think of me as a good candidate otherwise, I'm not fit material because of this.
>
> So how about that?! I guess I thought the Church was beyond this point. So I'm returning to lay ministry...I do so gladly yet there is a sadness, too.
>
> What I see here at the seminary among those who are gay and hidden is unhealthy behavior which greatly disturbs me. I guess I find that to be serious about a friendship with a man, it's important for me to lay my cards on the table so he knows who he's dealing with in an honest way. I just can't be hidden again and the trade-off is worth the price to me.[20]

Finally, in the same week, a sister in a top administrative position told me of a conversation she recently had with a bishop. In a moment of candor he had let his guard down and broke ranks to talk about issues of sexuality among the clergy. Speaking of priests—and bishops—who are gay he concluded that bishops tend to refuse to deal with the "gay issue" lest it blow up, possibly incriminating them.

Meanwhile, at another level, an increasingly aware public is commenting on the growing evidence of large percentages of gay men in seminaries and the clerical state. North American data suggests that among the clergy at least thirty percent are homosexual in their orientation.[21] On the other hand, these increasing numbers of men must remain closeted and repressed—denying who they are—because of the climate of homophobia that comes from the Vatican. When the various unhealthy symptoms in a closed, dysfunctional family dominate (no-talk rule, internalized feelings, unspoken expectations, entangled relationships) it is no wonder bishops and major superiors seem paralyzed by this phenomenon of ever-increasing numbers of homosexuals seeking admission to seminaries, priesthood, and religious life. They just deny the problem exists.

Another public manifestation of confusion around sexual roles of celibates, especially in Canada and various parts of the United States, is found in the highly publicized indictments and convictions of priests for sexual abuse of children. To date the best church-sponsored examination of this phenomenon is found in the Canadian *Report of the Archdiocesan Commission of Enquiry into the Sexual Abuse of Children by Members of the Catholic Clergy* (the "Winter Commission Report"). Written to examine allegations of pedophilia by a significant percentage of the priests of the Archdiocese of St. John's, Newfoundland, the Commission was asked to address "two fundamental questions about the series of events which occurred within the Archdiocese: what factors contributed to the sexual abuse of children by some members of the clergy, and why it took so long before the church became aware of the deviant behavior."[22] As to the first question, factors of power abuse related to the church "had a direct bearing on the occurrence of child abuse by priests of the Archdiocese." In Newfoundland clerical power had reached "a position of nearly absolute authority in everyday life."[23] Consequently, the victims were perfect codependents who could be controlled by addicted clerics. This phenomenon, the Commission insisted over and over, could not be isolated from the system itself.

> A patriarchal (adult-male dominated) system has been reinforced by the authoritarian Roman Catholic church. Historically, as such attitudes became institutionalized in the policies and structures of church and society, they provided a strong cultural and social support for oppression, where one person or group dominates those without power.[24]

As to the second question—"why it took so long before the church became aware of the deviant behavior"—the Winter Commission

> discovered that the Archdiocesan leadership did, in fact, have knowledge, since the mid–1970s, of deviant or sexually inappropriate behaviour among some Roman Catholic clergy in this Archdiocese. This was long before the victims publicly disclosed that they had been abused as children.[25]

Heading the list of reasons why silence became the rule by church officials was that they "denied the problems."[26] Denial is at the heart of the patriarchal clerical system, which is self-destructing (at least in North America) because of the addiction to the preservation of a male celibate clergy.

The priests noted above may be abusers; they are also victims. They are victims of a system that imposes celibacy without proper contemporary supports, so that its members often become sexual anorexics on the one hand or sex and love addicts on the other. It is hard enough not to be sexually anorexic when one embraces celibacy understood as a charism for service in the church; it is another thing to have it imposed by a hierarchy that can afford to be asexual because its identity does not come from relationships that are intimate and generative but rather from power and patriarchy.

The "don't think, don't feel, don't act" models of closed family systems are proving to be physically, psychologically, emotionally, and financially draining to the institutional church. Yet the papal and curial obsession with maintaining the male, celibate, clerical model of the church at all costs (personally and monetarily) continues for the local churches. Meanwhile the voices of bishops who do not support the preservation of the male, celibate, clerical model are silent or silenced. When asked their position on the issue of married priests and women priests, many bishops echo the Roman view; a few, like Archbishop Weakland of Milwaukee, have stopped being codependent and say something like, "The Holy Father has told us we are not to talk about this."

In 1988 Father Anthony Curran told parishioners that Pope John Paul II's stance on mandatory celibacy was "dead wrong." He explained that many problems plaguing the clergy, including drug and alcohol abuse, were rooted in mandatory celibacy. Before the week was out he had apologized "for the injudicious use of the phrase 'dead wrong' with regard to the Holy Father's stand concerning celibacy for the diocesan clergy.... I acknowledge that I was in violation of canon law in speaking publicly on the matter."[27] This public apology for criticizing the papacy's stand on celibacy took place the same year a Politburo member had to publicly apologize for criticizing a position held by U.S.S.R. Communist Party leader Gorbachev. However, later (and tentatively) the Soviet Union entered into recovery by admitting its disease.

Such recovery does not seem to be in the prospectus of the Vatican. Noting that "the presence of the priest is necessary for the maintenance and the development of local Christian communities," Pope John Paul II offered guidelines for "Sundays in Priestless Parishes" to the Congregation for Divine Worship instead of broadening the groups from which priests are currently drawn.[28] Instead of calling the parishes eucharistless the clerical mindset calls them priestless. Episcopal priests who are married are brought in; Catholic priests who get married are sent out. The result of such decisions, at least as they impinge on the Catholic church in the United States, is that the institutional addiction continues while the rights of the laity expressed in *The Dogmatic Constitution on the Church* get ignored: "The laity have the right to receive in abundance the help of the spiritual goods of the church, especially that of the word of God and the sacraments from their pastors."[29]

The above quotation from the Second Vatican Council speaks of the rights of the laity. Since women constitute half of the church, what rights do they have? According to the 1917 code of canon law women were viewed as potential temptresses to clerics.[30] This attitude flowed from a viewpoint of women as dependent on and subordinate to men. With the publication of Pope John XXIII's encyclical *Pacem in Terris* in 1963 and subsequent documents from the Second Vatican Council, the magisterium's teaching on women changed. The new code of canon law, promulgated in 1983, states: "In virtue of their rebirth in Christ there exists among all the Christian faithful a true equality with regard to dignity and the activity whereby all cooperate in the building up of the Body of Christ in accord with each one's condition and function."[31] However, the "condition" of women, according to the papacy and those writing canon law, makes them unable to function as priests. They are equal, but not equal. And, somehow, this confusing casuistry among curialists and canonists, which defines women as second-class within the system, is called "just."

The male clerical mentality often says more about the perpetrators than the victims. For instance, in 1989 thirty-five U.S. archbishops (chosen by Rome rather than selected by the National Council of Catholic Bishops) met at the Vatican with twenty-five top Curia officials and Pope John Paul II. There were several warnings about the rise of "radical feminists," who allegedly refuse to accept papal and/or curial authority. Asked to define "radical feminism," Cardinal Antonio

Innocenti, Prefect of the Congregation for the Clergy, mentioned the issue of women seeking priesthood. "Their desire is fed more by a search for power than a search for service," he said.[32]

The issue of power is very much at stake when considering the clericalized priesthood in Catholicism today. By some "tyranny of logic"[33] men are able to have this power but not women; somehow women seeking ordination are not seeking service but power. The psychological implications behind such thinking suggest many possible reasons why so many members of the hierarchy are opposed to women's ordination.

Much of the present rationale for Rome's attitude toward women seems to mask a male need to control them. Control constitutes the heart of addiction; addiction to control mirrors the clerical obsession. Such clerics do not want to be under the domination of women, but have no problem being part of a system that dominates and controls women, keeping them inferior. Women remain part of the institutional family, yet wonder why they continually receive little or no respect. As a young man once said to me, "If I were a woman, I'd never join a women's order." When I asked him why he would say such a thing, he responded, "Because it would mean my basic reality would always be defined by men."

A Dominican congregation of women had its new constitution critiqued and signed by a canon lawyer who happened to be a Dominican woman. With everything in order, the Congregation sent the constitutions to CICLSAL for approval. To their dismay it was returned with a list of corrections. Sensing sexism, the congregation employed a male canon lawyer. He made a few minor adjustments, signed the document, and returned it to Rome. It came back approved, carrying the blessing of CICLSAL.

Attitudes and practices of male domination over women are not limited to Roman congregations. They can be found in chanceries in this country as well. A woman (for obvious reasons her name will not be used) who worked for many years in a key position in a large diocese discovered a male peer was making ten thousand dollars a year more than she was. She appealed. It took over ten months for a response, which refused an adjustment.

Around the same time she began reading books by Anne Wilson Schaef and Gerald May on addiction, and she made some connections. As she notes:

> There was no "cause and effect" immediacy—it just came
> (probably after the ten months of frustration, reading, etc.).
> My father was alcoholic; I loved him a great deal. He was
> a wonderful father and man, but many nights at dinner his
> drinking became the focus of arguments or my shame (out-
> side the house) of his having had too much. Because he
> loved me, and I loved him, I thought I could get him to
> stop drinking. I never succeeded, and as an adult I stopped
> asking. In the past, I have reflected on some of this and
> worked at overcoming my need for approval, my unwill-
> ingness to trust those outside my family, the secrecy, etc.
> What came to me, however, was that in the church sys-
> tem, I was still that little girl *asking the church*—Father
> _____, my cleric supervisor, the bishop—*to stop being
> destructive, to stop drinking!* Once I had this insight, I felt
> different—I realized that this illusion of power/control was
> my addiction.

She wrote the facts of the salary injustice to the treasurer and sent copies to several others. That afternoon the supervisor came to her office, visibly upset, asking if she was planning to sue. She said no, that was not her intent, but that it was too bad that this was the threat that the church system responded to. The supervisor then proceeded to try to find out who told her about the differences in salaries; he wanted to "plug the leak." After more months of tension she finally did receive her adjustment. The incident helped her come to a new understanding of the addiction in the church:

> I am more centered . . . realizing that the system is dysfunc-
> tional and my piece was the little girl asking the alcoholic
> to stop drinking, believing that if I said it clearly—well-
> articulated—and over and over again, it would be heard,
> that I would be heard. I know now that I am talking to a
> drunk. I will still speak to the drunkenness, saying "you are
> drunk" but aware that I cannot make anyone stop drinking
> or stop an addiction.

Patriarchy in our clerical structures runs deeper than we imagine; it affects our deepest images of true religion. If it took a council to deal with the full equality in the church of Jew and Greek; if it took emancipation and civil rights legislation to help the church include former slaves with free *men* in the clerical state; perhaps it will take another council or dramatic events in the culture's story to show the untenability of the present position of institutional male celibate clerics on the issue of women in the church. Psychologists like Eugene Kennedy and theologians like Richard McBrien believe most critical conflicts in the church center around sex and power and how they intermingle. In today's church, power is determined by sex insofar as canon law limits leadership to *males* who profess *not to have sex*. The momentous issue facing the church at this time is whether or not it will deal with this conflict.[34] Until that occurs the present position continues to rely on an ideology supporting patriarchal clericalism such as that recently articulated in the priests' monthly, *Homiletic and Pastoral Review*:

> The patriarchal system has shown itself to be the proper one for the church, because of its efficacy. Two thousand years of existence and growth (not counting the thousands of years as a Jewish patriarchy) in a hostile world is a record demanding respect no matter what the ideology. The patriarchal system, as has been argued here, must be maintained, because it alone is compatible with man's nature and the social order which has evolved from it. Finally . . . the patriarchal system is necessary to preserve the idea of the sacred in men's minds. . . .
>
> For women to become priestesses is to concede to a worldly ideology, to obscure the distinction between the purposes of the world, to blur the distinction between the special function of the man and that of the woman, and to ultimately destroy the sacred in the minds of men altogether.
>
> The brief argument presented here advocates restricting the priesthood to men only. It also concludes that women must be prohibited from performing other functions closely associated with the sacred such as being altar girls and extraordinary ministers of communion. The argument does not rely on church doctrine but on "worldly wisdom," because that seems to be the ultimate authority for questions of psychology, social organization and even morality in some quarters. But, it is an argument consistent with the natural law philosophy of traditional Catholicism.[35]

The obsession with the conscious preservation of the male, celibate, clerical model of the church cannot be divorced from another phenomenon, which may be even more unconscious: The institutional church has yet to break adequately from its Western European roots and the mentality that keeps it a *white*, male, celibate, clerical system even as more non-white male celibates enter the clergy. According to Karl Rahner, the church today is not yet a world church precisely because of its ties to Western culture. "The result of the missionary work of the church in modern times, however unavoidable it may have been, was that the church was primarily a Western Christianity exported throughout the world. The church really remained a Western church with mission stations in other parts of the world."[36] The 1989 document from the Pontifical Commission for Justice and Peace, "The Church and Racism: Toward a More Fraternal Society," candidly admits that during the era of colonizations the interests of the Europeans who exploited the native peoples in the new lands were often allowed to outweigh the missionaries' efforts to bring those peoples the salvific message of the gospel. Colonists' efforts to dominate were even given encouragement "on the basis of false interpretations of the Bible."[37] The church submerged *the story* in order to reinforce the (Western) culture's story.

The roots of our ethnocentrism and racism run deep. Yet those outside our system—such as those colonized—can differentiate between what we say and what we are. When I was ministering among the Northern Cheyenne people in southeast Montana I learned that the word for *priest* in Cheyenne means "white man who stands between us and God." While the notion of priest as mediator may be correct, why does that mediator have to be white and male? It would be going against the definition for a Northern Cheyenne to be a priest in the Catholic church. So far there have been no Northern Cheyenne priests from Montana. How can a Cheyenne be a "white man"?

In the culture's story sexism and racism seem to flow from classism, which is grounded in money and avarice; in the church's story sexism and racism flow from clericalism, which is grounded in power and ambition. Yet, despite pontifical letters, a major letter on racism by the N.C.C.B., and another document from the black bishops, there are still those in leadership who are in denial about racism in the institutional church. One of these is John Cardinal O'Connor of New York. Noting that the issue of racism "won't be denied," he refused to call the institutional church racist because he identified the institutional church with the body of Christ itself. He told delegates to the national conference of the National Office for Black Catholics: "Of course there is racism, deep rooted and widespread. I do not believe the church is a racist institute. It is the body of Christ. But many of us are racist."[38]

Racism is an addiction that is destroying the body of Christ as surely as clericalism and sexism are destroying it. Like any addiction racism is rooted in fear and reinforces fear. As the Pontifical Commission's document on racism states: "Reprehensible attitudes have their origin in *irrational fear*. . . . Racial prejudices most often come from ignorance about others which. . . engenders fear."[39] If perfect love casts out fear, perhaps it will not be until white males stop being afraid of minorities (and women) and begin to love them as they love themselves that the church will be a true sign of Easter universalism.

The issue of racism in the church was highlighted in the 1989 decision by Edmund Cardinal Szoka of Detroit to close a large number of parishes, mainly in poor and black areas. People called his decision racist, and Szoka became the "identified patient." This approach overlooked the deeper racism of the church as a family with a disease.

What is happening in our central cities, mainly among blacks, is happening in another way throughout the United States with Hispanics. I am speaking about the phenomenal growth of the Protestant sects. The sects have been able to adapt former rigid mind-sets about Mary and the saints to include such popular piety in their approach to the Hispanic culture. The Catholic church, however, seems unable to turn from its bureaucratic approach. From the east coast to the west coast, the phenomenon is being repeated. A 1990 study initiated by the archdiocese of San Francisco revealed that lack of faith and the irrelevance of church doctrine are the leading causes for Hispanic conversions from Catholicism. At the same time, "dissatisfaction with priests and lack of significant involvement with the church also impel Hispanics to leave."[40]

In Latin America the story of Catholic conversions to Protestant sects continues as the institutional church remains wedded to the Western European, hierarchical, clerical model. Penny Lernoux notes that "not since the mass baptisms of Latin American Indians by the conquering Spanish in the sixteenth century has Latin America witnessed a religious conversion of such magnitude."[41] Lernoux believes one of the main reasons for this defection is the obsession of the hierarchy with the preservation of white "Eurocentric Vatican" interests instead of the real spiritual needs of the people.

Religion, Spirituality, and the Institutional Church

An old Dominican in the Alaskan wilderness, a recovering alcoholic, expressed dramatically how spirituality differs from religion. He said, "Religion is irrational. How else can you explain the craziness of so many of its practitioners? And how else can you explain their irrational need to control so many others in the name of religion?" In his own spirituality, nourished by his Dominican tradition as well as the Twelve-Step program, he had been led to experience God as his higher power. He didn't need anyone outside himself trying to bind up that God in a box that could be opened and shut at will. He could distinguish between spirituality and religion, as well as their manifestations.

Instead of stressing faith as a personal experience of God, religion warns us to be orthodox about our beliefs. Rather than help us in prayer we are told we sin if we don't say certain prayers. In place of a religion of the heart, we are told to be loyal to a magisterium in its definitions. Something has happened between the Acts of the Apostles and the actions of the Curia. Once she started reexamining behavior in the church, Anne Wilson Schaef began to recognize its part in the addictive system that enables us to deny our spirituality. She writes:

> Gradually I came to realize that the addictive processes of the promise, absorption, control, the external referent, invalidation, and dualism are all characteristic processes of the church. It was then fairly easy to see how the church actively inhibits and interferes with our ability to approach our own spirituality. . . .
>
> The church holds forth the promise of healing and spiritual growth, but neither is possible to achieve through addictive processes. The basic truths of the church are essential to the human soul, and the vehicles of their dissemination are the vehicles of the Addictive System and by definition can only lead to nonliving. It is sad that an institution with "life and life more abundant" to give chooses a process for delivery that denies life itself.[42]

When the church becomes an addict, spirituality is replaced by religion. In terms of its function, religion arises as a way to meet peoples' breaking points. It provides some sort of reference beyond one's self. It assists individuals in their adjustments to life's tasks and difficulties as well as providing moral legitimization for the social conformity of individuals in society. This is where it can be addictive as well as serve others' addictions. Authentic spirituality cannot be addictive. Indeed, the thesis of this book is that spirituality is the antidote for addiction.

It is precisely in religion's functional role as moral legitimator for social conformity of individuals in society that religion can be most addictive. I am not here speaking of religion as the object of peoples' addiction or of people being addicted *to* religion in the sense that religion becomes the addictive substance. This kind of religious addiction and abuse does not represent the main concern of this book. The way religion can be made to function by the leaders in the family and our codependent reaction to their functioning are the foci of my concern. I am concentrating on religion as the addictive process wherein key leaders addicted to power use religion to reinforce their power and where its codependents hook into it (and their power).

An example of how our religious leaders even try to control our religious experience through their definitions can be found in the Congregation for the Doctrine of the Faith's 1989 document warning about certain methods of prayer inspired by Buddhism, Hinduism, Zen, Yoga, and Transcendental Meditation and cautioning us to distinguish between physical exercises in prayer that produce pleasing sensations and "the authentic consolation of the Holy Spirit."[43] I could not help but see the document as a way to control of our prayer, but also to control how and whether we experience God! Rather than rejoicing that the presence of God can be found throughout all the traditions, it seems the Vatican needs to control even God.

CHAPTER SEVEN

The Church's Story 3

The Challenge to
Religious Leaders in Matthew 23

Conflict characterizes Matthew's entire gospel. This conflict rises at the beginning, plateaus after chapter 12, and then builds to a crescendo beginning with the conflict between Matthew's Jesus and various leaders starting in 20:17. By the end of this section all of the Jewish leaders are silenced (22:15–46). Then, with a fury unmatched elsewhere in the gospel, Matthew sculpts Jesus' exposition of the abuse of authority by the Jewish rulers and, ultimately, Jesus' rejection of Israel (23:1–39).

Approaching this passage from a form-critical viewpoint poses problems, especially if this acrimonious assault on the Jewish leaders is balanced with the passage immediately before about loving one's neighbor (22:38). One is tempted to conclude: 1) either Jesus was inconsistent in his teaching (saying with one breath to "observe whatever they [the scribes and Pharisees] tell you" [23:2] and then proceeding to challenge what they told the people in the rest of the chapter), or 2) he was unjust for implying that *all* in the Jewish leadership group should be condemned, or 3) he really addressed only a minority, or 4) he unfairly lumped into one group various factions among the Jewish leaders, who themselves differed greatly, or 5) such words never came from Jesus' mouth but were a Matthean creation from other sources.

Much has been written on these positions. David Garland, whose book *The Intention of Matthew 23* is seminal to the issue, notes that most scholars "have relieved Jesus of any culpability by ascribing the virulence of the discourse to either a nearly Jewish Christian community or to Matthew's community . . . . The basic assumption has been that the explanation for the polemical cast of chapter 23 can only be understood when the historical situation of Matthew is understood."[1]

The historical situation of conflict—between Jew and Gentile church members and between varying approaches to authority—gave rise to Matthew's gospel and his unique redaction of his sources. In an effort to make *the story* his church's story, Matthew seems to have combined new and old stories to shape his unique way of articulating his vision of authentic discipleship (12:52). His christology (*the story*) was to become the ecclesiology of the church's story. Facing issues in his community fifty years after Jesus' death and resurrection, he tried to highlight words and sayings of Jesus as well as accounts available about Jesus that would have particular relevance to his divided community, especially in those areas where authority seemed to be abused—even in the name of religion. According to Garland, chapter 23 "is not just a denunciation of Jewish leaders or Judaism; it is a warning to the entire Christian community. It is a *didache*, a polemic against the abuse of authority."[2] It stands as a polemic not only addressed to the community of Jesus, or to the households of Matthew, but to the church of our day as well.

Because the hierarchical principle of the institutional Catholic church seems to reflect the patterns Matthew challenged in chapter 23, it behooves us to return to it. The rest of this chapter will be spent reflecting on how the statements sculpted by Matthew's Jesus in chapter 23 can be addressed to the addictive patterns being practiced by the body of leaders in institutional Catholicism today. As this is done, especially when the application becomes quite specific, I ask the reader continually to keep in mind Matthew's original intent of fusing the two stories and how this invites a parallel approach in our era as well.

The Intended Audience of Matthew's Jesus (23:1)

The audience for Matthew's articulation of Jesus' words in chapter 23 is "the crowds and . . . his disciples" (23:1). Here, for the first time, the crowds and the disciples are clearly linked. From 21:1 on the crowds have not been seen in a positive light; they are united with the authorities against Jesus and will remain united until the end (27:20). By combining the crowds with the disciples (23:1) it seems that Matthew is predicating to his whole church the hardness of heart that came upon the people of Israel. The family had the disease, not just the "identified patient," that is, the leaders. In terms of addictive processes, the willingness of the crowd to support the behavior of the leaders, with their addiction to authority, says as much about the people as the leaders. The people are codependents, reinforcing a dysfunctional system in the critical stage of its disease. The codependency of the crowd actually feeds the addiction of the leaders.

Because addiction is a family disease, one cannot be addicted to power and control in a family unless members in the family feed that power by allowing the controls of the addict to take place. Such submission is reflected in uncritical subservience to the power and control of one or more others. This is a key notion when considering the clerical addiction in the church today. Addiction in the institutional leaders could not exist if church ministers and the laity did not allow it. Because addictive processes pass from generation to generation, the crowd in 23:1 becomes "this generation" (11:16; 12:39, 41, 42, 45; 16:41; 17:17; 23:36; 24:34), which also has gone astray.

As for the disciples themselves, they must hear the words about abuses in leadership because, precisely as leaders, they are "susceptible to the same spiritual cataracts that blinded the scribes and Pharisees."[3] Because Matthew's Jesus chose to confront the leaders in their disease, this kind of intervention points the way to hope and recovery for church leaders of any generation.

Scribes and Pharisees on Moses' Seat; *The Pope on Peter's Chair (23:2–4)*

As we saw in chapter three, after the fall of Jerusalem the Pharisees became the sole interpreters of the Law. The whole context of the first verses of 23 revolves not around the Law (23:2–3), but the way the leaders "tie up heavy burdens," hard to bear, and lay them on people's shoulders; but they themselves " are unwilling to lift a finger to move them" (23:4). The imposition of "heavy burdens" by the community's leaders on the members stands in direct contrast with the easy burden of Jesus' way of dealing with the Law and/or authority (11:30). Jesus' yoke "fits"; it makes sense. The leaders' yoke is burdensome and filled with contradictions.

As the section about Jesus' yoke is followed with concrete examples (in chapter 12) of Jesus' freeing people from interpretations of the Law that denied them their dignity, so the section about the leaders' yoke (23:4) is followed by one example after another of the way the leaders yoke people in the name of legislation that maintains their power. The issue for Matthew's Jesus was not that the scribes and Pharisees taught or legislated; it was how they unreasonably extended the sphere of their office or interpretation of passages into whole arenas of life with little or no authority in *the story* itself. Thus they became not the spiritual guides but the oppressors of the people, using religion as their ploy.

In meeting after meeting of Twelve-Step programs one hears people describing themselves as "recovering Catholics" or saying, "When I was bound up by the church's rules and regulations," or "When I was under the rule of the priests and nuns." They go on to describe heavy yokes laid on their shoulders in the name of their God; these yokes invariably reinforced various forms of oppressive religion and/or clerical control.

The image of binding here (23:4), in light of the binding authority given by Jesus to Peter (16:19) and to the church (18:18) can be a warning that those who insist on the authority of "the chair of Peter" might be just as abusive with authority as the scribes and Pharisees were from "the seat of Moses." When leaders become preoccupied with justifying their authority, the consequence can be an intellectual obsession, an emotional anxiety, and an addictive behavior, all geared to preserving that authority, which has itself become absolutized.

Today, statements and documents coming from Rome often revolve around 1) the need to maintain Roman authority over local churches, and 2) the need, within local churches, to maintain clerical control. Both are viewed as essential to the identity of the institutional church. Loyalty to authority becomes the shame-button pushed to keep members subservient to *the story* insofar as it is interpreted by the institutional church. Thus Pope John Paul II said to the United States bishops in his very first address to them as they gathered in Los Angeles in 1987: "There can be but one loyalty—to the word of God perennially proclaimed in the church entrusted to the episcopal college, with the Roman pontiff as its visible head and perpetual source of unity."[4]

The pope's speech to the bishops (not meant for them alone but for consumption by the "faithful"), mirrors the recent preoccupation by the papacy with the magisterium's power and rights: "The divine Redeemer entrusted this deposit [of faith] not to individual Christians, nor to theologians to be interpreted authentically, but to the magisterium of the church alone."[5] The faithful's role in the church is to accept the magisterial interpretation without question as a sign of their loyalty.

Without concentrating on the number of times the pope referred directly or indirectly to the centrality of the papacy in the church, it must also be remembered that the bishops' too, through their spokesperson and president, Archbishop May, stressed *their* power and prerogatives as well. In both clerical viewpoints—the papacy's and the national hierarchy's—the laity are to be subservient to clerical control.

Sometimes, however, the preoccupation of the Vatican for clerical control can go too far for the bishops themselves. An example can be found in the response of the Canadian bishops to the preparation document sent from the Council of the General Secretariat of the Synod of 1990 called to deal with "The Formation of Priests in Circumstances of the Present Day." Since forgetfulness is part of the addictive process, I found it interesting that, in their preliminary remarks, the Canadian bishops noted that the document represented an "apparent forgetfulness of the ecclesiological change of direction created by Vatican II (especially in *Lumen Gentium* and in *Gaudium et Spes*), ignoring the opportunities for a true ecclesial co-responsibility, and seemingly resurrecting the past."[6] In a powerful challenge to the addictive mind-set of the curial clerical consciousness, the bishops stated unequivocally:

> The document's major failing is related to its ecclesiological vision: the church model transmitted by the document is not the model of a church of communion as strongly recommended by Vatican II. The document's preconciliar ecclesiology creates the notion of a priesthood more centered on power than on service within the people of God; in this ecclesiology one must not be surprised to find few traces of the existence of co-responsibility. This intangible model with its emphasis on the hierarchical character of the institution leaves little place for contemporary questions increasingly more urgent: a limited-time ministry, ordination of married men, ordination of women.[7]

When the chair's authority gets exercised at the expense of the household's authority, and when an obsession is created in maintaining and justifying this control, definite signs of addictive patterns exist.

The Preoccupation with Externals,
Titles, and Rights of Clerics (23:5–7)

Matthew begins 23:5 by scoring the leaders for performing their deeds "to be seen by others." This parallels the way he earlier described the kind of almsgiving, prayer, and fasting that Jesus found repellent (6:1). In both cases (23:5 and 6:1) the external actions reflected hypocrisy and denied justice or right order. In both cases, true piety (that is, justice) was geared to gaining God's reward rather than human approval. The difference, however, between the hypocrisy in 6:1–18 and 23:5–7 is that the former is more general, while the latter indicates a specific legalistic rigidity that can be observed by others.

When human beings believe they alone have the power to interpret God's law, their legislation and traditions can be so controlling that they demand unquestioning obedience in the name of that God. An example is the 1989 requirement by the Congregation for the Doctrine of the Faith that future clerics "firmly embrace" whatever "is definitively proposed by the church regarding faith and morals." With seminaries and male religious orders reporting an increasing number of more traditional men entering the clerical state, it is not surprising that there was little public protest from the seminarians about this extension of magisterial power into their lives. Such submissiveness to others' control is a typical response of codependent people.

Besides observations about codependency, many seminary professors who were part of the dream of implementing the spirit of Vatican II and its more collegial and pastoral approach also have noticed among aspiring clerics an increasing preoccupation with externals, titles, and clerical rights. In some seminaries there seems to be no need to impose clerical dress codes; many candidates *seek out* those institutions that have them. The issue of dress is not limited to diocesan situations only. I know of the head of a major order of men, based in Rome, who feared to take off his habit in some of the houses of that order itself for fear that members of his own order might report him to the proper office in the Roman Curia. If that happened, he would inevitably be called to give an account of his actions; he would be shamed.

For many congregations of religious women, besides insisting on a hierarchical model of authority in the various institutes, another chief concern of CICLSAL revolves around appropriate, distinguishable "religious garb," even in those institutes that were founded with garb intentionally blending with the clothing of the culture. Constitutions are returned when nothing about clothing is mentioned. However, again, CICLSAL is only the "identified patient." One of the greatest sources of turmoil *within* many congregations since the Vatican Council has revolved around the issue of clothing. The dysfunctional situation is not only top-down; it spirals within as well.

In their defense, many leaders justify their right to impose new kinds of discipline as reminders of long-forgotten rules among the clergy. These rules are recalled or enacted with a real sense that these norms will enhance the church's image and bring about better order among its members. However, in light of Jesus' concern about externals, titles, and procedures among the religious leaders in his day (23:1–7), Matthew's rendition of Jesus' response to such ways of acting cannot be taken lightly either. In referring to the first seven verses of chapter 23, Wolfgang Trilling finds parallels between Jesus' words to the scribes and Pharisees and Matthew's church leaders:

> This introduction already contains a devastating condemnation which anticipates all that is to follow. Jesus pitilessly exposes the hollowness of a "justice" which is dominated nearly everywhere and is paraded with official authority, yet is rotten to the core, permeated with distortion, vanity and lies, is full of fine words but is dire hypocrisy. This is the ugly counterpart of the true "justice" described by Jesus (5:20ff.) and to which all are bound. The example of the Pharisees is meant to be a salutary warning to Christians and a check on their behavior.[8]

The "they" who parade their authority and insist on their titles did not pass away with the destruction of the Temple; "they" existed in Matthew's house-churches; "they" are alive and struggling for even greater control in the church today.

The Direct Referencing of Matthew's Community (23:8–12)

In verses 8–12, Matthew's Jesus stops talking about the scribes and Pharisees and directly addresses the crowds and disciples. The transition reveals not only a christological purpose, but even more, an ecclesiological message. The sudden shift in the direct audience (which still is gathered in the Temple) from the scribes and Pharisees to the disciples becomes a type for Matthew's own community. The words to the disciples—"you"—no longer simply reveal a polemic against the Jewish leaders' behavior; the broadened issue now involves rules for regulating the Christian community wherein there is place for but one rabbi, one father, and one teacher.[9]

The first item among these broadened rules deals with a rejection of the term *rabbi* because "you have one teacher, and you are all students" (23:8). At the time of Matthew, being a rabbi involved teaching; teaching involved a hierarchy. However, if Jesus is God-with-us in authority, he is the *one* teacher. Those failing to acknowledge Jesus as their Lord and teacher will appropriate the title to themselves, even though they receive the mission to teach from their Lord (28:18). They utter the necessary words about Jesus as teacher, but their preoccupation and behavior belie their words. In their minds, even in the presence of Jesus, *they* are the authoritative teachers. In Matthew, when anyone calls Jesus "teacher" it indicates insincerity (8:19; 9:11; 12:38; 17:24; 19:16; 22:16, 24, 36); only those who "talk the talk" but are unwilling to "walk the walk" call Jesus teacher. Matthew uses this to stress the fact that Jesus alone is the authority, the authoritative teacher.

Among the Jews teachers of special rank were sometimes called Father. In the house-synagogues to be called Father was a special honor. However, if under the one household authority—that of Jesus—*all* are brothers and sisters (23:8c; see 5:22–24, 47; 12:48–50; 18:15, 21, 35; 25:40; 28:10), there can be no patriarchal figure. In this light it becomes more understandable why Matthew's Jesus immediately says, "Call no one your father on earth, for you have one Father—the one in heaven" (23:9).

Matthew's unique use of the notion of God's singular paternity not only rejects earthly patriarchy but raises another model for household dynamics to be emulated: the collegial model.[10] In a more contemporary vein the rejection of earthly patriarchy means the rejection of a male, clerical model in favor of a basic community of equal brothers and sisters. Thus, for recovery to take place, the hierarchical addiction to clericalism must stop. A converting collegial community demands the end of patriarchy and its addictive ways.

This passage countermands with a deeper authority any effort to make legislation or teaching support a church's story that canonizes hierarchy and patriarchy at the expense of mutuality and collegiality.

Because Matthew's use of the words "you" and "your" in reference to the crowds and disciples serves as a referent for the church, he is offering a paradigm for how authority should be expressed in the community. Whether parent to children or master to servant, the new household of children and servants exists under but one head: Jesus Christ. Thus, Matthew's Jesus adds another admonition: "Nor are you to be called instructors, for you have one instructor, the Messiah" (23:10).

Besides the role of leadership in a household, an instructor also occupied a position of authority. Thus in this third rejection of a title Matthew's Jesus warns about abuses of authority connected with teaching. In this, as well as in the other titles rejected by Jesus as hierarchical, Matthew has a warning for the leaders of his own house-churches about adopting titles, especially insofar as these might indicate superiority over others. Church leaders are called to service, not power.

Finally, in a passage reminiscent of the exchange of Jesus with the mother of James and John—which is placed at the beginning of the series of critical conflict stories with the leaders (20:26–27)—Matthew uniquely combines notions contained elsewhere in his narrative (18:1–4; 20:26–27) to have Jesus say: "The greatest among you will be your servant. All who exalt themselves will be humbled, and all who humble themselves will be exalted" (23:11–12). The fact that Matthew alone uses this saying here presupposes a unique need in his community.

Woes for Hypocritical Teachers Who Believe They Alone Are Correct (23:13–36)

The "woes" in this section of Matthew (23:13–36) reveal the most sustained denunciation in all the gospels. The verses—found in both Matthew and Luke—seem to have come from a common source, which adapted less strident warnings in Mark 12:38–40. Comparing Matthew's first use of the word for "woe" in 11:21 with its sevenfold use in chapter 23:13ff, makes it quite clear that a whole infrastructure (if I can use the notion) is being addressed. The infrastructure is "this generation" (12:39; 23:36; see 11:20–24). The term referred to a total reality, whether it be Chorazin and Bethsaida (11:21) or Capernaum (11:23) or Jerusalem (see 23:37). Both in chapters 11 and 23 the woes are addressed to specific entities because of specific behaviors, which resulted from specific ways of thinking that can be called addictive.

Furthermore, in both cases the specific parties refused the intervention of Jesus and his invitation to convert (seek recovery). Finally, in both passages the judgment of God implies a rejection of the institution because of its failure to repent. The infrastructure, its institutions, its "isms," and its ideology stand condemned.

The connection of the woes with the appellation of the scribes and Pharisees as hypocrites indicates that the woes reveal much more wrath and anger than sorrow or grieving. Yet, as with any intervention wherein those intervening realize they will not be successful, while the woes do mirror deep indignation, their inner core reveals grief and anguish. In this sense, and because Matthew's Jesus referred to himself as a prophet (23:34), the woes can be considered a prophetic proclamation against a clerical consciousness—a last-ditch call to life in the face of an environment of death. As such they represent Jesus' final intervention toward the religious leaders inviting them to embrace a spirituality of wholeness instead of the process of addiction.

The leaders had used their position of power to turn images of life (the realm of heaven, vocation recruiting, the Temple, the altar, tithing, purity, justice, and Jerusalem) into figures of death (shutting off the realm of heaven, proselytes who become mirror-images of clericalism, money more important than the sacred, injustice, impurity, hypocrisy, and Gehenna). Consequently, the woes were addressed to them.

With the stereotypical formula: "Woe to you, scribes and Pharisees," the leadership group is identified collectively under one characteristic—hypocrisy (23:13, 15, 23, 25, 27, 29). Matthew alone uses this term for the leaders. The contemporary dictionary definition of *hypocrisy* is "a feigning to be what one is not or to believe what one does not; *esp*: the false assumption of an appearance of virtue or religion."[11] It implies conscious duplicity, an effort to mislead, a kind of phoniness. Today, people are called hypocrites when they pretend piety or deceive others. Another nuance—closer to the meaning in the first century—is being an actor. Matthew's use of the word did not refer so much to the mask worn by an actor, but to the way an actor *interpreted* the story.

That the leaders are called blind in 23:15, 17, and 19 implies that any misleading they may have done was unintentional. Furthermore, 23:23 does not imply any insincerity and 23:29 does not accuse them of feigning to perform religious acts. Earlier Matthew's Jesus made it clear that hypocrites might be quite oblivious to their own sins

(7:3–5). Thus any notion of conscious pretense seems deficient. We need to probe deeper for the meaning of hypocrisy. As we do, we will find that it revolves around notions that are interconnected: justice as the heart of the law, and interpretations of the law that do not promote and/or reveal justice.

In Matthew, justice represents the right order of people in house-holds and the right way of sharing their resources; hypocrisy reveals a dynamic that perpetuated disorder or dysfunctionality in the household or family system. As both 6:1ff and 23:13ff make clear, the leaders of the households were called hypocrites because the "order" they demanded disrupted the household and promoted injustice even as it ensured the Law's observance as the leaders interpreted it in their legislation and traditions. For instance, in 5:20 Matthew's Jesus de-manded a justice that exceeded the justice of the scribes and Pharisees. Then he applied this demand for inner order, justice, or righteousness to six cases (antitheses) where the leaders' interpretation of the Law said one thing but Jesus' interpretation of justice demanded another (5:21–47). He concluded the antitheses by saying that authentic justice (5:20) demands a perfection that reflects the dynamics of the reign of God (5:48).

In Matthew, justice, bearing fruit, fidelity to God's will, and do-ing good indicate parallel notions.[12] Since justice and doing good interrelate, injustice involves doing evil. Matthew's unique word for "doing evil" is *anomia*. He uses it four times. In 7:23 it means non-involvement in the face of evil. The second use occurs in the parable of the seed on good and bad ground; the evildoers (13:41) will be cast from the reign of God. The third use is in this section. It connects directly with hypocrisy (23:28). The final time refers to the end times. That verse states, "Because of the increase of lawlessness, the love of many will grow cold" (24:12). The increase in doing evil adversely affects relationships of love and familiar relationships of love assume reciprocal justice. In this sense, the first notion of hypocrisy involved disordered or unjust family dynamics that reflected the dysfunctional, evil behavior that was disrupting the family of disciples.

Another notion of hypocrisy used in Matthew's time which prob-ably influenced his story can be found in an extra-biblical source of the culture's story—the documents of Qumran. Considering them-selves to be righteous or just, the members of Qumran accused their antagonists—probably the Pharisees—of "seeking after smooth things."

The image does not refer to persons who seek an easy way out, but to those who give false interpretations of scripture.[13] While a sense of flattery, deceit, and lying may be present, the notion mainly involves false counsel and interpretation of the law; it involves a misunderstanding of God's Law, which misleads God's people. Precisely because the Pharisees came to view themselves as *the* interpreters of the Law, and since their interpretations often reflected those of people in power who interpret legislation to promote their own unconscious interests, Jesus repudiated them. Furthermore, that they tried to bind people to their interpretation of the tradition was doubly wrong (23:14). Subjectively they might be saved due to their ignorance and hardened conscience; objectively their obsession with their interpretation and making sure the community abided by their interpretation alienated them from God's reign.

This understanding should help us when applying the passages in 23:13ff to the leaders of the church today. To think that one could read their hearts would be presumptuous. To believe that they are consciously duplicitous and insincere would be rash. To put every leader of the institutional church into the same category would be simplistic. The sincerity of the leaders is not being questioned; rather, the dogmatic and legalistic interpretation of *the story* by key leaders, combined with the public silence of the other leaders in face of those interpretations, does not measure up to the reign of God announced by Jesus Christ.

When the charge of hypocrisy was leveled against the leaders, the basis for the charge stemmed from the leaders' faulty interpretation of the Law. Over and over Matthew's Jesus charged the leaders with misinterpreting the meaning of Jesus and his mission (9:3, 34; 12:24, 38; 16:1–4; 21:15). Because of their blindness they honestly believed what they declared to be of God was true; however, in light of another vision of God's nature and reign, they were simply wrong. According to Garland, "The Pharisees are condemned in the Synoptics only as their teaching stands in opposition to the will of God and Jesus' mission."[14] They were unjust and rejected because they misinterpreted God's will and thus perpetuated evildoing.

Matthew's use of the term *hypocrite* serves a pedagogical function for church leaders until the end of the age; the behavior rejected by

Jesus in *the story* should be recalled so that it will not repeat itself in the church. Since the scribes and Pharisees were leaders in the religious family, their self-serving use of power undermined the faith of the other members; thus they endangered the ultimate destiny of those they viewed as dependent on their teaching. They made themselves woe-ful. The woe-warnings serve as a challenge to church leaders of any generation.

Donald Senior notes that "this list of indictments is not merely to pass judgment on past generations of Israel's leaders, but to scorch false leadership in the *Christian* community."[15]

> **But woe to you, scribes and Pharisees, hypocrites!**
> **For you lock people out of the kingdom of heaven.**
> **For you do not go in yourselves, and when others**
> **go in, you stop them (23:13).**

One cannot imagine a more severe criticism of the leaders of a religion ordered to facilitate entrance into the reign of God than that they create obstacles to that entrance. The facilitators become the stumbling blocks. The image of shutting off the reign of God may suggest the power of the rabbis to bind and loose. It may also refer to the casuistry (and possibly the practice of excommunication after Jamnia) enacted by the Jewish teachers. Because the Jewish leaders corrupted the Law with their teaching (16:12), Jesus transferred the power to bind and loose to Peter (16:19). And because Peter became a stumbling block (16:23) that same power to bind and loose was given the community as well (18:18). Since binding and loosing involve authority, the institutional leaders have interpreted these passages to make 16:19 dominant and to virtually exclude 18:18. Acceptance of this limited interpretation helps create and perpetuate a church of codependent people whose self-understanding of discipleship depends on the self-serving interpretation of the addictive leaders.

One of the gravest dangers facing teachers and leaders is the tendency to use their role of power to proscribe legislation or teach doctrine that is self-serving. Another danger revolves around their effort to control information so that those dependent on them for that information will not be able to question their authority. Thus, if the church of Matthew 16 can be interpreted in such a way as to reinforce hierarchy and patriarchy and if God and God's reign can somehow be construed in patriarchal notions, the issues of women and collegiality need never be addressed. But they *are* being questioned today. The obsession of the curial leaders with preserving a male, patriarchal God, however, is evident in the way they have tried to shut out the idea of God as female as well as male.

When, in an address to 900,000 people in 1978, Pope John Paul I said that God "is a father, but even more mother," no mention of the feminine idea of God was included in the official paper of the institutional church, *L'Osservatore Romano*. It printed the speech on September 21, 1978, but the parts referring to God as female were censored. The curial teachers tried to shut off the papal teaching when it collided with their patriarchal image. They shut off information about God and God's reign that might make the disciples ask questions about ways patriarchy is being used to reinforce, on earth, a church that does not reflect the reign of God—who is neither male nor female.

The Vatican also reveals its preoccupation with controlling thought within the church by trying to shut off any teachers whose teaching does not reinforce its own. This refers not just to individual teachers, but to whole seminaries where the pastoral approach does not reflect that of those who define themselves as official teachers. This has been particularly evident in seminaries in Brazil.

The obsession with shutting out certain images of God or theologies is not limited to those at the top of the clerical hierarchy. The patriarchal perspective and prerogatives get promoted throughout the system, sometimes subtly. At a meeting of our provincial leaders several years ago Sister Francis Borgia Rothleuber, then president of the Leadership Conference of Women Religious, spoke about sexism. She showed how we Capuchins, as well as the institutional church as a whole, discriminated against women in leadership, liturgy, and even in our very language about God. When she finished, one of the men who had just finished his graduate studies in theology was livid.

"What's the matter?" a couple of us asked him.

"It's her talk," he replied angrily. "It's just not true. This idea that God is male/female is just totally untheological. She's just wrong. God *is* male."

"You've got to be kidding!" we said, almost in unison.

"Never! God is male. It is revealed. God is Father; God is Son. That's simple revelation," he countered.

"But," I said, "if God is just Father and Son without being equally Mother and Daughter, there is discrimination in God and that's incompleteness. And you wouldn't accept incompleteness in God."

"But it is *revealed* that God is Father and God is Son," he argued back.

He had shut his understanding of the reign of God from being inclusive in order to preserve an exclusive male, clerical model of church. Why was he so obsessed with the definition? Why was he so angry about the human interpretation of the revelation? Was he really that convinced that God was male? Or was it because, for him, God *had to be male*? Was that the only way this male cleric could maintain his elite position in the patriarchal institution? Yet, if he had analyzed the way dogmas about God's sexual identity had evolved into ideology, he would have found that those who made the definition at such places as Chalcedon and Nicea were all males.

I left that conversation, as I leave many similar conversations and interpretations, thinking that the issue really has little to do with good theology; rather, it bespeaks how theology can be used to promote the power of the theologizer. In this case it was being used by my confrere to shut off access to a share in the power of God to any but celibate male clerics. Those clerics who have the power to define can interpret the definitions in their own interests. Whenever they misinterpret God and God's reign, the translators and interpreters become hypocrites.

> **Woe to you, scribes and Pharisees, hypocrites! For you cross sea and land to make a single convert, and you make the new convert twice as much a child of hell as yourselves (23:15).**

The word *convert* is used in the gospels only once—this time in Matthew. At the time Matthew wrote his gospel, Palestinian Judaism, especially the Judaism of the Pharisees, demanded full acceptance of the whole Jewish Law as they interpreted it. Because their interpretation did not always promote the underlying purposes of the Law, hypocrisy again resulted. Consequently, this woe does not speak against the effort of the community's leaders to make converts. Rather, it chastises their obsession with making of those converts clones who parrot *their* interpretation of the Law. Such converts, rather than becoming children of God's reign (8:12; 18:3), become double children of hell, worse than their recruiters.

Whereas the Pharisees' disciples were expected to mouth the interpretative teachings of their recruiters and submit to their authority, the disciples of Jesus were to submit to his authoritative teaching by putting it into practice (28:18–20). To be a convert of the Pharisees is to become a hypocrite as they are; to be a disciple of Jesus is to submit all interpretation of the Law and the prophets to his words and example.

The preoccupation of the Vatican with naming new bishops who are clones of the papal and curial interpretation of church and church teachings has become increasingly a cause of dismay. Many of these proselytes seem to be even more addicted to the preservation of the male, celibate, clerical model of church than those who named them. Whereas under Popes John XXIII, Paul VI, and John Paul I the bishops named were generally pastoral and collegial, intent on implementing the Second Vatican Council, the new proselytes have been chosen because of their willingness to stress orthodoxy and patriarchy and support the effort of the papacy and Curia to ensure their prerogatives in teaching.

Responding to Pope John Paul II's early 1990 appointment of Thomas V. Dailey as the new bishop of Brooklyn, Richard McBrien, chairman of the University of Notre Dame's theology department, wrote an op-ed piece for *The New York Times* entitled "A Papal Attack on Vatican II." Noting that Dailey's appointment "fits into a pattern of institutional change in the Roman Catholic Church over the past decade or so," McBrien offered an extended analysis of the obsession of Pope John Paul II and his Curia to ensure a Matthew 16 model of the church:

> Since his election in 1978, Pope John Paul II has been determinedly appointing a certain type of cleric to important archdioceses and dioceses all around the world.
>
> These bishops tend to be uncritically loyal to the Pope and his curial associates, rigidly authoritarian and solitary in the exercise of pastoral leadership and reliably safe in their theological views. (That is, their understanding of the faith is untouched by, if not hostile to, the most significant developments in theology and biblical studies since the '50s.)
>
> Although the pattern of appointments is clear everywhere—Austria, Brazil, Canada, the Netherlands, Peru,

West Germany—nowhere is it more apparent than in the
U.S.

Since 1980, with the exception of the Archdiocese of
Chicago (where a pastorally credible, middle-of-the-road
Archbishop Joseph Bernardin was needed to put out the
fires ignited by the scandal-plagued administration of the
late John Cardinal Cody), every major appointee has been
more hard-line than his immediate predecessor.[16]

After giving clear examples of places from Boston to Los Angeles and New York to Denver where more hard-line bishops have been
appointed, McBrien notes that these appointees are part of the "post–
1978 Vatican strategy aimed at restoring the church to the institutional
state which existed prior to Vatican II." He also notes that the episcopal appointees being enlisted in this restorationist effort tend to have
two things in common: a simplistic theology, and an unquestioning
institutional loyalty. He notes the homeostatic consequences efforts to
"restore" the pre-Vatican II church of Matthew 16 are having on the
body, consequences which reflect addiction in a family:

> The Vatican's pattern of episcopal appointments is lower-
> ing the morale of the church's most engaged and effective
> priests, nuns and lay members, many of whom are edging
> to the conclusion that the church's present leadership is ir-
> relevant, if not even inimical, to their deepest religious and
> human concerns.
>
> There are hundreds of such Catholics in Brooklyn who,
> for several decades, have been struggling against enormous
> obstacles to keep the church alive and effective. They were
> undoubtedly waiting to work with their new bishop in a
> common pastoral cause. His opening press conference must
> have been discouraging.
>
> Bishop Dailey has a favorite expression: "You never
> say 'no' to the church." He will have to learn very quickly
> that *they*, and not just the hierarchy, are the church.[17]

As McBrien stated, the obsession with appointing clones is not
limited to the United States. In July 1986 Pope John Paul II bypassed
all the auxiliary bishops and the entire archdiocesan clergy to choose as
archbishop of Vienna an obscure Benedictine, Hans Hermann Gröer.
Following this he created a military ordinariate for Austria (a neutral
country) against the wishes of pacifists and neutralists. Then, in 1987

he named a conservative theologian—a man with links to Opus Dei who stressed the need for obedience to the hierarchy and discipline in the church—as auxiliary bishop of Vienna. In early 1989 Wolfgang Haas was named coadjutor to Chur, Switzerland, in an act that outraged the people's sense of justice.[18] In early 1989 he named a conservative village priest archbishop of Salzburg.

Whether ignoring the names of three candidates proposed by Catholic leaders and appointing Joachim Cardinal Meisner, the conservative archbishop of Berlin, to Cologne, or wearing down the efforts of the church of Matthew 18 in Ireland to propose their candidates by imposing a conservative metaphysician as Dublin's archbishop, or installing a long-time Vatican official as Primate of Brazil, the obsession with insuring like-minded bishops is clear.

In January 1989, 163 Catholic theologians from Austria, Switzerland, West Germany, and the Netherlands, strongly critical of such tactics by the Vatican and the pope, signed a document called the "Cologne Declaration." They were later joined by two hundred other signatories. Their principal grievances were threefold: 1) The Vatican has been appointing bishops throughout the world "without regard for the recommendations of the local church and without respect for their established rights"; 2) qualified male and female theologians were being refused official church permission to teach in a way that represented "dangerous interference in the free exercise of scholarly research and teaching" as well as an abuse of power; and 3) the "theologically questionable attempts to assert the pope's doctrinal and jurisdictional authority in an exaggerated form." The declaration concluded:

> It is not part of the papal office to sharpen conflicts of a secondary nature without any attempt at dialogue, to resolve such conflicts unilaterally and by official decree, and to turn them into grounds for exclusion. If the pope does what does not belong to his office, he cannot demand obedience in the name of Catholicism. Then he must expect contradiction.[19]

> **Woe to you, blind guides, who say, "Whoever swears by the sanctuary is bound by nothing; but whoever swears by the gold of the sanctuary is bound by the oath." You blind fools! For which is greater, the gold or the sanctuary that has made the gold sacred? And you say, "Whoever swears by the altar is bound by nothing; but whoever swears**

> by the gift that is on the altar is bound by the oath." How blind you are! For which is greater, the gift or the altar that makes the gift sacred? So whoever swears by the altar, swears by it and by everything on it; and whoever swears by the sanctuary swears by it and by the one who dwells in it; and whoever swears by heaven, swears by the throne of God and by the one who is seated upon it (23:16–22).

Upon a casual glance, the above passage might indicate that Matthew's Jesus is concerned about cultic matters dealing with the Temple and its altar. However, again, the issue of the woe revolves around more misinterpretations of the teaching of the Law by its teachers. Besides showing how their casuistry had allowed secondary issues to become primary, this passage reveals a deeper approach to oaths. In 5:34–36 the leaders were told, "Do not swear at all, either by heaven, for it is the throne of God, or by the earth, for it is his footstool, or by Jerusalem, for it is the city of the great King. And do not swear by your head, for you cannot make one hair white or black." In reference to the apparent contradiction between 5:34–37—which demands no oaths—and 23:16–22—which implies that all oaths are binding even when God's name is intentionally avoided—it should be clear that all oaths ultimately involve God. The issue is not oaths per se but the hypocritical approach to them.

Despite its insistence that the magisterium alone can determine with certitude *the story*—which rejects oath-taking (5:34)—the Congregation for the Doctrine of the Faith in 1989 imposed a new formulation of the profession of faith and a new oath of fidelity for those who assume offices in the church (from cardinals and bishops to pastors and deacons, seminary professors and theology teachers). In addition to the former profession of faith, which included the Nicene Creed, along with an acceptance of those doctrines of faith and morals "defined by the church's solemn deliberations or affirmed and declared by its ordinary magisterium," the new oath was extended so that the oath-taker would have to vow: "I firmly embrace and hold all and everything which is definitively proposed by the church regarding faith and morals."

When the document appeared, a Holy Office consultor explained that this kind of truth "proposed by the church regarding faith and morals" included the papal teaching on birth control as contained in the encyclical *Humanae Vitae*. If his interpretation was true, heretofore undefined teachings would be considered definitely proposed—and required to be embraced.

The fear of challenging either the oath of fidelity or the refusal to allow public dissent by theologians in the Catholic church became clear to me in June, 1990 when I attended a conference of 150 justice and peace ministers who gathered to anticipate the centenary of Catholic social thought since Leo XIII's *Rerum Novarum*. At the gathering I led a workshop entitled "Justice in the Household of the Faith."

During the gathering the Congregation's "Instruction" disallowing public dissent became public. The whole group voted to have a committee of four theologians, including myself, draft a response. Despite the overwhelming endorsement of the response, it became clear that the participants did not want their names or group affiliation to be public. Fear of recriminations, fear of "a repeat of 1984" [the dynamics that were used by the Vatican against those who signed *The New York Times* statement on abortion], and fear of their communities being identified with their actions dominated. When it came time to have the press conference, I was the only cleric who would give my name as one of the group who dissented.

> **Woe to you, scribes and Pharisees, hypocrites! For you tithe mint, and dill, and cumin, and have neglected the weightier matters of the law, justice and mercy and faith. It is these you ought to have practiced, without neglecting the others. You blind guides! You strain out a gnat but swallow a camel (23:23–24).**

Matthew's version of this "woe" makes it clear that the scribes and Pharisees again were misinterpreting the Law. Because they did not distinguish between trifling concerns and weightier matters, key elements of the Law were neglected. As the leaders of the institutional church interpret church law and practice today, the two issues about not distinguishing the small from the great and leaving critical matters neglected are evidenced in the lack of accepting a hierarchy of truths and in the way the basic sacraments of the church are being denied in order to preserve the *raison d'eglise*.

When I was in the seminary I studied from a universal catechism imposed on the church as a result of the Council of Trent, in order to ensure orthodoxy. Today's effort by the Congregation for the Doctrine of the Faith to impose its interpretation of the church's faith in the first universal catechism in the church in more than four hundred years has proven to be another example of the curial obsessive control over thinking, feelings, and behavior in the Catholic church.

Joseph Cardinal Ratzinger, head of the commission writing the catechism, told students that the draft being circulated for responses, which bore the stamp of "secrecy," was a "marvelous work," although "imperfect." What he considered remarkable various national hierarchies rejected as basically flawed in content as well as in purpose. As Matthew's Jesus condemned the scribes and Pharisees for not distinguishing between primary and non-primary issues, the "conservative-oriented" N.C.C.B. committee responding to the catechism rejected it because, among other things, it failed to distinguish between peripheral beliefs and central dogmas of the faith and even equated theological opinions still open to debate with established Catholic doctrines. The vision of morality presented, committee members said, reads as if "morality is fundamentally a matter of observing the law, rather than a matter of discipleship."[20]

Probably the most critical application of this woe to contemporary church practice revolves around the insistence of the papacy and Curia on preserving of the male, celibate priesthood, even when the weightier matter of the regular sacramental celebration of reconciliation and the eucharist remains undone. Due in large part to the obsessive refusal of the Vatican to open the ranks of the priesthood in the Western Catholic church beyond male celibates almost half of its members do not regularly celebrate these two essential sacraments. At the same time that the Vatican proved heroic in insuring food for those in Africa who were starving because of what meteorologists and geographers might call an act of God, it did nothing to alleviate the eucharistic famine there, and in so many other parts of the world. In fact, it was *responsible* for this eucharistic famine. The inability of Catholics to regularly celebrate the eucharist is no act of God; it is an act of humans with hardened hearts.

The limitation of the priesthood to male celibates has no grounding in *the story*. To deny it in the name of the non-resurrected Jesus Christ, who was a male celibate, when his members cannot be fed, represents that injustice that is concerned about bread but doesn't recognize the body. It reveals a hardness of heart among church leaders who are willing to lose millions of Catholics to other denominations in favor of a law that has absolutely nothing to do with *the story*.

> **Woe to you, scribes and Pharisees, hypocrites! For**
> **you cleanse the outside of the cup and of the plate,**
> **but inside they are full of greed and self-indulgence.**
> **You blind Pharisee! First clean the inside of the cup**
> **so that the outside also may come clean (23:25–26).**

Wolfgang Trilling shows that this woe can be interpreted three ways. A literal interpretation stresses the purity of vessels and their contents. A figurative explanation contrasts the external behavior of the Pharisees with their hidden motives. A third interprets both literally (the first verse) and figuratively (the second verse).[21] In light of the stress on inward purity by Matthew's Jesus (see 5:20–48), it would seem the latter interpretation must be used in understanding the meaning behind the above words.

Building on the previous woes, this lament of Matthew's Jesus does not refer as much to rituals of washing as to behaviors related to the Law's misinterpretation. The religious leaders failed to see the weightier issue of moral purity because they obsessed about levitical purity. They showed more concern about ceremonial matters than moral rectitude. Garland repeats the fact that the woe attacks the scribes and Pharisees for their failure as teachers:

> As the guides of God's people they are blind.... Their
> hypocrisy is not that they simply pretend to be pure while
> actually being full of robbery and extortion; rather, they
> have failed in their responsibility to make clear the will of
> God.[22]

One of the deepest disappointments I have experienced in my ministry of corporate responsibility in the Catholic church since 1973 has been the lip-service paid the effort to bring the church's teachings to bear upon the marketplace, accompanied by a reluctance, if not outright anxiety, of getting involved for fear (unfounded) such a ministry might affect the "bottom line" of dioceses. As of this writing there are fewer than twenty dioceses in the United States doing what the bishops themselves declared in their letter on the United States

Economy *must* be done by every Catholic institution having stock in United States corporations: "As part owners, they must cooperate in shaping the policies of those companies through dialogue with management, through votes at corporate meetings, through the introduction of resolutions and through participation in investment decisions."[23]

The contradictions between what is said and what is done get even clearer when considering the Vatican and its finances. The Banco Ambrosiano scandal, which today is still mired in secrecy and intrigue, has created a sense of cynicism over curial fiscal alliances.[24] This cynicism heightens when one recalls papal denunciations of apartheid in South Africa at the same time (1982–1985) the Vatican Bank participated in eight bond issues totalling $251.9 million for three South African government entities.[25]

Inconsistency also exists between words and actions by church leaders involved in the Vatican's behind-the-scenes politics and its legislation on clerical involvement in politics. The statement about non-involvement is clearly stated: The outside of the cup and plate get cleansed; internally all sorts of power plays are happening. One example of this duplicity is action in Chile during the late '50s, '60s, and early '70s, where the institutional church worked behind the scenes to promote the Christian Democrats despite its protestations about neutrality.[26] Pope John Paul II warned priests in Latin America, Africa, and Asia to stay out of partisan politics. But in his native Poland, Catholic priests introduced Solidarity candidates during Mass and hosted get-acquainted rallies with them afterward with no sanctions.

The underlying issue in the above cases has little to do with partisan politics; rather, it involves ecclesiastical politics and its institutional self-interests. This was made clear in November 1988 when a priest in Pakistan, Rufin Julius, was elected to the country's national assembly. The following March he was named to head the Ministry of Minorities. Despite the celebrated public shaming by Pope John Paul II of Ernesto Cardenal for accepting the Ministry of Culture in Sandinista Nicaragua, the Vatican viewed the election and appointment of Julius as acceptable. As one Curia official declared: "Pakistan is a completely Muslim country, where there are no lay Catholics to defend the interests of the church."[27] Wherever the "interests of the church" will be promoted, even if against its own previous interpretations, those interests take priority.

> Woe to you, scribes and Pharisees, hypocrites! For
> you are like whitewashed tombs, which on the out-
> side look beautiful, but inside they are full of the
> bones of the dead and all kinds of filth. So you also
> look righteous to others, but inside you are full of
> hypocrisy and lawlessness (23:27–28).

At the time of Matthew's gospel, graves were marked at a certain time of the year to warn pilgrims, especially priests, so that they would not be defiled by inadvertently coming into contact with these homes of the dead. The marking of graves was not just to keep people from defilement; it involved the task of guiding Israel in the way of justice. Just as we have seen that hypocrisy involved a misinterpretation of the norms of justice in people's behavior or teaching, so iniquity— the *anomia*, the lawlessness—represented injustice as well. Garland concludes: "This woe once again is related to Pharisaic failure in the stewardship of the Law, although it, more than any of the other woes, also attacks the inner existence of the Pharisees."[28]

I already have shown, and will show in the next chapter, how *anomia*, besides being connected to justice, involves a kind of mean-inglessness. This *anomia* is especially evident among priests to the detriment of their morale. Yet there is no united effort that is known on the part of the United States bishops to change the inhumane ways priests are filling in the gaps due to declining numbers and the perpetuation of an unjust system that denies people the sacraments. Outwardly the institutional church expects that its statements about justice will be heard by those to whom it speaks. It fails to see how it represents in its inward behavior a contradiction to its own message.

At least ten years ago I attended the annual shareholders' meeting of Marshall & Ilsely, a large bank in Wisconsin. I attended on the proxy of the Milwaukee Province of the School Sisters of Notre Dame, who had filed a resolution questioning the bank about its mortgage practices, especially "redlining" poverty areas. I asked Mr. Puelicher, the chairman of the board, why the bank had no minorities or women on its board of directors. Since women, like the Sisters I was serving as proxy, represented a sizeable part of the bank's customers, I suggested that women should be represented at every level of the bank, including its top management.

"Sir," he replied, "aren't you a member of the Roman Catholic clergy?"

When I answered affirmatively, he countered: "Don't you have the same problem in your organization?"

As the shareholders laughed loudly, I couldn't help but think of the statement about justice in the institutional church from the 1971 Synod of Bishops: "While the church is bound to give witness to justice, she recognizes that anyone who ventures to speak to people about justice must first be just in their eyes. Hence we must undertake an examination of the modes of acting and of the possessions and lifestyle found within the church herself."[29]

Addicts dare not examine themselves critically if that examination will indicate the need to change their modes of acting and of the possessions and lifestyle which they manifest. Their denial undermines their stated values. Such behavior and denial reinforce in the institutional church an inconsistency between teachings and behavior. It also reveals institutional addiction. As Fassel and Schaef note: "Organizations themselves function as addicts, and become key building blocks in an addictive society, even when this dramatically contradicts their espoused mission or reason for existence."[30]

> **Woe to you, scribes and Pharisees, hypocrites! For you build the tombs of the prophets and decorate the graves of the righteous, and you say, "If we had lived in the days of our ancestors, we would not have taken part with them in shedding the blood of the prophets." Thus you testify against yourselves, that you are descendants of those who murdered the prophets. Fill up, then, the measure of your ancestors. You snakes, you brood of vipers! Can you escape being sentenced to hell? Therefore I send you prophets, and scribes, some of whom you will kill and crucify, and some you will flog in your synagogues and pursue from town to town, so that upon you may come all the righteous blood shed on earth, from the blood of righteous Abel to the blood of Zechariah son of Barrachiah, whom you murdered between the sanctuary and the altar. Truly, I tell you, all this will come upon this generation (23:29–36).**

In this passage Matthew's Jesus employs an interactive hermeneutic. He is saying, in effect, that the "story" of the ancestors and their efforts at promoting justice in unjust religious institutions is becoming "this story." Those challenging the leaders will be victimized because they are threatened by the challengers' thinking, their passion, and their demands for institutional conversion. The addition of the word *dikaios*, "just" (four times, in 23:28, 29, 35 [2x]) indicates that those who used the notion of justice to reinforce their unjust interpretation of the Law continue to persecute others in the name of justice.

By raising monuments to just people martyred in the past, the leaders tried to disassociate themselves from any part in their ancestors' past. But the sin was intergenerational. Garland shows that the clear emphasis placed upon "you" throughout this passage indicates that the issue being addressed is "definitely a contemporary one and not a problem regrettably bequeathed by unrighteous ancestors."[31] Its emphasis on "you" applies to all those religious leaders in any religious institution of any generation who reject those who call for a change of unjust systems and structures.

I can think of no better example of today's leaders erecting tombs for those treated unjustly by previous church leaders while they undermine parallel efforts in the church than the women's issue. The same leaders who glorify and venerate St. Clare of Assisi reject a woman like Sr. Theresa Kane. They conveniently forget that Clare of Assisi *refused* to obey legislation for her Order given by the papacy while they call Theresa Kane "disloyal" for merely asking for dialogue on the role of women in the church. The persecution of the prophets continues.

The Desolation of the Church and Grief for Its Disease (23:37—24:1)

In the face of all these forms of hypocrisy, Matthew's Jesus concluded the woes with a lament about Jerusalem that also can be addressed toward Rome: "Jerusalem, Jerusalem, the city that kills the prophets and stones those who are sent to it! How often have I desired to gather your children together as a hen gathers her brood under her wings, and you were not willing" (23:37). Despite the pain being caused, despite the evident contradictions, despite the pleas that the leaders change, addictive thinking and acting continue in Catholicism. Like other unrecovered addicts, the leaders "were not willing" to recognize their visitation, their divine intervention, and change.

More and more, as bishops become embarrassed by the papal and curial addiction, as priests break from the load left by others who have died or resigned, as religious women and men stop participating in the liturgy, and millions of people are denied participation in the eucharist because "you were not willing" to change a human law to enable a divine command to "do this" in memory of Jesus take place, as more and more informed Catholics "drop out" and refuse to protest except by their absence from church life, the next words of Matthew's Jesus ring clear: "See, your house is left to you, desolate. For I tell you, you will not see me again, until you say, 'Blessed be the one who comes in the name of the Lord' " (23:38–39).

Immediately after this verse Matthew drops the reference to the poor woman at the treasury, which follows in Mark 12:41–44 and Luke 21:1–4. Instead, after saying "your house is left to you, desolate," he says that "Jesus came out of the temple" (24:1). Matthew's unique redaction indicates the abandonment of Judaism for Christianity.[32] If this is so, we might ask if the same might not be taking place in the abandonment of institutional Catholicism of Matthew 16 for another kind of community-based Catholicism of Matthew 18.

In concluding this third chapter dealing with the church's story, I cannot deny that I have a feeling that I have been "disloyal" to the pope and the hierarchy. However, what I have said is true; the sources attest to the accuracy of my statements. So why the feeling? Does our codependency make us so fearful that we can't allow Matthew's Jesus to challenge us and the leaders in our church again? Or have we become so intellectually hardened of heart and so dogmatic that we read any attempt to apply *the story* to the church's story as a misuse of *the story* or an example of fundamentalism? Or might we have become so accustomed to the disease of clericalism that we no longer get angry and deny our ability to grieve over Rome?

Justice in the Catholic church demands a serious examination of the modes of acting we find in our church. For me, the recollection of Jesus saying that John's message of justice was not believed by the leaders, but was believed by the tax collectors and the harlots who repented (21:32), and the knowledge that this statement is followed by the parable of the wicked stewards of the household (21:33–46) is ominous. Even more ominous is the way this pericope ends: "Jesus said to them"—church leaders everywhere and the rest of us in the church as well:

"Have you never read in the scriptures: 'The stone that the
builders rejected has become the cornerstone; this was the
Lord's doing, and it is amazing in our eyes'? Therefore
I tell you, the kingdom of God will be taken away from
you and given to a people that produces the fruits of the
kingdom." When the chief priests and the Pharisees heard
his parables, they realized that he was speaking about them.
They wanted to arrest him, but they feared the crowds,
because they regarded him as a prophet (21:42–46).

CHAPTER EIGHT

Biography
Story and My Story

In sculpting *the story* of the first gospel, Matthew examined how the Jesus story was lived out fifty years before in a way that indirectly challenged the culture's story and directly challenged the religion's story. He showed that the Jesus story contained the fulfillment of *the story*, especially the Law and the prophets.

By making his christology his ecclesiology, Matthew made Jesus *the story* that was to be fulfilled in the lives of his disciples. The commission to "make disciples of all nations" would involve sharing in *the story* through baptism and living it out by observing everything that Jesus commanded (28:19–20). This was to be done not only in the house-churches but "always, to the close of the age" (28:20). Each disciple's biography/story must be the fulfillment of *the story*, which must be expressed in the church's story ("make disciples" [28:19]) and the culture's story ("all nations" [28:19]).

Each person is a story in himself or herself, since every person's identity revolves around his or her story: "Tell me your story, and I will know who you are." Each person's story longs to be told in such a way that he or she will be understood. Only when a person believes he or she is understood can community begin. Otherwise alienation continues.[1]

Each person's story begins, not with the self in isolation, but the self in community. I am "we" before I am "I." We experience our identity through a world with a certain order and cohesion that is communicated through language. Language reveals meanings; it reveals a story or narrative that becomes the basis of each individual's personal story. In some unique way, the heart of the universal story

147

as it tries to describe the human condition is birthed with each of us as we enter the world. However, very soon every person begins to experience barriers indicating that I am not "we." There is an I and a Thou. And sometimes there is a Me. What was once other-oriented becomes self-centered. When this happens, we erect barriers to defend our*self* from what we perceive to be invasions. For some, these barriers become balanced boundaries; for others, walls get erected.

Especially when walls get erected, the person's original transcendent aspirations surrender by degree to conformity, apathy, and lack of meaning. The result is the impairment of love. The effect on *the story* is that what was created by God to be a love story becomes painful alienation from God, others, and self. In addiction terms, this wounded self is called a codependent person, someone who is powerless over such relationships, and whose life has been and is deeply affected in negative ways by interaction with significant others. Codependent people's intellectual, emotional, and behavioral condition interacts with rules (overt or covert) and relationships that are ordered to control and/or prevent the open expression of their own or others' thinking, feeling, and acting.

Building on these preliminary notions from symbolic interactionism and codependency, I can now trace my own story as the desire and effort to be free of my walls and to enter love's embrace. As I do, I have some embarrassment, some sense of feeling ill-at-ease. First, I am not used to sharing intimate reflections from my past and present for public consumption. The embarrassment also comes because I know that the sharing of stories that is essential to a Twelve-Step process is not always appreciated by others; in fact my embarrassment increases when I realize I may be criticized for taking "a familiar confessional pride in their disorders, as if every addiction were a crucible. The disease of codependency is probably millennium fever. Everybody wants to be reborn, and in recovery, everybody is."[2] My embarrassment and lack of ease is somewhat mitigated when I realize the reader can skip these pages. However, they are pages that must be written if the interactive hermeneutics of *the story*, the culture's story, the church's story, and my story is to balance.

My Story in Light of the Other Stories

I remember listening to a retreatant who had come for a private conference. "When I go to your talks all I hear is how much God loves me and how we ought to love God and one another. It's so hard for me to listen to you say that because I don't feel as though God loves me." She was in turmoil over the lack of love in her life. Her words hit me like a bolt of lightning. Why?

First of all, I became powerfully aware of God's power to enable people to hear what they need to hear. She had *heard* me talking constantly of God's love for us and our response. Yet I had never talked about God's love for us or about our love of God and others. I realized that day that I hadn't preached on love once, and that the reason was because I didn't really sense that I loved God. I was preaching a retreat on Jesus' Beatitudes in Matthew, yet I couldn't preach on the first and greatest command of God, which Matthew's Jesus said is the foundation for the whole story of the Law and prophets (22:40): "You shall love the Lord your God with all your heart, and with all your soul, and with all your mind. This is the greatest and first commandment. And a second is like it, You shall love your neighbor as yourself" (22:37–39).

I did not know it at that time, but I was unable to love God with my whole heart, my whole soul, and my whole mind because I had a "hole in the whole"—the core of codependency. I did not know either that the main reason why I found it so hard truly to love others (as much as I desired to and tried to) was because I was only able to love God and others *as* I loved myself. And I did not love myself well. My lack of love affected the way I viewed God and others (my thinking), the way I ran from intimacy with God and others (my feeling), and the way I related to God and others (my acting). For me the prophecy of Isaiah was fulfilled: "You will indeed listen but never understand, and you will indeed look, but never perceive. For this people's heart has grown dull, and their ears are hard of hearing, and they have shut their eyes so that they might not look with their eyes, and listen with their ears, and understand with their heart and turn—and I would heal them" (13:14–15).

Listening to this retreatant became an invitation for me to listen to my heart, to discover the hole in my heart that made it a stony heart instead of one of flesh, and to begin to change my heart with the grace of God's loving care.

I was in my mid-forties when that sister came to see me—a living example of what the books about the mid-years say. Despite a life that others would consider quite successful, that "something wrong"—that hole in my heart—revealed chapters in my story that any skilled reader would interpret as revealing an increasing sense of meaninglessness.[3] While I was told I was *doing* good, I didn't *feel* good. And while I believed I was interpreting God's word correctly, especially God's word about doing good and practicing justice, something felt empty inside. This sense of emptiness brings me to the fourth and final time Matthew used the word *anomia*—"doing wrong."

After discussing the end times and the resulting upheavals, Matthew's Jesus prophesied: "And because the increase of *anomia* the love of many will grow cold" (24:12). In my own story the passage could be translated, "Because of the increase of meaninglessness in my life, my heart was growing cold." I sensed something wrong not just with my heart; something seemed to be wrong with my *self*.

According to therapists like Rollo May and Viktor Frankl, the sense of meaning is central to human existence and to interpersonal relationships. Frankl found that people could be very successful and seem to have all their needs met, but if they lacked meaning, many would attempt to stop the narrative of their biographies—they tried taking their life. He also discovered that many times the suicide attempt happened despite therapy. He concluded that this occurred because therapists didn't focus on the central role of meaning in life:

> It had been overlooked or forgotten that if a person has found the meaning sought for he is prepared to suffer, to offer sacrifices, even, if need be, to give his life for the sake of it. Contrariwise, if there is no meaning he is inclined to take his life, and he is prepared to do so even if all his needs, to all appearances, have been satisfied.[4]

To all appearances, my needs had been met—at least my power and prestige needs. Although I was from a working-class Irish family, we always had food on the table and clothes on our back, even though my mother had to return to teaching when I was eight years old. I had twelve years of private Catholic schooling. I entered the Capuchin Order at nineteen and was one of the first Capuchin seminarians to write not just one book, but two books while still in the seminary.[5] *Origins* had featured a chapter from a pamphlet I wrote on corporate responsibility; it became for quite a while "the bible" for Catholics involved in using church investments for social change.[6] One of my subsequent books, *Spirituality of the Beatitudes*, published by Orbis Books, had gone through many reprintings and had become the basis for a ten-part video series and renewal program used throughout the English-speaking world. I had served two terms on the Provincial Council of my Province of Capuchin Franciscans and was a member of many of its significant committees. And yet I knew my heart was growing cold (24:12).

According to Frankl when a sense of meaninglessness pervades a person's life—and he or she does not commit suicide—that person orders his or her life in one or more expressions of what Frankl calls the "neurotic triad": depression, aggression, and addiction. I believe I experienced all three. I tried to deal with them by letting their symptoms control me and by denying their power over me.

I didn't have a deep depression. Rather, I experienced the low-level depression that results from feeling powerless over relationships (with God, others, and myself) as well as a sense of being out of control—of my life and my relationships with others. The depression was reinforced by my sense that religious life as we know it is dying and that many who have stayed have given up hope. It was further reinforced when good men left our brotherhood. Many were close friends; their separation created a real void.

I had Frankl's aggression too, expressed in my Type-A personality. I drove myself and competed with others. Yet after twenty-five years in the Order, when there was nothing left to compete for, the hole in my heart grew larger.

Then there were the addictive patterns, which went beyond workaholism and perfectionism. Although I never came under the control of alcohol or drugs, I knew I had other addictive traits. I had stopped smoking—over two packs of cigarettes a day—in 1972. Five months later I had gained fifty-three pounds. My addictions were not limited to substances; I sensed something amiss in my relationships as well. Being in my mid-years, I was beginning to become obsessed with issues of intimacy and sexuality, and celibacy and genitality as well. This often got triggered when I saw a man my age or younger with a child. A real pain would begin gnawing inside of me.

I don't recall if I knew then about codependency. I thought my pain at seeing a man with a child was my body's way of telling me I never would have a child of my own. That may have been so, but I later learned that the pain was not just about losing a child of my own "out there"; the gnawing also came from the muffled cry of my own child "in there," inside of me, looking for me to stop my compulsive running.

Thus, as my depression, aggression, and addictive patterns increased my sense of meaninglessness, so did my diminishing love. As much as I wanted to love, I didn't feel I could. I couldn't love because something deep inside me kept me from experiencing God's love for me. Something was wrong in the way I thought, felt, and acted toward God and others that revealed lack of understanding (in a Matthean sense) with my heart. Again, I didn't know it at that time, but if I was going to love others, it had to be grounded in self-love; if I was going to love God, it had to be grounded in the love of others as well.

After getting my master's degree in economics in New York in 1985, I went to Berkeley to pursue the Ph.D. in theology. Deep down, as I travelled west, I knew I was leaving a way of life behind to pursue something that had been eluding me for most of my recent years—friendship.

While I still feel close to my high school friends—very close in fact—a problem developed for me after high school. I spent my college years and theology years in seminaries of my Capuchin Franciscan Province. One by one, over a period of years, most of my Capuchin friends left. They had followed the inclinations of their hearts and were leaving. I found myself saying good-bye to them knowing I had not initiated the separation and that I wasn't allowing my heart to act on the same feelings. Furthermore, when I returned for visits after schooling outside the Province, some of the men I had thought of as friends were in other relationships that didn't include me. There was physical presence, but psychological good-byes. I hadn't initiated these either. I was becoming powerless over my relationships.

So, in going to California to pursue the Ph.D., I also went to pursue friendship, if possible. At the same time I also was seeking to experience God's love for me, especially at prayer. Soon after I got to Berkeley I met a young priest whose name was Paul. We enjoyed each other's company and were concerned about similar issues. We started playing racquetball and talking about our lives.

At prayer I was trying to change my image of God from a kind of energy to a more personal presence. Even though I had beautiful parents, I was not able to image God as father or mother. And if God weren't mother or father, I didn't have many options. In seeking to experience a more personal God, I changed my mantra at prayer from "Be in the name of Jesus" to "Live on in my love," which I knew was from John's gospel. I had also taken courses from Ernest Larkin, the Carmelite, on John of the Cross and from Jim Finley on Thomas Merton. At Berkeley I was taking a course in prayer and meditation taught by Dan O'Hanlon, which used various rituals as aids in prayer, including Zen and Yoga.

One day during this period I had a racquetball game with Paul. In the middle of one game we had a volley that seemed to go on forever; it was the longest volley I had ever had. As it continued, the intensity between us grew; it became electric. Finally, when the volley came to an end, we spontaneously gave each other a great embrace. In that embrace, something happened. We were not just two men charged by a game's competitiveness; we were friends.

That afternoon I went to my prayer and meditation class. We were handed scripture passages to use for guided meditation. Mine was John 15:9–17.

> As the Father has loved me, so have I loved you; abide in my love. If you keep my commandments, you will abide in my love, just as I have kept my Father's commandments and abide in his love. I have said these things to you so that my joy may be in you, and that your joy may be full.
>
> This is my commandment, that you love one another as I have loved you. No one has greater love than this, to lay down one's life for one's friends. You are my friends if you do what I command you. I do not call you servants any longer, because the servant does not know what the master is doing; but I have called you friends, because I have made known to you everything I have heard from my father. You did not choose me, but I chose you. And I appointed you to go and bear fruit that will last; so that the Father will give you whatever you ask in my name. I am giving you these commands that you may love one another.

I was struck by the fact that this passage from John was the basis for the words that had become my new mantra: "Live on in my love." So I started to reflect on the passage. When I got to the phrase "You are my friends," one of those experiences that lasts but a few moments but is worth a lifetime happened. That morning's embrace with Paul turned to my afternoon's embrace with God. In that union I came to understand God as friend and myself as God's friend.

In that experience I learned that, just as I had discovered the friendship between God and me *after* the human experience of befriending, the usual way we experience God builds on human encounters. This helped me understand that if I would love God with my whole heart, I would have to experience God's love for me, but that love probably would be contingent on my love for others and, even more for me at this point, my experience of their love for me.

Despite growing friendships with people like Paul, my work addiction kept me from taking the kind of quality and quantity time to develop relationships and to deepen my intimacy. I said I wanted deeper relationships, but my behavior and work addiction showed otherwise; work had a deeper hold on me than relationships. However, an experience in August 1988 moved me another step toward a recovery of love.

I was giving a week on Franciscanism at San Damiano Retreat in California with two other Franciscans. One was Sr. Janet Sullivan from Tampa. Toward the end of the week Janet gave a sermon in which she told of her own struggle with God and her battle with self-surrender. She concluded by saying something facetious like, "We have come a long way when we no longer think we need God to be our savior."

Another bolt of lightning! At least five years after the experience with the retreatant, I sat there struck, convicted, by her words. I began asking myself: When was the last time I thought of God as my savior? The very name Jesus means "savior," but I never think of Jesus as my savior; what's the matter with me? Have I moved so far into creation-spirituality that I no longer have any room for redemption? Am I so proud that I don't need a savior? What kind of a follower of Francis am I if I am so proud? Why am I thinking such novitiate-sounding thoughts?

After the flood of the questions and a parallel surge of guilt feelings, I decided to embark on a search to understand and to experience salvation. I began by reading about it; nothing seemed to click. I asked others, "What does it mean to you to be saved?" A systematic theologian responded, "We don't consider that any more." My Capuchin brother Dan told me that it meant modelling our lives on Jesus, who saved others from their sins. That had been my approach, too, but somehow, I felt I needed to be saved from *my* sin. A friend involved in the charismatic renewal gave me the standard answer I had come to expect from charismatics. No reply seemed to resolve my dilemma. My search continued quite obsessively through the next weeks.

In a classic work-addictive pattern I had planned back-to-back meetings and talks over a ten-day period that took me from Chicago to Milwaukee to Santa Fe to Chicago to Minneapolis to Milwaukee to Fond du Lac to Dubuque and back to Chicago for meetings and workshops. By Dubuque I was overextended, concerned about defending my dissertation in a week, and had developed a cold. At the meeting I asked for something to keep my nose from running. A nurse-infirmarian brought me an antihistamine, which worked rapidly; my nose was cleared.

Two hours later, driving my rent-a-car to my last engagement in Chicago the antihistamine proved to be more powerful than I expected. At one moment I realized I was getting sleepy and thought I ought to stop for a rest; the next moment I recall being pulled from the car. It had been totalled.

I was told not to move while the rescue squad rushed me to a hospital twenty miles away. On the way I wondered if I'd be able to move my neck again, or my back, or be able to continue my speaking engagements. For some reason, possibly shock, the fact that I might be an invalid for the rest of my life didn't really bother me. After X-rays, which revealed only a broken ankle, I received over twenty-five stitches around my right eye. Then a policeman came and told me something like: "You went off the highway into a ditch, came out of the ditch back across the highway, hit a culvert, and bounced off. Then you went across the road again and across the yard of a church, stopping when you hit its front steps."

Hearing his report brought an immediate, spontaneous reaction from deep within me: *You have been saved.* At the same time tears of understanding welled in my eyes. However, almost as soon as I experienced myself as *saved*, I felt a deep sadness that I couldn't say that *God* saved me, or that *Jesus* saved me. I wanted to *feel* saved; I wanted a personal experience of God, of Jesus as my savior as well as my friend. I wanted redemptive theology and incarnational theology.

My car accident made my search for salvation more poignant, but it didn't stop my work addiction. Despite the cast on my ankle and crutches I returned to Berkeley two days later, successfully defended my dissertation, and continued my speaking engagements. I was proud that I had to cancel only one commitment. Meanwhile I began developing chest pains, but I attributed these to my chest's adaptation to the crutches.

A month after the accident I returned to Wisconsin for a provincial meeting. On Thanksgiving morning my chest pains became so severe that my brother Dan took me to the hospital. I had blood clots on my lung. I needed five days of absolute bed-rest—or else. This time, more than the accident in Illinois, I realized I actually might die.

After celebrating the sacrament of the sick I began to experience more than my usual share of the Irish guilt that has hounded me throughout my life. If I die, I thought, what is God going to challenge me about? Instead of thinking about areas of my life where I did sin consciously, my first reaction was to realize that I would be challenged for not allowing myself to become intimate with anyone.

Upon returning to Berkeley and getting off my crutches, I had dinner with a friend. My heart had been trying to tell me that I was attracted to her; my intuition told me she might be attracted to me as well. I went to our dinner wanting not to close down the feeling again. During our time together we discovered we shared mutual feelings about each other as well as a desire to spend more time developing a relationship. However, she said, "It's a little hard, Mike, to develop any kind of relationship with you when you're running all over the country. We need to take more time if anything's going to develop in a relationship." Although I was still over-committed, I promised I'd refuse more commitments for the next year and a half and, despite a still-hectic schedule, our relationship, our care, and our love began to develop. At the same time I began sensing a change in my relationship with God, my sense of God's care, and my understanding of God's love as well.

I began looking for a spiritual director with a "contemporary" understanding of salvation, knowledge of the affective dimension from both sides of the brain, sensitivity to celibates in intimate, non-genital relationships, and the ability to help me in my desire to experience God in prayer. I found this kind of sensitivity in a Jesuit in Berkeley.

After giving him a brief overview of my past, I focused on my prayer and the desire to come to experience God's love. He asked, "What do you do when you go to prayer?"

"I just try to detach myself of thoughts so that I come to be empty before God," I responded.

"Do you ever ask for anything to happen?"

"No," I said, "because that would mean I would be wanting something when I should be wanting *nothing* before God."

"Well, St. Ignatius said that we ought to begin our prayer asking God for the fruit of what we'd like to see happen in prayer, so why don't you think of asking God for the fruit of prayer that you desire."

Although it went against years of past practice—to be nothing and to want nothing before God—I began to ask God "that I might experience your intimate love for me more personally, to live in that love, and to share that love more intimately with others." The first time I used this little asking prayer it came to me that to ask is to depend on the one being asked. I had not asked when I prayed before because that would make me dependent, dependent on God. And I unconsciously had not wanted to depend on God for anything, even in prayer.

At the same time these very positive things were occurring in my life, my food addiction was stimulated. I found myself eating more and more, especially chocolate ice cream, and not just for evening dessert. I started gaining weight. When I approached my former peak of 191 something happened inside me. I gave myself over to the idea, the feeling, and the decision that I would get fat. I knew I was powerless over food, but that didn't change my decision to eat more and more, even though I knew I would have negative thoughts and feelings about myself. I rationalized that people who loved me or thought I had something to say would accept me and/or my words even if I was fat. And if they didn't, that was *their* problem. At that point I stopped weighing myself but began feeling the changes in my body—and in my belt.

This decision to give in to my addiction didn't last long. A sudden appearance of cold sores on my mouth and then in my mouth worked like an "intervention." Unable to eat for four or five days I began losing weight. With the rapid weight loss, my attachment addiction toward food turned to a kind of aversion addiction. I stopped eating and, when I started again, I began dieting seriously for the first time in eighteen years. When I finished I had lost twenty or twenty-five pounds and was thinner than I had been since quitting smoking. I congratulated myself for having such will power and drive.

During my dieting I also thought I had been recognizing my poverty and need or dependency before God in prayer. But the limitations in the way I interpreted that soon struck me as well. I was giving a retreat on Matthew's Beatitudes at Presentation Center in Los Gatos. During the conference on the poor in spirit I explained that, when we sit down to pray (or whatever we do with our bodies), I realize I am poor in spirit because I know I cannot determine my experience of God; I depend on God to be revealed to me on God's terms, not my own.

Making the retreat was a diocesan priest who had been a late vocation. He had been a union organizer and civil rights activist, had gone into treatment for alcoholism, and was ordained recently. When he came to see me he said, "I'm having a hell of a time with the third step, especially the part about turning my life and my will over to God." Again his words hit me like lightning. Here I was the retreat director giving a retreat on being poor in spirit. I had identified being poor in spirit with turning my *prayer* life and will over to God. And sitting before me was a retreatant who was struggling with turning his *whole* life and will over to God! In the depths of himself he was struggling with becoming poor in spirit. The contrast could not have been more stark. Here I was still in control, if not of my prayer, of my life; I was listening to another priest who struggled with giving up his need to control.

I made a step that day in giving up trying to control God, but it was a baby step. A few weeks later I gave a retreat on the Jersey shore. I had decided to get up early to watch the sun rise on the Atlantic. As I came to the beach, the sky was a gorgeous bright pink with lavender and just a hint of clouds. The beach was virtually empty of humans but filled with sea gulls and sea shells. As I began walking I started my new routine for prayer: "Dear God, let me experience your intimate love for me more closely, let me . . ." Before I could complete my intercessory prayer, I sensed God saying, "Come on, Michael, if I were any more explicit in showing you my love than in what you see right before your eyes, I would have to deny your freedom because it would take that to overpower you."

It had happened. God's love was revealed to me in that moment. I could only be present before that love in awe and deep gratitude. At the same time I didn't need philosophically to deduce this love from effect to cause to uncaused cause. God was just there. And, thanks be to God, a sense of that presence has remained, even though it definitely isn't at the forefront of my thoughts, feelings, and behavior to the degree it might be.

Around this time I began to be aware that I had to do something about my codependent relationship with the institutional church. I had started going to CODA (Codependents Anonymous) meetings in Berkeley. But I sensed I needed something more; I needed some kind of treatment to achieve any real recovery. While giving the Beatitude retreat at Los Gatos I read a brochure announcing a residential treatment program for codependents run by a group called CODACARE. Based in San Jose, CODACARE had John Bradshaw on its board and was linked to other places treating codependency. Immediately I felt this would help me deal with my codependency in the church; I made plans to enter.

Meanwhile, the more I read about codependency, the more confused I became. I knew that if the theory was correct, I was codependent insofar as I was part of the church family whose "identified patients"—the hierarchy—were addicted to power. This made me, as a minister in the church, not only codependent but part of the addictive process, especially as a white, male, celibate cleric. However, my confusion revolved around my past. By most accounts that I read a true codependent comes from a dysfunctional family setting, which launched the person into the church's dysfunctional family. But my family of origin was not that dysfunctional, especially in my early formative years. Furthermore, the more books I read, the more it seemed codependent people were "pleasers," who found their whole identity in trying to heal the "identified patient." While I wanted the healing part, I didn't see myself as a pleaser; I was a challenger. By the time I came to Los Gatos I knew I would not be dealing just with myself as a white, male, celibate cleric; I was going to deal with my *self*.

Presentation Center is located in the Santa Cruz mountains in the midst of huge eucalyptus trees and redwoods. The very environment invites recovery and healing. CODACARE's holistic approach took advantage of the environment to invite a unification of past, present, and future into the *now* as well as a unification of our heart, mind, soul, and body *here*. A full-time ritualist, along with two therapists, invited the participants (three of us) to dip into the psyche as well as our bodies.

In the early morning of the first full day I walked along the nature trail. Halfway down the path, which I identified with my "journey," I saw a perfectly shaped pine cone about four inches tall. Right in the middle of the path. Thinking it might represent some kind of sign, I stopped to pick it up. However, once I picked it up I discovered that it had a big chunk missing inside. Just as I was about to throw it away—who would want to keep something with so big a blemish?—I realized it represented my *self*. I was someone who looked very good to others but who had a big chunk missing, a big "hole" in the "whole."

During the input sessions that morning we began learning about codependency and how it functions. We were given the "definitive" definition of codependency that Pia Mellody and others in the field recently hammered out: "a pattern of painful dependence on compulsive behaviors and on approval from others in an attempt to find safety, self worth, and identity. Recovery is possible." Things were beginning to make sense. Insights came quickly in the group work with our therapists.

That evening I began reading John Bradshaw's *Healing the Shame That Binds You*. As I read the first pages I could identify with his insights:

> When shame has been completely internalized, nothing about you is okay. You feel flawed and inferior; you have the sense of being a failure. There is no way you can share your inner self because you are an object of contempt to yourself. When you are contemptible to yourself, you are no longer in you. To feel shame is to feel seen in an exposed and diminished way.
>
> When you're an object to yourself, you turn your eyes inward, watching and scrutinizing every minute detail of behavior. This internal critical observation is excruciating. It generates a tormenting self-consciousness which Kaufman describes as, "creating a binding and paralyzing effect upon the self."[7]

Reading this passage I did something I don't recall doing before. I made a note in the margin—"me growing up." Sensing I was on to something, I turned the page. My intuition was confirmed as I read:

> It is crucial to see that the false self may be as polar opposite as a superachieving perfectionist or an addict in an alley.

Both are driven to cover up their deep sense of self-rupture, the hole in their soul. They may cover up in ways that look polar opposite, but each is still driven by neurotic shame. In fact, *the most paradoxical aspect of neurotic shame is that it is the core motivator of the superachiever and the underachiever, the Star and the Scapegoat, the "Righteous" and the wretched, the powerful and the pathetic.*[8]

Reading this passage began to penetrate my walls. I began sensing that, somehow, those walls had been built because of shame. In Bradshaw, shame is the root and fuel of all compulsive/addictive behaviors. Consequently, internalized shame constitutes the heart, the essence of codependency.

Bradshaw distinguishes between shame and guilt and, within each, between healthy shame and guilt and toxic shame and guilt. Building on his ideas, I would say that healthy shame is an emotion that signals us about our limits and when we have reached them; it invites conversion and liberation. By contrast, toxic shame, the shame that controls and binds, makes us feel limited and incomplete in our *selves*. Healthy shame arises from what we do; toxic shame descends to who we are. Healthy guilt is the awareness that we have failed to meet the mark, that we have made choices that have separated us from God, ourselves, and others. It too invites conversion through confession. Toxic guilt results from addictive behaviors such as workaholism and perfectionism, as well as other addictive processes.

When I went to bed that night, I reread those passages. In the middle of the night I awoke thinking about the passages; I read them again. When I got up in the morning I read them once more. As I read them this time I sensed that this day would be special for me. After my early morning walk on the nature trail, our guided meditation in the midst of four redwoods, and breakfast, I decided I would return to the path. I had walked the trail the night before; I had also walked it early that morning. It was in the middle of isolated mountains in a private place; there was no way that any outsider could have been there since the times I was there earlier. However, just as I turned onto the path I saw a balloon, the kind that people give for special celebrations or take to airports as a greeting. The helium was gone. The side with the message was face down. Only the balloon's blank, silver side faced me, a little ribbon dangled from its end. Wondering what the message might say—might it have something to say to me?—

I picked it up. There Snoopy the Beagle and his buddy Woodstock gave a greeting—"Happy Birthday." "Isn't that nice," I said to myself as I put the balloon back. "I wish there had been something on it for me."

I hadn't walked more than ten feet when something in me said, "You dummy, that's exactly the message for you. Today is going to be your birthday. You are going to be born today!" I couldn't get back to that balloon quickly enough! I picked it up and brought it back with me to the input session, which began right away.

At the input session Linda Voorheis, one of the therapists, began sharing the theory about the shame-core that exists in each of us. When we are born we are "we" before we are "I." At that time we are bonded with our primary care-givers. They mirror our goodness, uniqueness, value, and selfhood. We sense ourselves as good. However, being human and imperfect, there comes a time in our development when our care-givers no longer give us unconditional positive care but begin to communicate messages to us that indicate we are not good enough. Somehow, a little hole opens in our heart so that it no longer is quite whole. Needing to protect our *selves* from these invasions of our boundaries, which were once experienced as good, results in the creation of defenses—our walls.

We begin to build defenses to protect ourselves from further wounds and from having more violations of our boundaries. Our defenses take one of two directions. We either tend to *submit* and take a "lesser than" approach in our successive thinking, feeling, and acting. Or we tend to *rebel* by appropriating a "better than" approach to others in our thinking, feeling, and acting. Both extremes bring us to codependency. The chart below (see p. 163) shows how our shame-based self-esteem gets expressed in normal, interdependent ways as well as in the two extremes of codependency.

Linda started by making sure we understood that a "better than" way of coping with our shame-base reflected dependent thinking, feeling, and acting as much as a "less than" approach. The fact that much of the literature stresses the latter had kept me unclear about my codependency. As she continued, the pieces started to fall into place. By the time she got to "No Higher Power" in the "better than" column, I knew this column could have been entitled "Michael Crosby." I could feel my heart stirring. I raised my hand and asked Linda, "Please slow down. You're describing me! I've got to understand what you're saying." By the time she concluded I had reached what Matthew's Jesus called understanding, a combination of grasping a teaching and personal application.

REACTIONS TO BOUNDARY INVASIONS
BY CARE-GIVERS

"BETTER THAN"	"GOOD ENOUGH"	"LESS THAN"
(Codependent)	(Interdependent)	(Codependent)
Grandiose	Acceptable	Unimpressive
Overachiever	Modest	Underachiever
Perfectionist	Good	Mediocre
Invulnerable	Vulnerable/Protected	Too Vulnerable
Competitive	Cooperative	Yielding
Arrogant	Appropriate Self-Esteem	Deferring
Needless	Needs in Order	Too Needy
Wantless	Wants in Order	Wantful
Controlling	Non-Controlling	Controlled
No Accountability	Accountable	Culpable
Overly "Mature"	Mature	Immature
No Higher Power	Has Higher Power	Seeks Power Over
No Spirituality	Spirituality	No Spirituality

Building on the morning's insights, the afternoon's group work took us to that shame-based place where we could discover and share with that child within who had been wounded. Returning to meet that child, for me, began the process of healing the "hole" in my whole mind, my whole heart, and my whole soul. Returning to the child, for me, was a significant step in my recovery. It enabled me to turn from the addictive process that had ruled over me and to turn toward the reign of God. Before I had *thought about* the reign of God and had written and lectured about it; now I had an *experience* of the reign of God. It had happened because I had become more one with my child within. For the first time in my adult life I entered a little into the saying about becoming a child in order to enter the reign of God. As I began to experience my child, I began to *experience* God's reign, God's love, in me. "Truly," it had been said unto me: "unless you change and become like children, you will never enter the kingdom of heaven. Whoever becomes humble like this child is the greatest in the kingdom of heaven" (18:3–4). Now, being "better than" truly meant being "less than" and wanting that with my whole mind, my whole heart, my whole soul, my whole self.

For me, my beginning recovery from codependency and my addictions has continued to make sense only by remaining in conscious contact with my child. This child is poor in spirit and to such is given the reign of God (5:3). In experiencing God's reign, I am beginning to experience God's love. Now I am no longer anxious about what it means to be saved. I am saved and my salvation *is* God's reign of love within me. Life now means to remain in that love, being like a child and, like a child, being friends with my child—my *self*—God, and those around me.

As our input sessions continued I came to understand better the two main ways codependency occurs. Like it or not, I had developed a "better than" approach and I was its victim. How did this become central to my story? Did *the story*, the culture's story, or the church's story facilitate the development and nourish the codependency in my story? Anne Wilson Schaef sees the cultural context that invites us into codependency nourished and "supported by three of our major institutions—the family, the school, and the church."[9] Perhaps a deeper examination of these early care-givers might help me understand how my boundaries were invaded and how I reacted by building up my defenses.

I grew up in Wisconsin during the 1940s and 1950s. I attended twelve years of Catholic grade and high school during which time I went to St. Patrick's church for Mass, Tuesday evening devotions to Our Lady of Perpetual Help, First Fridays, First Saturdays, Tre-Ore, Forty Hours, and Parish Missions (which further convinced me I would go to hell if I stepped out of the path even once). I was a likely candidate to become hooked into the addictive process because the three institutions of family, school, and church were deeply enmeshed in my formative years. I was never away from the other two when I was actively a part of the third. They reinforced one another.

To my knowledge there was no alcoholism or other substance abuse in my parents or their parents. However, it was in my grandmother's family. Her brother died of the disease. While alcoholism didn't directly affect my nuclear family, we did live by a certain rigidity of expectations. The Crosbys were to be better.

I was the third of four boys. Despite the fact of hand-me-downs and often being dressed similarly as children, we were never compared to one another by my parents, which can happen in such a devastating way that the cage of codependency gets reinforced. While I don't recall my parents giving me the script called "less-than," it became the basis of my self-understanding, especially as a result of comparing myself to the first, second, and fourth children of the Crosby family. Thus my feelings of being "less-than" and my codependency had roots in the comparisons *I* made of myself with my brothers. I never felt I was as good as they were, especially in the various fields where they weren't just average or even good, but were better, if not the best.

First there was Pat. He was the hero of our family. He excelled in looks, personality, and sports. He was tall—over six feet—and had size thirteen shoes. He was prom king, received the first major letter in baseball given a sophomore at his Jesuit high school, and received a basketball scholarship to Rockhurst College in Kansas City. I was only average in looks and height, had normal shoe size, got the job of planning for the prom, played right field in baseball when the others allowed me to play, and messed up the one shot I had when I played CYO basketball after sitting on the bench all season.

Dan was the family saint. He broke up the fights I invariably began with Pat or my younger brother. He took the name Aloysius in honor of the young Jesuit who was noted for his purity. He was the brains of the family and received a two-year scholarship from St. Patrick's grade school to the local Catholic high school. He left after one year to go to the seminary. When he got there he was called "holy Dan"— by the seminarians no less! When he joined the Capuchins he edited the college quarterly periodical and the theological journal on Franciscanism. He graduated summa cum laude. I was never considered holy by anyone, except perhaps a "holy terror." Not only did I not graduate summa cum laude, but I didn't get honors. Dan too was over six feet and wore size thirteen shoes. I didn't feel I measured up to his personality, his brains, or his holiness. And I still wore size tens!

Jerry was the fourth boy. He too would grow to over six feet and develop a great personality. I always thought he possessed the best of Pat's and Dan's gifts. Like frosting on a perfect cake, he had a good sense of humor and a great memory. It was especially his humor that made him the life of the party. While I liked to party, I always felt surprised to discover people might actually want to invite me! In my early formative years I considered Jerry the best of the bunch. Consequently I continually picked fights with him when I was young, somehow figuring that I better get my licks in while I could.

Given the talents of Pat, Dan, and Jerry, I became the family "scapegoat," who got blamed for starting fights with my brothers, or the "mascot," who acted crazy. With such exceptional brothers (as I viewed them), I didn't have many other options! As I compared myself to them I didn't feel I belonged; I felt apart and alienated. I was deeply angry for not excelling like them; I deeply resented who I was. I wasn't good enough. I was just normal, and for a Crosby that wasn't good enough. Somehow, I thought to myself, my parents had given me these defective genes, which gave me so much pain. So to return some of my pain to them, I rebelled. The fact that, at various times, Pat or Dan or Jerry suggested I check my birth certificate to make sure I really belonged to this family didn't help. I already believed there was something really wrong with me.

While at home I was the center of family tensions and its "identified patient"; in school I became a model student and a class leader. At home I would often be reminded of my Jekyll and Hyde personality. This only made me worse.

My earliest memory of school was kindergarten. I remember waking up the second day, having come to the conclusion that school was worthless. I announced to my mother that I didn't want to go anymore.

"Why?" she asked.

"It's the second day of school and I can't even wead or wite," was my rationale, typical of a perfectionist.

My next memory is visiting the speech therapist in first grade at St. Patrick's. She tried to help me pronounce my "r's" and to say "st" instead of "ts." Having people laugh at me when I was in the school play, taking the role of one of the Magi, and saying my line—"I see a tsa ova tha"—contributed to my working hard to conquer my impediment.

Although I don't have many memories of grade school, I do remember the fear I developed when the sisters insisted that Our Lady of Fatima had warned that blood would flow down Wisconsin Avenue in Milwaukee by 1960 if we didn't repent from our sins. And Jesus was really angry with us too. Only Mary holding his arm back was keeping him from throwing that huge whatever-it-was that would destroy the earth.

In many ways high school days at St. Mary's Springs Academy were among the happiest of my life. I had great friends and great times out of school, often quite illegal and invariably involving alcohol. But I was a model student in the school and about my opposite way of living at home nobody knew—except Sr. Loretta Anne. I was to teach her class as part of Future Teachers of America day when I was a junior. After school the day before I came to her homeroom and asked what I should do. She told me that there was no way I would teach her class on so little preparation. She added that she was sick and tired of my hypocrisy; she knew what I was doing after school at home and about the drinking too. Sr. Loretta Anne wasn't alone. My parents were worried about what was happening to me. They started talking more about taking me to see the parish priest. I feared that more than anything—that he would know what a phony I really was.

I did go to see a priest when I was a sophomore in high school, but not to deal with worries about my *self*. Rather, I was concerned about my future. I felt I was *supposed* to become a priest, that God wanted me to become a priest; since seventh grade I had had this sense of what I was supposed to do. My overwhelming image of God at that time was a God of retribution. If I did anything wrong or didn't do what God wanted, I would be accountable. So I became quite concerned about doing what God wanted me to do and how to do it perfectly—which I thought meant being a priest.

But I didn't want to be a priest. So I went to a Catholic high school rather than the seminary Dan attended, in good part to "lose my vocation." I began to go steady in my freshman year, got into the group which I considered the "best" crowd of guys in the class, and began what we called "serious drinking" between my freshman and sophomore years. Midway in my sophomore year I sensed I was disobeying God by not going to the seminary. That's when I visited the priest-chaplain of the high school.

He told me that he entered the seminary after high school and, as far as he was concerned, didn't think God cared at all whether I went to the seminary after high school or not. That was all I needed. In those days the priest was God's mouthpiece. I had gone, ready to submit to what he said. Now "God" said it didn't matter; it was up to me. So, with this revelation of God's will for me, I decided I had a couple more years to "lose my vocation." I did things that made me ashamed, then went to confession every Saturday, afraid of being exposed as a terrible sinner.

The closer I got to graduation, the more agitated I became. I had to make a decision and hadn't been able to shake the idea of going to the seminary. Finally, in the spring of my senior year the day of decision erupted upon me through a most peculiar incident. I had been at a beer party on a Friday night. Of course that was not what I told my parents when I had asked for my mother's car. Early Saturday morning they woke me up to go to Mass and communion for "First Saturday."

As I drove my mother and dad to Mass, loud, clunking sounds came from the trunk of my mother's car. My parents kept asking what it was. I said I didn't know but would check it at the service station where I worked, a few blocks from the house. Returning from church I stopped in the middle of the street in front of our house to let them off. As I started driving away, Dad yelled, "Stop that car." When I did, he pointed to the trunk and said "Open it." There was the empty beer keg and its pump. "Get into the house," was all he said.

Once in the house we went to the kitchen. Silence ruled—the normal tactic employed by many parents as a prelude to a serious question about life. As they prepared breakfast together, quietly talking to each other but not to me, I stood near the counter, my head on my hand, knowing I was going to need a pretty good response to the forthcoming question. On the one hand I could decide finally to go to the seminary. Or, although there probably were many other options, I could go into the military. So, as the silence continued, I went back and forth between "the seminary" and "the service." Finally the silence was broken and the anticipated questions came: "Michael, what is going to happen to you? When are you going to get your life in order? What are you going to do with your life?" My only response was a somewhat muffled: "I'm going to the seminary." The words were out. For some reason my parents forgot about the beer keg.

The night before I went to the seminary there was a going-away party. All of us were entering service or college. That was the way it was in 1958. The girl I had been dating did not come. Although I felt abandoned, I was relieved that I didn't have to see her. In the middle of the party a deep sense of impending loneliness and fear about my future came over me. I went into the washroom and wept, saying something to God such as: "Why are you doing this to me, making me so unhappy? I want to get married and have babies and none of these are going to be possible because of what you want me to do."

When I got to the seminary I met a group of fine classmates. I fit in immediately. And I liked it, to my surprise. I read *The Confessions* of St. Augustine and immediately made his story my story. I developed deep shame and guilt about the pain I had caused my parents and brothers. I felt I had to do penance for my past, which I thought was truly evil even though, in reality, it was quite normal for an adolescent with a negative self-image. I promised myself I would make it up to them, especially my parents.

I decided that I would join a religious order's seminary so that I would be a religious priest. I studied "Guidepost," which had one-page summaries of the various orders. I thought I might be good working with high school students, that I could save them from the "evil things" I had done. So I started concentrating on the Salesians and Oblates of St. Francis de Sales, two groups who had many high schools. At the same time I read about St. Francis of Assisi and was affected by his spirituality. Dan, who had joined the Capuchin Franciscans, told me that the Capuchins said their purpose in life was "to live the gospel." That sounded appealing too.

By the day of decision the three possible orders had become two: the Oblates and the Capuchins. I drove to our parish church. There I made a quick visit to the blessed sacrament and then went where I thought I'd really get results—to the Blessed Virgin's altar. After more prayers I recalled that the Capuchins' purpose was "to live the gospel." I knew this is what I wanted. I wanted to make my story the gospel's story. I would join the Capuchins.

If I was a budding codependent when I entered the Capuchins, its corporate culture at that time provided just the right environment for my codependency to reach full bloom. As I look back, my thirty years in religious life have been, on balance, very good years. But the early years, before the changes in religious formation really took place in the church and my Province, were another story that deeply affected my story.

Diane Fassel and Anne Wilson Schaef say that the third sign determining the possibility of viewing the institutional church as addictive, is when the organization itself provides the "fix."[10] They also say that another indication of how addictive an organization can be happens when people—like me—become addicted to its mission and promises.[11] Having entered with a drive to make up to my parents and brothers for all the harm I had done, the mission of the religious life—to offer me a way of perfection—and its promises—"if you do all these things I promise you eternal life"—fit my need for instant salvation from my past. I was ripe for the organization I entered; I would be loyal and submissive.

Before I rebelled; now I repressed any rebellion in me. I submitted to the will of the superiors because I was told they represented God; their will for us was God's will. By obeying them, I had my salvation ensured. In submitting to them and their interpretation of God's will I lived out the characteristics of the person addicted to the organization in its mission and promises: "A person addicted to the promise of the organization is willing to endure any amount of bad experiences to hold onto that promise, which can be anything from 'life everlasting' to a sense of belonging to a community or being accepted."[12]

But that is hindsight. Returning to my early years in the Order, I recall that my trip to the novitiate was great fun. The majority of us who were to constitute the class of thirty-one novices took a bus from the Fond du Lac area to Huntington, Indiana. I was nineteen years old. We began immediately with an eight-day silent retreat, during which I was introduced to the various rituals of the Order and its prayer. In the name of being mindful of the passion of Jesus we "took the discipline"—a thrice-weekly practice of beating our bare behinds with a chain as we recited the penitential psalms. While I know now that this was physical abuse forced on us by the institution, I never questioned it. However, the abuse I *did* know I was experiencing— emotional and psychological pain—came from one of the superiors. But this was one of the things we didn't talk about.

I know now that this man abused and invaded our sexual boundaries with his persistent questions about our practice or non-practice of celibacy before and during novitiate. As a class we would wait silently in fear each day when he came to teach us or give us our work assignments; on Sundays the fear bordered on anxiety as we went for our hour-long spiritual conference. At these times one of us would inevitably be singled out for public shaming. The year-and-a-day for novitiate seemed unending. (I have since discussed this with him. He believes he did the best he knew how. He too was a victim of the system.)

Between ending the novitiate and beginning philosophy studies, I was able to go home to celebrate my parents' silver wedding anniversary. My mother saved the holy card I gave her for this occasion. It could not be a more clear indicator of the kind of shame-based self-image that controlled me at that time. On the back of the card I wrote: "For being the best and loving the most in putting up with the worst. I'm offering the month for you."

Having had a year of college, I only needed three years at our philosophy seminary at Crown Point, Indiana. Once there I immediately descended to the bottom group of my class academically. Going to my brother Dan for help in studies only made me feel more inferior. Within that first year I began to have a dramatic loss of hair. I asked to go to the doctor to see what was wrong. I was told that I was being vain and shouldn't worry about my looks. I was bald by the time I was twenty-three.

I started publishing articles during that time. Some appeared in quite respected journals such as *America* and *Emmanuel*. In my second year I also started to improve in my studies, having learned how to memorize the Latin syllogisms for the Thomism we used for philosophy. Yet the fear I had every time I had to knock on a professor's door or go to confession or to monthly spiritual direction made me feel like jelly inside. Rather than diminishing as I got closer to solemn vows, it seemed to increase.

By March 7, 1963, I had advanced academically enough to be chosen as one of three presenting a formal paper for the annual St. Thomas Aquinas Day lecture. My topic dealt with the way ideas get into our heads. I don't know what I said, but I do know that one of the things I did do was question a point about a position held by the Angelic Doctor. In anger the head of the philosophy department, rather than explaining why I was wrong, simply declared: "If you don't like it, you can get out." With less than three months to go before graduation I was afraid I had received my walking papers. I went to the Director of Clerics to find out what was going to happen. He assured me I would not be expelled.

I went home the next month to be with my dad, who was dying. He had been failing for the previous seven months, and we knew he was dying. I was not allowed to visit, except once, despite repeated requests to do so. Whenever I would ask to be with him, my superior would say, "No, you can't go just because you want to go. You can do

more good for your father by obeying than by doing your own will."
I had entered the Capuchins wanting a clear way to perfection; I had
been told all along that if I obeyed my superiors—even their slightest
desire—I would be doing God's will. It hadn't been too hard to do
that up to now; in fact, it was getting me many graces to make up for
my past wickedness to my family. But now I was home.

That first night Dan began telling me what had happened to me
as a Capuchin, that the system had made me an automaton, a zombie
whose identity was totally defined by the institution's overt and covert
rules and expectations. His sharing proved to be a kind of intervention
for me. I began to step apart from the system that had proved to
be the largest influence in enabling me to become codependent. The
institutional church and the Order's participation in it had become my
addictive substance—making me a classic codependent. What Fassel
and Schaef describe about the organization becoming the addictive
substance fit me as though they had me in mind when writing it:

> The organization becomes the addictive substance for its
> employees when the employees become hooked on the
> promise of the mission and choose not to look at how
> the system is really operating. The organization becomes
> an addictive substance when its actions are excused be-
> cause it has a lofty mission. We have found an inverse
> correlation between the loftiness of the mission and the con-
> gruence between stated and unstated goals. When this lack
> of congruence exists, it is more probably that the organiza-
> tion will enter into a rigid denial system with concomitant
> grandiosity.[13]

Dad died on Easter Sunday morning, April 14, 1963. As I got
into the car to return to Indiana the day after his funeral I remember
thinking: "I have only six weeks left in the seminary. I'm coming
back and you'll be able to control my behavior, but never again will
I let you or anyone else control my mind."

During that summer—at our theological seminary in Wisconsin—
I wrote my first book. It detailed what the modern popes (those since
Pope Leo XIII [d. 1903]) said the Franciscans must be and do in
the institutional church and society. Needless to say my unquestioning approach to papal statements and declarations has been adapted
somewhat between then and now! At any rate, submissiveness in the
name of spirituality was evident as I tried to address those who might

not agree with what the popes had said. Rather than thinking papal pronouncements might not be absolutely correct or might be ill-advised, I found no problem in accepting them; the members of the Order who would question were the ones who needed to rethink their positions!

> In certain places it may seem the popes emphasize points not usually stressed. It may also seem they overstress particular points or stress things which may even appear alien to our spirit. If this seems to be the case, let us not jump to the conclusion they have been wrong. As Francis did regarding studies, let *us* rather look to our genuine spirit. If we do, we can only deduce that our life is to be lived at the feet of these popes, not only listening to their words of counsel for us, but eager to put them into practice.[14]

Since writing those words I have taken more steps forward and many steps back into my disease. For one thing—as should be evident from this book—I can no longer unquestioningly submit to any human or institutional authority except the full authority revealed in Jesus Christ (28:18). Furthermore, while the institutional church has become more hierarchical, my Province has struggled to become more collegial. With the changes in the Province that began in conjunction with the Second Vatican Council I have been both helped and hindered as I walk, but the overall journey has provided me with a deep source of gratitude for the way my recent superiors have supported me. Thanks to them I can now name my disease and work toward further conversion and recovery.

PART III

RECOVERY

Recovery is for the addictive process what conversion is for the spiritual life. Both involve an alternative process of leaving something behind and turning to something else.

Recovery thus involves two dynamics. The first involves stopping the addictive process. Many people think that stopping drinking ensures recovery. What it ensures is that drinking stops. Unless the second stage in the process is embraced the likelihood is that nothing will change except the object of the addiction. A new way of thinking, feeling, and behaving is demanded.

In Part Two on intervention I wrote that I follow the school that believes an admission of addiction only comes when the presentation of the data about present behavior is overpowering. As of this writing, there seems to be no data to indicate that those caught in the addictive process of preserving the male, celibate, clerical model of the institutional church have admitted the exact nature of their wrong. Therefore hope for recovery at this time is not possible. However, since this institution is also a family, and since these leaders are merely the "identified patients," the following pages on recovery are addressed to codependent Catholics, those of us who have been caught up in the family disease but now want to become involved in recovery's two processes: to stop our participation in the controls of the addictive process, and to begin thinking, feeling, and behaving anew.

CHAPTER NINE

The Spirituality of Becoming Wholehearted
(Mt 6:19–34)

Recovery from the addictive process involves a change of objects of our heart's thinking and consideration, its feeling and desires, and its behavior. The change will be from earthly-based objects, relationships, and processes to heavenly ones. These will indicate where our treasure is—and where our treasure is, there will be our heart. When recovery is authentic it moves from the addictive process into the process of wholeness or perfection. Recovery, like spirituality, involves a transformative journey of the heart.

While we have traditionally been aware of the need for a transformation of our own hearts, it has only been recently that we have spoken of the need for a transformation of structures. In 1986 the bishops of the United States wrote in their pastoral letter on the economy:

> The transformation of social structures begins with and is always accompanied by a conversion of the heart. As disciples of Christ each of us is called to a deep personal conversion and to "action on behalf of justice and participation in the transformation of the world."[1]

If conversion of individuals, groups, and institutions is to take place, there must be a change of heart in their perceptions, their emotions, and their behavior. There must be a movement from being under the control of one power to another, higher power, a conversion from one spiritual force to another. If institutional Catholicism suffers from the addictive disease of patriarchal clericalism, only if it submits to a higher power will it be able to recover from its pathology. Only if it converts from its addiction to power to its higher power will it be able to experience the peace and joy of the reign of God.

After showing his audience how easily it was caught up in obsessive thinking, anxiety, and behavior related to what to eat, drink, and wear, Matthew's Jesus says:

> "Therefore do not worry, saying, 'What will we eat?' or 'What will we drink?' or 'What will we wear?' For it is the Gentiles who strive for all these things; and indeed your heavenly Father knows that you need all these things. But strive first for the kingdom of God and his righteousness, and all these things will be given to you as well" (Mt 6:31–33).

This passage presents Jesus' treatment program for recovery from addiction according to Matthew: 1) *Stop* the addictive thinking, feeling, and behaving around the addictive objects, which have taken authority over life and body; then 2) *Strive for* God's reign and God's way of justice or right ordering in our thinking, feeling, and behaving.

In probing why some Catholics need a program for recovery and others don't, I have been helped by the distinction between Culture One Catholics and Culture Two Catholics made by Eugene Kennedy in *Tomorrow's Catholics/Yesterday's Church: The Two Cultures of American Catholicism.*[2] Culture One Catholics constitute part of that reality which "emphasizes, stands by, and works diligently to protect the institution and its lines of control over the church at large. *Institutional* might be a word well added to the list of the distinguishing characteristics (one, holy, catholic, and apostolic) that the church has traditionally claimed for itself."[3] Culture One Catholicism is "official Catholicism that remains the absorbing, sometimes obsessing, First Culture environment."[4] As such, this institutional Catholicism need not be limited to those leaders who are absorbed and obsessed with preserving that environment. Culture One Catholics are also those who by their own choice or by temperament are controlled willingly or unwillingly by the family disease that is merely identified in its institutional leaders. As such they are codependent Catholics. I am one of them.

Culture Two Catholics have moved from the shadows of institutional Catholicism to recognize that they are the people of God.

Kennedy finds these kinds of Catholics "widely deployed, finding their center of gravity in America at large rather than within the handsomely fenced churchyard of ecclesiastical structure. . . . These Catholics are impressed when their bishops leave institutional concerns behind them in order to address major societal problems,"[5] but because they are almost totally involved with their families and work, with troubles and challenges enough of their own, they somehow have been able to be free of the obsessive preoccupations of the institutional leaders. For example, even though my Capuchin brother Dan is a minister in the institution, he is a Culture Two Catholic. He is not obsessive about the role of the institution and doesn't feel the need to react to its control as I do.

The next chapters of this book are not meant for the institutional leaders who see no need for conversion. Neither are they addressed to church ministers, like Dan, who seem to be free of the church-family's disease. They are for myself and others like me, codependent Catholics who know all about Culture Two Catholicism but remain hooked into Culture One Catholicism. These chapters will talk about *our* recovery, not theirs.

As we begin our journey from the addictive process into the process of wholeness, I will treat the three essential elements that constitute both the addictive process and the process of wholeness—the intellectual, emotional, and behavioral dimensions. Each will be examined from the "negative" way it might be expressed—in disordered forms that must "stop" if we are not going to move into addicted ways of thinking, feeling, and acting. Then I will investigate the ways we can seek alternative ways of perceiving, emoting, and behaving. Finally, I will show how each of the three ways manifests itself in a particular virtue which, combined, constitute the underlying way of wholeness or perfection: faith, courage (hope), and dedication (love).

From "The Lie" to Truth and Faith

In "Alcoholics Anonymous: From Surrender to Transformation," David Berenson details three ways conversion takes place. Berenson speaks of first, second, and third order changes. He shows that AA is arranged so that people can stop their addictive behavior by education, therapeutic change, or transformation. First order changes happen, for a small percentage of people, when they attend an AA meeting and hear the information presented about alcoholism as a disease. However, for most people, simple *intellectual comprehension* is not enough to bring about spiritual understanding. Second order changes are used by therapists in recovery. They stress *intervention* in the addictive process by being aware of such issues as transference and family systems and suggesting alternative responses to past stimulation. However here, as in first order changes, the behavior alterations may fail to affect the depths of a person's being. Third order changes, however, involve *transformational change* and a profound reorganization of a person's life: "In a transformational shift there is a radical reorientation in one's view of what's real. What happens is not a reframing of reality as happens in therapy but a seeing that here is a reality beyond all frames."[6]

When Matthew's Jesus says, "Therefore, I tell you, do not worry about your life, what you will eat or what you will drink, or about your body, what you will wear" (6:25), it might be considered parallel to the nagging spouse who tries to get the partner to stop drinking. Not much is accomplished by the nagging. So Matthew has Jesus move to the first order of possible conversion by getting his hearers to change their thinking about their addictive behavior. He uses an image from nature: "*Consider* the lilies of the field. . ." (6:28). The first thing to be considered is disordered thinking.

The addictive process, which is sustained through denial, feeds on disordered thoughts, perceptions, and considerations. For recovery to take place for church codependents, we must "get honest." In addictive institutions and systems, dishonesty—"the lie"—is normative. Anne Wilson Schaef has noted: "Like the drunk, the Addictive System is fundamentally dishonest; it is just more subtle about it."[7]

In my work in corporate responsibility, I have found many subtleties in the way corporations try to mislead people's thinking about their products and corporate practices. For the 1990 annual meeting of shareholders of Philip Morris, my Midwest Capuchin Province and the Adrian (Michigan) Dominican Sisters co-filed a shareholder resolution that would require the company to become smoke-free in its production and marketing by the year 2000. The heart of Philip Morris' business is tobacco. Feeding its institutional addiction to profits by exploiting the nicotine addiction of consumers, Philip Morris responded and sent us a proposed statement in opposition to our resolution. Its statements included these: "The proposal is premised primarily upon a number of unproven assertions about the alleged health consequences of cigarette smoking," and "Despite years of effort and expense, medical science has been unable to determine the specific causes of many diseases, including those which are statistically associated with cigarette smoking," and "Based upon unproven and unsupported scientific and economic assertions, the proposal implies that the appropriate 'solution' to the smoking and health issue is to impose a virtual ban on smoking by forcing manufacturers 'to stop cigarette production.' "[8]

Reading Philip Morris' response, I had further discussions with a lawyer and the Provincial. I informed Philip Morris, through the lawyer, that my Province was prepared to sue the company unless it changed its "distortions of truth" and "misstatements of fact" about cigarette smoking and health. Our threat of a lawsuit became like a minor intervention. With the threat of our lawsuit over its attempt to manipulate people's information about cigarettes and health, Philip Morris had a "change of heart." It dropped everything in its statement of opposition dealing with smoking and health and merely addressed the financial conflicts that might accompany shareholder approval of our resolution.

"Misstatements of fact" and "distortions of truth" are other phrases for "the lie." For an addict, the lie is first to one's self about the way one is thinking, feeling, and behaving; second, to those in the family; and third, to the world. I believe the institutional leaders in the Catholic church perceive patriarchal celibate clericalism in much the same way that the managers of Philip Morris perceive cigarette profits. For the church leaders, the addiction involves processes and relationships; for Philip Morris, the addiction is to substances and relationships. The addiction has become so normative that dishonesty around the issue becomes standard. When the leaders' last refuge for support for male, celibate clericalism as the norm in the Western Church appeals to Jesus as a male celibate, the argument becomes quite weak indeed.

Codependents easily get hooked into the dishonesty of the addicts. As in all addictive families, members, according to Schaef, "are expected to support the lie they live. They get confused and crazy and gradually come to distrust their own perceptions. They lose their ability to distinguish between truth and lying, and the potential for honesty becomes even more remote."[9] The consequence is inaction—and the addictive process continues. The only way to stop the addictive process from infecting those of us who are family members in the church is to intervene in the thinking patterns and ways of perception. This demands a passion for truth as the main opponent of the dishonesty. Unless the dishonesty is checked, it will lead to obsessive thinking that reinforces the lie as well as the addictive process. We will begin thinking in the same way as the addict and use dishonesty to rationalize it as well. The only alternative is to stop the dishonest patterns and begin to seek entrance into the process of wholeness through a new order grounded in truth.

The process of conversion from disordered thinking and dishonesty begins by stopping its control and by seeking truth so that faith can be ensured. To do nothing is to be part of the lie; to be part of the lie is to descend into corruption. W. H. Auden once wrote: "As a poet there is only one political duty, and that is to defend one's language from corruption. And that is particularly serious now. It's being so quickly corrupted. When it's corrupted, people lose faith in what they hear, and this leads to violence."[10] Since the basis of a collegial community rests upon the faith its members have in one another, to have one's language abused, manipulated, or controlled by those in power creates disruption. This manifests violence.

In what seems to have been his last work before he left communist Russia with its obsession with thought-control, Alexander Solzhenitsyn asked: "Is there really no way out? And is there only one thing left for us to do, to wait without taking action? Maybe something will happen by itself?" He responded to his own questions by saying the effort to control the way we think must stop:

> It will never happen as long as we daily acknowledge, extol, and strengthen—and so not sever ourselves from—the most perceptible of its aspects: Lies. When violence intrudes into peaceful life, its face glows with self-confidence, as if it were carrying a banner and shouting: "I am violence. Run away, make way for me—I will crush you." But violence quickly grows old. And it has lost confidence in itself, and in order to maintain a respectable face it summons falsehood as its ally—since violence can conceal itself with nothing except lies, and the lies can be maintained only by violence. And violence lays its ponderous paw not every day and not on every shoulder; it demands from us only obedience to lies and daily participation in lies—all loyalty lies in that.[11]

In response to Roman obsession with controlling the way the entire church thinks along with the equal obsession to have everyone submit to some "objective truths," ministers and members in the church can silently acquiesce and become enslaved in the same addiction, or we can stop our participation in the dishonesty and the lie.

A recurring theme, especially in Pope John Paul II's writings, is "truth." His first encyclical, *Redemptor Hominis*, revolved around the notion of the "truth of man" [sic]. For him, promoting the "truth of man" is at the church's heart:

> The church wishes to serve this single end: that each person may be able to find Christ, in order that Christ may walk with each person the path of life, with the power of the truth about man and the world that is contained in the mystery of the incarnation and the redemption and with the power of the love that is radiated by that truth. Against a background of the ever increasing historical processes, which seem at the present time to have results especially within the spheres of various systems, ideological concepts of the world and regimes, Jesus Christ becomes, in a way, newly present, in spite of all his apparent absences, in spite of all the limitations of the presence and of the institutional activity of the church.[12]

It is precisely in its obsession with controlling peoples' minds in the name of "truth," in demanding unswerving obedience to those "truths" in the name of loyalty, that "the institutional activity of the church" makes many feel that Jesus Christ has become absent in the church. In a church that considers absolute obedience the hallmark of loyalty, what Solzhenitsyn concluded for the Soviet Union applies. He writes: "The simplest and most accessible key to our self-neglected liberation lies right here: personal non-participation in lies."[13]

In the face of the violence that is done to the people of God, who are denied the sacraments and their just rights to participate fully in the life of the church, the way to recovery begins in non-submission to the lie. Non-participation in lies reveals the first step in the process. It demands that the dishonesty stop. The next step involves our effort to seek reordered thinking in the form of truth that is free of the obsession to control its expression. These two processes constitute our initial recovery in thinking. If we maintain fidelity to this twofold way of recovery we will find ourselves moving into faith itself.

Part of the addictive process for many codependents is such that one's whole faith as a person involves a relationship with the addictive agent or dynamic in such a way that the person's trust revolves around that relationship as the object of his or her addiction. One is obsessed with maintaining one's supply. If conversion—moving *from* the addiction *to* another way of living—is to take place, the former power and strangle hold has to be relinquished under the persuasion of a higher power, in whom the recovering codependent has a newfound faith. For believers, the ultimate higher power is God.

Outside the church there is much controversy in the field of addiction about the notion of the higher power. In 1985 Jonas Ellis published an article that was very critical of the Twelve-Step program's spiritual component and recommended that the steps referring to God or a higher power should be deleted.[14] This position was supported by many within the drug dependence treatment field and in the recovering community. Many saw it as merely transferring faith in one substance, relationship, or process for another; changing a dependence on something for a dependence on something else. In considering such a statement we need to observe the behavior of church leaders, ministers, and members and ask who their higher power really might be.

I noted previously that one of the main forces keeping me from having faith in God or Jesus as my savior revolved around my self-centered preoccupation with maintaining control. Yet, during all this time, I thought I had faith. I thought I believed in God and had a relationship with God; yet my underlying belief was in myself, and my relationship with God was centered in myself. For those caught in the addictive process, self-centeredness is the norm. There can be no real faith in anyone else, including God. The implications of the last statement for the addicted institutional leaders in the Catholic church is telling. If they are their own "higher power," they don't need God. They have become the higher power; they alone are infallible.

As we move more deeply into our addictive ways, we move into a parallel crisis of faith. Yet the very presumption of the leaders, the ministers, and members of the church ("the faithful") is that they have faith. But this assumption needs articulation in thinking, feeling, and behaving, a discovery I made years ago when I was part of the leadership group in my own Province.

Month after month, the name of one brother kept coming up in personnel discussions, connected to one negative situation after another. After one month too many I asked, "How can he do this? Doesn't he have any faith?" The response of the Vicar Provincial was immediate: "Mike, we can't just presume the faith of the men." Religion *assumes* faith. Spirituality *manifests* faith. There is a big difference. Religion can be addictive; spirituality cannot. Part of the difference involves faith. Such faith goes far beyond submission to "truths."

Faith in both the secular and religious sense involves four steps: 1) *persons* enter into 2) *relationships* that engender 3) *trust* to such a degree 4) that they are willing to make a *commitment*. The centurion entered into a relationship with Jesus, trusting that he was able to heal his slave. He committed himself to Jesus, which in turn engendered Jesus' response: "Truly, I tell you, in no one in Israel have I found such faith" (8:10). Peter walked toward Jesus on the water in trust and declared, "Truly you are the Son of God" (14:22–33). Genuine spiritual faith involves submitting to a higher power. It means moving from self-centeredness to God-centeredness.

Such faith is shown in the willingness to share that faith with others. Not only does faith-sharing represent the essence of the Twelfth Step, which entails communicating the good news about recovery to others and listening to others' stories of faith in their higher power, in their God, which in turn reinforces one's own faith, but it also becomes the basis for healing communities. Grounding in this kind of faith enables codependent Catholics to consider how their emotions can cage them in fear and keep them from freedom and a life of courage. This brings us to the second step in moving from the codependent way of feeling in the addictive process to the process of wholeness.

From Fear to Freedom and Courage

Matthew's gospel shows us that our heart's emotions and desires are oriented to what or whom we treasure (6:21). These emotions and desires can be ordered or disordered regarding what or who will satisfy the longings of the heart. As such they can contribute to positive or negative spirituality. One way or another, desire is at the core of the process for addiction or wholeness. All desire ultimately represents a longing for the ultimate. Gerald May writes:

> After twenty years of listening to the yearnings of people's hearts, I am convinced that all human beings have an inborn

desire for God. Whether we are consciously religious or not, this desire is our deepest longing, and our most precious treasure. It gives us meaning. Some of us have repressed this desire, burying it beneath so many other interests that we are completely unaware of it. Or we may experience it in different ways—as a longing for wholeness, completion, or fulfillment. Regardless of how we describe it, it is a longing for love. It is a hunger to love, to be loved, and to move closer to the Source of love. This yearning is the essence of the human spirit; it is the origin of our highest hopes and most noble dreams. . . . If we could claim our longing for love as the true treasure of our hearts, we would, with God's grace, be able to live these commandments.

But something gets in the way.[15]

That "something" is fear. Fear represents the apprehension engendered by some specific person, object, or situation that is perceived as a threat to one's well being. Unless reordered, fear can easily lead to anxiety, the apprehension that arises when some *un*specified person, object, or situation becomes perceived as a threat to one's very existence or self-understanding.[16]

Perceived physical threats don't cause us as much apprehension as psychological dangers. Some people who seem fearless in the face of physical dangers become quite disordered in the face of psychological threats. Psychological threats involve relationships, and these affect one's self-concept. It is not surprising, then, that AA defines addiction as self-centered fear, a disordered dependence on one's self.

Because it is so basic, no one can be free from fear. Fear is a natural emotion; it is God-given and, therefore, positive. In face of impending danger Jesus manifested fear (26:39), probably not just of betrayal but of being left alone (26:40–46). Perhaps this fear of being lonely, abandoned by others, constitutes the basic human fear.

Existential loneliness is that loneliness each of us experiences, yet which can never be fully understood or completely shared by others. Loneliness constitutes part of life's fabric; it too is good and cannot be avoided. Fear seems to be the emotional reaction that arises at that point in an infant's life when he or she realizes that the "I" is no longer the "we," but is, indeed, quite alone. At this point of existential loneliness, there are two possible journeys to take. The first, which begins from a sense of feeling precious and free, continues that way and is influenced by healthy shame and guilt when deviations are made. The second way, taken by those who experience themselves as toxically shamed or guilty, progresses into various fears; the person moves further into anxiety and the addictive process as an active addict or co-addict.

For people on the second journey the fear of loneliness leads into obsessive thinking about their condition, anxious feelings about their alienation, and addictive behaviors to forget about their loneliness. However, I am not dealing with these final levels in the addictive process here; I am considering their primary stages. The primary stage of emotions and desires in the face of loneliness, if we speak of "negative" spirituality, is fear; if we speak of "positive" spirituality it is freedom leading to courage.

A parallel fear that keeps many codependents in the disease involves the fear of intimacy. If shame is the core of codependency, the fear of intimacy expresses the manifestation of that shame. This fear was a major reason for my own work addiction and perfectionism.

In many ways fear of intimacy results from lack of faith. Without personal relationships of trust there can be no commitment. And commitment involves a degree of intimacy. Without faith, there will be fear of intimacy. If celibates have faith only in themselves and not in any higher power, there can be no genuine intimacy. Emotional intimacy involves persons who have relationships of trust. It requires honesty and truth; it breaks down where there may be dishonesty and lies.

In response to the leaders of the church and their authority addiction there can be many fears, especially for those ministers who depend on them for their very livelihood. One of these fears deals with fear of rejection, especially by those we consider significant in the institutional arrangements around us; we fear that we will be unacceptable to the leaders of the institution. The intensity of this fear corresponds quite closely to our view of ourself. Where self-esteem is positive, the fear will be less; where it has been harmed, the fear will be greater. The intensity of the fear will also correspond quite closely to the degree we see ourselves and our livelihood identified with the institution. For instance, I have never feared writing my concerns about questionable behavior to political leaders or corporate executives. Yet, when I write CICLSAL registering my concerns about its activities, I often feel deep fear, bordering on anxiety. Why do I fear our religious, canonical leaders and not our political and economic leaders?

Another fear deals with change. Many codependents in the church can be highly critical of its teachings and the behavior of our leaders, yet, deep down, fear any real change. Another fear dealing with change involves the assumption that it is better to deal with the devil we know than with the one we don't. Some people remain in their fear and choose to remain in destructive relationships and situations rather than risk getting into a worse situation. Fear of change in dysfunctional settings keeps us in a dependency state; we become that system's victims.

One of the fears that has held me in bondage too many times is fear of failure. Having worked at being perfect and having competed with others, just the idea that I might fail, or that others will know I have failed, is enough to paralyze me. Peter Orlando notes that anytime we act like the one who asked "Mirror, mirror on the wall who's the fairest of us all?" we are revealing the shadow side of ourselves.

> The need to be "the greatest," to be seen in a certain light, and to avoid mistakes is the largest contributor to anxiety that I have discovered. There is no disgrace in finding ourselves upon the "floor of life"; the only disgrace is not getting up. It is a delusion to think that our worth comes from the contribution that we make or the gifts we are given.[17]

When we begin to center life around ourselves, fear of failure, of change, of intimacy, of loneliness can become self-destructive and lead into addictive behaviors. When we fail to recognize that fear can be our emotions' invitation to deepen our relationships with others rather than to rely on ourselves, we can easily be controlled by the fears and remain codependently fearful. This kind of fear keeps us and others from the conversion and transformation we seek.

A final fear facing many people accustomed to clerical control in the institutional church involves fear of freedom. Just as the spouse becomes immobilized thinking of the possibility of separation from the addictive partner, so many of us codependents in the church get paralyzed in our thinking and feeling when we try to imagine life separated from clerical control. For many, especially very progressive groups of women religious, the fear that they might lose their canonical status and, thus, their property, keeps them psychologically unfree, afraid to make a canonical separation that would free them from unwarranted papal or episcopal controls.

The opposite of fear is freedom. Fear of freedom deals with being bound or loosed. According to Michael Cavanaugh, fear of freedom

> is the fear of being bound by significantly less restraints or by no restraints. . . . It is a very subtle fear because most people realize that they fear the imposition of restraints and "naturally" assume that they would welcome its opposite, namely, freedom. But this assumption is invalid for many people. The more freedom we have, the more free rein our impulses have; the more we have to set our own limits; the more we must carve out our own existence; the more we have to assume responsibility for our own behavior; and the more we are left alone by others.[18]

Codependency is characterized by control. By definition, control denies freedom. Thus one's fear of freedom might, in reality, be a disordered desire to be controlled or to compulsively keep trying to control others. I have found in my own life that my obsessive need to control—myself, God, my Capuchin province, people I work with, and even the pope and Curia—reflects a lack of true freedom on my part.

True freedom means freedom *from* the need to control and freedom *to be* who I am, to allow God to be who God is, and to rejoice when other people are who they are. The fully functioning person, the person who is free and part of the process of wholeness, manifests that integrity by the various freedoms which relate to human power: the power/freedom to think and perceive, to sense and feel, to will and choose. When these freedoms are frustrated by others, relationships become dysfunctional; when they are denied by systems they might be submerged but will keep resurfacing.

In the "welcome" at meetings of CoDependents Anonymous a promise of freedom is made if people apply the Twelve Steps and principles found in CODA to daily life and relationships. That freedom can be experienced as an alternative to self-defeating lifestyles. The "welcome" ends: "No longer do you need to rely upon others as a power greater than yourself. May you instead find here a new strength within to be that which God intended—*precious and free!*"

In Matthew, the phrase for "have courage" can be translated "take heart." Many people give up seeking their treasure because they lose heart; they fail in courage. Many people stop seeking God's reign and God's way of justice and stop insisting that it be translated into the institutional church because they lack courage. They fear the consequences of being free. Instead of living out our desires in freedom which makes us courageous we remain locked in our cages of fear.

As I reflect on my approach to life, I realize I was grounded in self-doubt and loaded with fears. When I was challenged at the way I promoted justice in the world and in the church, I began to slack off, fearful of rejection. Yet I denied my fears and kept acting as though I were perfectly in control. I became the kind of person controlled by fears who has been so well-described by Brendan Callaghan:

> At some unreflective level, we believe ourselves to be not only immortal, but also practically omnipotent. We censor our experiencing of failure and death, and block out from our consciousness these reminders of our limited mortality. But by so doing, we make ourselves their prisoners; by denying that it is there at all, we render ourselves unable to face what we fear; by denying that we have fear, we make cowards of ourselves. The inability to face these simple facts of our own humanity can be seen not simply as a model of our other imbalances and inordinate attachments, but as lying at the heart of them all. So it is of considerable importance, if we are trying to come to some fuller understanding of the workings of the Spirit of God in our hearts, that we face up to this question of our fears, and find the courage to examine our cowardice.[19]

Courage that flows from true freedom enables us to face our fears and name the cowardice that can bind us; it gives us the assurance, grounded in faith, that we are secure. Although Matthew's Jesus does not use the Greek word for courage, he sees it as a condition of one who is secure in the heart. Since to "take heart," for Matthew, means to have courage (14:27), if one's treasure indicates where one's heart is, and if the treasure is secure, the heart will be courageous.

Courage cannot be understood apart from faith. Without courage, faith has no expression. Without courage, faith is hollow. Faith is faith only when it gives courageous expression to its convictions. The manifestation of faith is one's commitment in trust to risk the comforts of life in courageous love, which rises from giving one's life to the higher power who is God. According to Rosemary Radford Ruether:

The courage of faith is based, then, not only on conviction of truth, but also on ultimate trust in God. This ultimate trust is possible because the Christian, in the words of Tillich, already has made the final act of courage, which is to accept one's own acceptance by God. Christian courage, then, is rooted in grace. It is not something that one strives to attain on some ladder of merit, but something that is given by God. Having been given the gift of acceptance by God, "just as we are," the Christian is freed from anxiety. Fearlessness or courage is based on this grace of being both upheld by God and placing our trust in God. It is precisely this trust in God that enables one to speak truthfully and act justly without regard to those worldly vested interests that have a stake in lies and injustice.[20]

In the institutional Catholic church, with its addictive power over us, one of the greatest obstacles keeping us from challenging it to truth and internal justice revolves around lack of courage. St. Thomas writes that we should pray for the virtue of courage. He says so, not because it might be a virtue in itself, but because he sees courage as the virtue *needed* for the promotion of justice. In other words, many codependents fail to speak up for justice in society and in the church, because we are not fearless, because we lack courage. Courage gives us the grace to speak for justice. It enables us to seek first God's reign and to be committed to that justice which reveals God's reign.

From Attachments to Detachment and Commitment

Before I got involved in addiction studies, attachment seemed like a positive virtue. In some ways, it is. However, when considered as part of the addictive process, attachment reveals a form of behavior that parallels dishonesty (to the intellect) and fear (to the emotions). It manifests a kind of disorder of the heart that indicates a lack of detachment, a kind of "wealth in spirit," that keeps us from being committed to the reign of God. Attachments are behavioral disorders that can enslave desire and undermine clear thinking. While developing attachments is part of the human condition, when these attachments become disordered they easily lead to anxiety and addictions.

Once I mentioned in a group of Capuchins that I really enjoyed a mixed drink. In other words I was saying that I had some kind of attachment to alcohol. One member of the group was a recovering alcoholic. He looked at me somewhat skeptically. Not long afterward the

Provincial, who was known to be concerned about excessive drinking in the Province, commented that he had heard about my comment. He made it clear that I should be careful because my attachment might lead to an addictive pattern of behavior. I know he is right, given my past, and I must be careful.

In themselves attachments are not bad; however, because they are geared to objects, relationships, and processes that can be addictive, they always represent the possibility of addiction. Ministers can be very attached to the institutional church and yet be free of being *addictively* bonded to it. The church has been the object of our attachments, and rightly so. However, when we find ourselves becoming obsessive in our thinking and becoming anxious in our feelings about issues in the institutional church and what the institutional leaders do or don't do, we are close to stepping over the fine line between attachment to the institutional church and codependent behavior, making it as an end in itself, as what ultimately most concerns us.

Martin Luther said the object of our attachments will become our god. Whatever is most important will be our treasure. Where our treasure is will indicate where our heart is also. Whether Luther or Matthew's Jesus, the great spiritual traditions make it clear that disordered attachments reflect processes that can reveal a heart that is compromised.

The addictive cycle starts when we perform an action or enter a relationship that gives pleasure; it either alleviates pain or produces a positive stimulation. When subsequent behaviors are initiated to repeat or increase the pleasure, an increasing attachment to the objects of those behaviors is not far behind. Thus, if we do not actually *stop* the behavior, we must be disciplined lest it turn into an addiction. At the same time we must begin seeking ways to ensure that we can become detached from our attachments; otherwise we will probably be heading toward addiction.

In almost all the great spiritual traditions, detachment initiates the process into wholeness or perfection (19:21). Climbing the mountain in the psalms involves having clean hands and a pure heart (Ps 24:4). The Beatitudes of Matthew's Jesus begin with a blessing for those who are poor in spirit (5:3). The Benedictines demand a vow of renovation of life; the Carmelites seek *nada*; the Franciscans desire marriage with Lady Poverty. Buddhists concentrate on the Four Noble Truths: 1) suffering is a fact of life; 2) suffering is caused by attachment; 3) liberation from suffering and the reestablishment of human freedom happens only through detachment; and 4) human effort toward detachment must involve all aspects of one's life in a deeply spiritual way. When the Four Noble Truths are combined with the Eightfold Path[21] detachment is not far behind. A way of becoming detached from patriarchal clericalism can be found in the approach of some feminists, who have adapted the Four Noble Truths to create the Four Noble Feminist Truths: 1) suffering exists under patriarchy; 2) the cause of this suffering was prehistoric man's inability to confront the reality of death and pain without aversion, and life and pleasure without craving; 3) there is a cure; and 4) the cure is the Eightfold Path integrated with the Twelve-Step Feminist Program.[22]

The reference to the Twelve-Step program recalls the way of detachment, which is at the heart of the recovery program for addicts ever since the founding of Alcoholics Anonymous; it has come to serve as the context for recovery for other addicts and codependents. Beginning with the first three steps one gradually comes to realize the centrality of detachment from the addictive process by "letting go" and "letting God." What Al-Anon and Alateen say about detachment in reference to people living with addicts within a diseased family can apply equally to ministers and others affected by addicts within the diseased institutional family called the church: "We let go of our obsession with another's behavior and begin to lead happier and more manageable lives, lives with dignity and rights; lives guided by a power greater than ourselves." Authentic detachment flows from the refusal to be dishonest; it involves the embrace of truth and faith in the sense we have described it. This kind of detachment is not controlled by fear but is free and courageous because its approach to life is spirit-based.

If in the addictive process to be "given over" to the object of addiction or codependency manifests addictive behavior, to be "given over" to the reign of God instead of some form of mammon-reign reflects the opposite of addiction. This dimension of a spirituality of wholeness reflects commitment or dedication. The final result of reordered thinking and perceptions, feelings and desires, behavior and actions builds from faith to courage to commitment. Thus, despite his "little faith," Peter had the courage to walk on water and to realize it was not his power but a higher power that enabled him to do so.

When he admitted this higher power as the source of his life, he could make a commitment—"Truly you are the Son of God" (14:33).

Whether it be *the story* with its covenants, the culture's story with its "individualism and commitment in American life,"[23] the church's story with its commitment to discipleship, or my story, all of history and all biography can be narrated in terms of addictions or commitments. As Margaret Farley notes: "At the heart of this history, however, lies a sometimes hidden narrative of promises, pledges, oaths, compacts, committed beliefs, and projected visions. At the heart of any individual's story, too, lies the tale of her or his commitments—wise or foolish, sustained or broken, fragmented or integrated into one whole."[24]

Faith results from rightly ordered thinking and relationships. Courage or hope expresses rightly ordered desires. Commitments reflect rightly ordered behavior, which is grounded in positive self-love, love of others, and love of God. Commitment means intimacy with self, others, and God. If addiction and codependency reflect disordered, self-centered love, commitment reveals properly ordered, other-oriented intimacy. If first order recovery involves education, and second order conversion revolves around therapeutic change, then commitment to intimacy reveals the heart of third order transformation. This transformation revolves around intimacy, which grounds it in that kind of love that fulfills the first and second great commandments.

A great difference exists between infatuation and intimacy—as much as addiction or codependency differ from commitment. This difference can be known by who or what gets center-stage attention: one's self or the other. When one considers others or things in terms of seeking pleasure or alleviating pain, it is more than likely those others or things will be centers for infatuation or codependency. But when the others are loved *as* the self, reciprocity results. Commitments can be sustained.

Seeking First God's Reign

The process of religious conversion involves the same dynamics as economic conversion (or any other kind of conversion). In Matthew, the process of conversion to the reign of God is outlined in parables. These parables tell stories about different kinds of conversions and different steps in the conversion process. Some parables tell stories about people *seeking*, others narrate *findings*, still others describe people *selling* this or that while others *buy*. In 13:45 Matthew's Jesus brings the four steps of conversion together in one little parable: "The kingdom of heaven is like a merchant in *search* of fine pearls, who, on *finding* one pearl of great value, went and *sold* all that he had and *bought* it" (emphasis added).

Matthew's Jesus uses the same terms to describe the process for religious conversion of disciples that advertisers implement in seeking economic conversion of consumers. Seeking, finding, selling, and buying the pearl of great price or the treasure in the field as images of God's reign (13:44–46) are at the heart of the gospel.

In 19:16–30 Matthew tells the story of the rich young man who sought to enter the reign of God but failed because of the addictive power of his wealth. He contrasts this lack of conversion with that of Peter who said, "Look, we have left everything and followed you" (19:27). The rich young man and Peter embody two different approaches to the conversion process of seeking, finding, selling, and buying. Peter sought Jesus;[25] so did the rich young man. Both found Jesus. Peter was willing to "sell," but the rich young man was not. He could not "buy" into the reign of God because he would not reorder his life on behalf of the poor by letting the reign of God's justice dwell in him (19:21–22; see 6:33).

Why, we might ask, could Peter enter into conversion and not the rich young man? Somehow the young man's great possessions had an addictive force over him. His possessions are the consumer items in our culture's story. They might also be the hierarchy's power in the church's story. Or they might even be our codependent obsession with trying to control both the culture's story and the church's story to conform to *the story* and our story.

Conversion implies a change of loyalty, a change from the reign of one god to another. It involves "selling" in order to "buy." But one will never sell unless what is bought is perceived as better. The rich young man could not make a commitment to Jesus because he did not experience Jesus as better than his possessions. Our culture will never change, nor will the institutional church, until one or the other or both come to experience a higher power than the possessions and power that are now craved addictively. The institutional leaders of the Catholic church—and all of us who minister in it codependently— will break with the addiction to the preservation of the male, celibate,

clerical model of the church to the degree we experience the risen
Lord, who is neither male nor female, come under that higher power,
and start ordering our lives and our ministry in the church in a way
that manifests that power. That will happen when the obsession with
power and control is converted to service and care. It will happen
when intimacy replaces addiction.

Our recovery process as codependents demands detachment in
order to enter and remain in the care of God as we understand God
to be revealed. How this detachment takes place will be the subject
of our next chapter.

CHAPTER TEN

Seeking Purity of Heart in Order to See God

(Mt 6:22–23)

The eleventh step in the Twelve-Step program for recovering addicts and codependents states that we seek "through prayer and meditation to improve our conscious contact with God as we understand God, praying only for the knowledge of God's will for us and the power to carry that out." Probably the main reason for the rich young man's inability to leave his possessions rested in the fact that his conscious contact was oriented toward them, not to Jesus. His contacts with Jesus had not been significant enough for him to reorder his priorities and become a disciple of Jesus. What had happened in the lives of Peter and Andrew, James and John had not happened in his life. Remaining addictively fixed to his possessions had more power over him than discipleship with Jesus.

Recovery from the addictive processes in our lives—whether expressed in addictions or codependency—necessitates staying in conscious contact with God as our higher power. The consequence of not remaining in that mindful attention to God is that the thinking, feeling, and behavior of the addictive process will again manifest themselves in our lives. Their power will supplant the authority of God in the risen Christ and their Spirit.

Only the realization and/or experience of a *greater* power can free a person from the power of addiction. When we apply this insight to our culture's story, we can see that only a power greater than the market's addictive hold on us can enable our conversion. The same conclusion can be drawn in the church's story about the addictive force of the institution's ways of thinking and acting. However, where *possessions* constitute society's addictive substance, *power* represents the addictive force in the institutional church. Only experiencing a higher power will enable those institutional leaders addicted to power to begin the process of their conversion. Only the experience of a higher power will free from addiction's enslavements and empower ministers and members of this church, especially if they are Culture One Catholics, who have been subservient and submissive to that power.

A brief survey of the greatest contemplatives in the church shows that they did not allow themselves to be seduced by the dishonesty, the fears, and the attachments of the leaders of the institutional church. Whether Teresa of Avila or Catherine of Siena, John of the Cross or Thomas Merton, contemplation, which brought them under the authority of a higher power, also enabled them to challenge abuses of authority of clerical power.

The first steps in the Twelve-Step conversion process show that the beginning of recovery occurs in one of two ways. According to the first way, addicts become increasingly disillusioned with the contemporary thinking, desires, and behavior exhibited in their lives; similarly codependents become increasingly disillusioned with their effort to control the thinking, desires, and behavior of the addicts around them. Admitting they are powerless over those addictions and/or relationships and that, consequently, their lives have become unmanageable, they "bottom out." This realization opens them to something or someone else to be "given over" to. Addicts stop "running after" the former object of their addictive processes, such as what they will eat, drink, or wear; the codependents stop "running after" the person(s) or organizations they have been trying to control. This enables them to seek another power in life, which, when found, provides new meaning for life.

The second way of recovery involves finding a power with more authority than the one that currently addicts or makes one codependent. The only way to achieve this is through an experience whose force is so great that the deficiencies of the former way of thinking, feeling, and acting are unmasked. This is usually called a spiritual awakening.

While both ways of recovery involve grace on the part of the recovering person, they also demand continually seeking to be touched by God in prayer as well as by seeking only to do God's will. Conversion involves being given a share in God's power to carry out God's will through actions that bear fruit in justice.

The experience of faith is the experience of finding God's reign within and around ourselves. This experience is contemplation. Living in a sense of consciously seeking contact with God's reign is contemplative thinking, desiring, and acting. Contemplation and a contemplative approach to God's reign represent the deepest experience of faith humans can have—the antithesis of obsessions and a compulsive approach to life.

All humans have faith in something or someone; this faith involves them in relationships and gives them enough trust to make a commitment to that "other." One's ultimate faith is that which constitutes the object of his or her concern. For many, this ultimate concern constitutes an addiction, which can only be altered if one begins to believe in something or someone more significant. Thus, Matthew's Jesus chided the members of his house-churches on their "little faith" in the care of their heavenly father and urged them to seek the experience of God's reign and order in their lives and relationships (6:26–32). Then their "little faith" would begin to grow and become their ultimate concern.

While contemplation is pure gift, for us, fidelity to the contemplative experience begins with seeking the reality of God's reign and God's order in our life. It is expressed in resting in that reign alone. Contemplation is facilitated when we examine where our treasure is to signify where our heart also may be. When our treasure reveals an addictive object, relationship, or process, detachment from that "treasure" becomes necessary in order to have a pure heart, an undivided self.

The following sections will examine the process of becoming pure of heart; that is, the process of seeking first God's reign in order to see God and enter into the care and justice that is at the heart of that reign. A Matthean context for the discipline that this examination entails is found in 6:22–23: "The eye is the lamp of the body. So, if your eye is healthy, your whole body will be full of light; but if your eye is unhealthy, your whole body will be full of darkness. If then the light in you is darkness, how great is the darkness!"

Since contemplation involves moving from darkness to light, from illusion and dishonesty to truth and faith, from worry and fear to freedom and courage, from affinities and attachments to detachment and commitment, we start moving toward contemplation by examining the eye as the lamp of the body. This is the first stage. When the eye's lamp reveals darkness or unsoundness, we must discover the exact nature of that unsoundness. Understanding the control this darkness can have over us, how the culture's story and the church's story of our generation can contribute to reinforcing the darkness, and how they can contribute to the addictive process, we can move to the second stage: detachment from our unsoundness by hearing the call of provident care. We enter the third stage when we respond to the call by seeking God's reign of justice and care in our thinking, desires, and actions. This third step involves two processes. In the first part—which is pure grace—we enter God's reign through contemplation. This experience of being contacted by God moves us to the second part, in which we strive to maintain conscious contact with God in all the processes of our life, especially in our promotion of justice as a sign of our participation in the reign of God and God's way of justice.

Addictive "Looks"

Richard Byrne describes various "looks" as unhealthy attachments which keep us from seeing God.[1] Byrne's "looks" represent Matthean impurity of heart, addictive dynamics, and treasures that serve as stumbling blocks rather than blessings on the journey up the mountain. While we will always have some obstacles to seeing God, to the degree our attachments move to addictive "looks," to that same degree our hearts will be impure, our inner light will be darkness. The issue is not that we have the "looks," for these attachments are part of the human condition; the concern is how they reveal the addictive process from which we must become detached.

The first "look" Byrne describes as an obstacle to experiencing our higher power is the "curious look." This does not represent normal curiosity, such as interest in how a machine works. Rather, it indicates a kind of addictive curiosity or anxiety regarding past and future situations or issues that keeps us from living in the present moment. Because it can be so forceful, a curious look inhibits our ability to experience the caring presence of God. It is best expressed by Matthew's Jesus in the parable about the seeds falling on various kinds of ground. The seed sown among thorns which "grew up and choked them" (13:7) represents addictive anxieties as well as worry associated with money: "As for what was sown among thorns, this is the one who hears the word, but the cares of the world, and the lure of wealth choke the word, and it yields nothing" (13:22).

The curious look is full of cares, anxious about many things. Certainly we have to think, we have feelings, and we have to do certain things, but the curious look represents an approach to all these that is obsessive. According to the philosopher Martin Heidegger, obsessive curiosity is one of the chief characteristics of the inauthentic self.[2] He points to three characteristics of the curious look: not tarrying, distraction, and never dwelling anywhere.

People with the curious look who never tarry are preoccupied with the past and the future. Advertisers play on this curious look. They continually invite us to the "new and improved," implying that something is wrong with what we have now. The institutional leaders also can manipulate this tendency in us by making us wonder if we've been forgiven for our past sins or by making us depend on the institution for our future. The only way to be freed from the fears and anxieties connected with these issues of salvation is to live in the present, in the care of God. If we codependently allow these institutionally determined threats of hell or promises of heaven to control our thoughts, emotions, and behavior, we fail to accept ourselves as beloved children in whom God is pleased and as sinners who experience forgiveness when it is requested.

The distraction dimension of the curious look is an occupational hazard in patriarchal and hierarchical systems. It can even come to the fore when there are collegial situations that call for leadership. One time I was at a Chapter of my Province. Before the elections of our leaders, I was walking with another Capuchin whose name had surfaced for one of the leadership positions. Because I thought he would be good for the office, he had my vote. However, as other brothers came walking toward us, I could *feel* him leaving me psychologically to be with them, anxious about whether they would vote for him or not. I said: "You really want to be elected, don't you?" "What do you mean?" he asked. "I can feel your distraction," I told him. "You are preoccupied wondering if you will be elected or not."

If this happens with a collegial group like ours, what must be said when the whole bureaucracy of the institutional church is identified with hierarchy and upward mobility? Career-building keeps people obsessed with the curious look, wondering who they need to know in order to get the position they covet. Once that position is ensured, the anxieties begin about the next position or the next person that must be won over.

The result of never tarrying and being distracted—if they are obsessive attitudes—is to be "outside of ourselves." I have discovered in my recovery that, when I live in my disease, I live from the shoulders up. I get cerebral and short of breath. When I am not so preoccupied, I can be in touch with my own child, with the reign of God within, and live more from my center-self. In the disease we are outside of ourselves; in recovery we are centered. Outside of ourselves there is no ground to our being. The word might come, but it finds no home. Filled with cares, we fail to experience care. Our cares and the cares of the culture's and church's stories choke out God's care. We remain at the surface level, unable to move beyond it in order to experience the reign of God.

Byrne's second "look," the lustful look, involves us at our body level and at the pleasure-pain level of a child. As such it keeps us at the surface so that the word is unable to find root. At this level we can get preoccupied with seeking pleasure or avoiding pain. These preoccupations keep us from purity of heart; since our sights are centered in self, we cannot see God. Matthew's Jesus warns: "For out of the heart come evil intentions—murder, adultery, fornication, theft, false witness, slander. These are what defile a person" (15:19–20).

The seeking of pleasure and avoidance of pain characteristic of the controlling force of the lustful look are reinforced by our generation as well. Advertisers play on our lustful look by promising us instant relief from our pains when we take a certain medication. They promise us instant success when we use certain kinds of mashed potatoes and frozen foods. Pain becomes negative, with no redeeming qualities. Rather than recognizing it as an invitation to growth, it becomes something to be denied or numbed. Or we seek the person or object, the organization or relationship, that will ease our pain. Then, having had immediate pleasure, we feel guilty. The pain begins again, and we seek relief again. The addictive process takes over.

Among the leaders in religion, the tendency to be controlled by the lustful look takes the form of an obsession with getting and maintaining power. Matthew's Jesus shows the mother of James and John—and James and John themselves—as the type of people and church leaders who can become preoccupied with a combination of the curious look and the lustful look (20:20–28). The lust was for power; the curiosity kept her wondering when the power would come.

When power is achieved, it can easily make itself felt over others in such a way that feeds into and sustains others' codependency. The lustful look feeds into and sustains the dependency many people have on outside forces, especially other people, for control. The leaders' obsession with control is futile unless it is paralleled by the ministers' and members' equal obsession about being controlled or trying to change that control.

Given the preoccupation of many celibates in the Curia not only with control but equally with issues of sex and generativity, perhaps the lustful look is more dominant than is admitted. When celibacy is not freely chosen, it creates the curious look. It makes of its victims sexual anorexics who spend an inordinate amount of time struggling with issues of intimacy and sexuality. When celibacy is imposed ("controlled"), or when it is not integrated with genuine care, it is quite likely to create addictive patterns. The huge number of priests who have left active ministry to get married indicates one of the things that can happen when people live at the level of the lustful look because of the imposition of celibacy. Even when celibacy *is* freely chosen, the tendency for sexual anorexia is never far from the surface because it goes against a person's sexual constitution to be non-genital.

The lustful look need not be limited to sex. Because it reflects the child-level of pleasure and pain, it can control our thinking, feeling, and behaving in such a way that our approach to life, relationships, and even God, is controlled by the seeking of pleasure and the avoidance of pain. If the emptiness that accompanies the search for God becomes too painful, I may quit trying to pray. Or I may approach prayer unconsciously trying to appropriate certain feelings that give me deep pleasure and a sense of God's presence.

I have discovered a signal that lets me know when I am more controlled by my lustful look than is normal when I experience pain and depression. This insight came to me many years ago when I met a sister in a beautiful print dress. When I noted how great she looked in the dress she said that she had bought it because she had been depressed. The awareness of Matthew's Jesus about the dynamics of the lustful look can be seen when he noted how concerns at the body level make us preoccupied with what we wear, drink, or eat. Clothes, food, and alcohol used often to alleviate pain and give temporary pleasure can evolve into the addictive process.

Even religion or God can become obsessions of the lusting eye. Both are sought after, not freely, but to meet some insatiable needs either for control or codependency. As one young women said to me: "I think I am codependent on God." When a person is into the disease of addiction or codependency, and the object of the disease is "God," this god is not the God who has been revealed in care and in healthy relationships, but a god who satisfies one's unhealthy needs. Often the lustful look frustrates our prayer because we enter prayer seeking a form of religious experience. This is not wrong as such—Ignatius said we should ask for various fruits of our prayer—but when we insist this is what *must* happen, our prayer is not contemplative but controlling.

Another "look," the ideal look, mistranslates the call to perfection (5:48; 19:21) into a demand for perfectionism. It is the occupational hazard of codependents because it serves as a continual reminder that we, as well as others, never measure up, are not "good enough," and can always be or do better. As such it becomes obsessive and even has been immortalized in the ditty many learned in their early formation days in religious orders: "Good, better, best; never let it rest/ Until the good is better and the better is best."

Advertisers also play on our ideal look. Certain expectations are communicated about what is right and what is wrong if you want to be seen as a success ("You've arrived"), as a caring person ("When you care enough to send the very best"), or as someone better than others ("Compare and Conclude"). Such appeals can be very influential to codependent people because they play to our identity and security needs. They reinforce a competitive approach. If I am or have the "best," it means that I am "better than."

Hierarchical systems feed on peoples' ideal look. When I entered the Capuchins I entered because I thought it was the way to perfection. Once I had entered, the leaders made it clear to me what path to perfection I should take, at least insofar as the vow of obedience was concerned. Our novice master told us over and over: "Ours is not to reason why; ours is but to do and die." If we met the ideal of dying to ourselves, somehow we would be on the way to perfection. As Anne Wilson Schaef notes, "This nonacceptance of ourselves and our humanness supports the illusion of perfectionism."[3]

When an addictive system promotes perfection as a possibility, the result is perfectionism, which reveals the futility of such a position at the same time the person displays an obsessive effort to make it happen. Schaef writes: "Something that is not defined by the system cannot (by definition) exist, and if something does not exist one does not have to deal with it. One can choose to deal only with those things that protect one's perfect, all-knowing image."[4]

For codependents like me, struggling with high ideals and their shadow-side in superachievement, perfectionism can be the chief obstacle in experiencing the higher power. This is so because my own or another's notion of perfection becomes our norm. And we never measure up. Consequently words like "should (not)," "ought (not)," and "must (not)" become part of our thinking, our approach to our feelings, and our critique of our behavior and that of others. The codependent dreams of being perfect, hoping that then the shame will somehow evaporate. Dominic Savino notes that perfectionism is one of the ways adults mask their shame: "The perfectionist fantasizes that it is not possible to blame or shame a perfect person."[5]

If codependency depends on outside forces for the meeting of our needs, it is no wonder people like me entered religious life, which promised salvation and a path to perfection outlined in our rules, constitutions, manuals of discipline, and superiors' orders. And while many of us have become free of that kind of codependency, we transfer our addictive behavior to our subtle interpretations of God. God, being perfect, expects the same from us. Somehow there is something very wrong with us when we don't measure up. Thus we "should" do this and "ought" not do that. "To be perfect, as defined by the institutional church, is to be like God the controller," Schaef notes in her book on codependency. She explains:

> If you are perfect, you not only have yourself under control, you also have everything and everyone else under control. Now this makes for an impossible dilemma. Since it is not possible for us to control absolutely our own lives— much less the lives of other people—striving to do so is a prescription for failure. Yet the institutional church expects its members (and its priests and ministers) to strive for perfection. If you should be able to and cannot, then you can only be a failure. Failure is depressing, and perfectionists are depressed.

> And not only does the church set up an impossible goal,
> it also makes itself indispensable by promising to help the
> individual achieve that unachievable perfection.[6]

Because the ideal look is based on perfectionism, it looks at others comparatively. There is no such thing as good enough. We must be better than, if not the best. Comparisons breed jealousies; jealousy is characteristic of the ideal look. We actually become jealous when someone does better because, somehow, this reveals that inadequate self about whom we are not pleased but ashamed. This leads easily to Byrne's fourth "look," the look of resentment.

The look of resentment is much more subtle and hidden in our culture, which has an ideal look that says, "You should not get angry." Yet the culture's ads play on the resentful look effectively. An advertisement for a top-shelf liquor says: "Living well is the best revenge." Another ad unites the resentful look with the ideal look: "If peer pressure has kept you from getting a Saab, get new peers."

While forgiveness is at the heart of the Christian life and recovery from the resentful look, leaders in the institutional church can play on our desire and need for forgiveness by regularly reminding us about the need we have to confess our sins (to its clerical representatives) and letting us know that they *alone* have the power to forgive. Bishops can excommunicate if we do not agree with the interpretations of teachings defined by the institution. At other levels deep resentments can result when church leaders abuse the confidence placed in them by people seeking their help. One of the resentments I had as a teenager was toward the priest I confided in while I struggled about whether I was "supposed" to go to the seminary. Whenever I saw this priest, I thought he looked at me as though he knew some dark secret about me that he just might tell. I felt embarrassed.

In the parable of the laborers in the vineyard, the workers who hired on early had resentment because the owner not only was just but was good. In this case the resentful look was connected with a sense that the early workers should have received more. Thus a comparison was made which involved the ideal look as well. When we think that we do not get enough of what we deserve, if we are living at the surface level of life, we easily become resentful, cynical, or angry. Whatever, these inner attitudes or "looks" are forms of violence that Matthew's Jesus connected to murder, the destruction of the self:

> You have heard that it was said to those of ancient times, "You shall not murder"; and "whoever murders shall be liable to judgment." But I say to you that if you are angry with a brother or sister, you will be liable to judgment; and if you insult a brother or sister, you will be liable to the council; and if you say, "You fool," you will be liable to the hell of fire (5:21–22).

When anger controls us, we remain at its level of control and cannot experience God's care. Control blocks care. Recovering addicts and codependents regularly make a moral inventory of our lives. We admit to God and others our wrongs and are willing to make amends to all we have harmed. We actually make amends when it will not harm. And we make this a regular practice in a way that evokes the further step Matthew's Jesus said must be taken when we know someone has something against us:

> So when you are offering your gift at the altar, if you remember that your brother or sister has something against you, leave your gift there before the altar and go; first be reconciled with your brother or sister, and then come and offer your gift. Come to terms quickly with your accuser while on your way to court with him, or your accuser may hand you over to the judge, and the judge to the guard, and you will be thrown into prison (5:23–25).

Anger can reflect positive or negative emotional expressions toward others. If it is grounded in care it is positive; if it is the reaction to control or the vehicle of control, it reflects the resentful look. At Twelve-Step meeting after meeting, people speak of their need to let go of their resentments and to "hand it over." They talk about "letting go" (of the resentments) and "letting God" (deal with the situation).

This notion of "letting go" and "handing it over" brings us to the second stage in contemplation: detachment. However, before moving to this second stage, I want to make it clear that we *all* have the above looks. The difference in whether they are addictive or not depends on the degree to which we are controlled by their dynamics or are detached from them.

Detachment

The addictive power of the looks is so great that the only way we can become detached from their force in our thinking, feeling, and acting is by "giving over" to a more powerful look. Controlled by these looks, we cannot see. Neither can we hear or feel. We remain in our disease; we stay unconverted. Somehow we must stop the looking and seek to see. In this sense, Matthew's Jesus said to the disciples:

> "For this people's heart has grown dull, and their ears are hard of hearing, and they have shut their eyes; so that they might not look with their eyes, and listen with their ears, and understand with their hearts and turn—and I would heal them." But blessed are your eyes, for they see, and your ears, for they hear (13:15–16).

The process of coming to purity of heart demands that we move beyond the addictive process and its surface obsessions, anxieties, and addictions and codependencies to be grounded in authentic cares. This process begins by looking in a new way at ourselves, others, and God. However, this can only happen when some kind of intervention takes place to begin reordering the previously addictive process. For most of us, the experience of care comes in one of three ways—from a divine intervention, from our own discipline, or from others.

In the first way the intervention may come from simple reflection, such as a recollection of Jesus as the providence of God's care as an alternative to anxiety over what will be eaten, drunk, or worn. Or the intervention might be a powerful experience of God. This kind of divine intervention happens but rarely.

The second way people can begin to become detached from the looks is by developing alternative ways of thinking, feeling, and acting that parallel the ways the addictive process began in the first place. Then the process of recovery is a process of reprogramming; that is, of replacing faulty and destructive information with information that can lead to wholeness and a meaningful, satisfying life. This kind of reprogramming might be called a way of developing "understanding with our hearts."[7] This demands a new way of thinking and feeling, of seeing and hearing, so that we might understand in a way that enables us to convert (13:15).

The process of understanding with the heart involves six stages. Making them work in our lives demands Matthean *understanding* rather than just listening, that is, putting into practice the teachings we have appropriated. The process includes 1) *hearing* in our heart what is seen; 2) *seeing* in our heart what one does; 3) *doing* from our heart what one says; 4) *saying* with our heart what one receives; 5) *receiving* in our heart what must be observed; and 6) *keeping* with our heart what has been understood. This way of understanding with the heart (13:15) reflects the Matthean sense of Jesus' question to the disciples: " 'Have you understood all this?' They answered, 'Yes.' And he said to them, 'Therefore every scribe who has been trained for the kingdom of heaven is like the master of a household who brings out of his treasure what is new and what is old' " (13:51–52). The steps of the model are well-presented in Luke's interpretation of the way Mary heard, saw, did, said, received, and "treasured all these things in her heart" (Lk 2:51). Through the exercise in understanding, one discovers that where the treasure is, there truly is the heart.

The third way we can become more detached from the addictive power of the looks comes by our associating with others, especially others who also are serious about their recovery and conversion. I often hear people doing Twelve-Step work say that the group, or various individuals in the group, are the ones who have shown the care they have needed to be faithful to their recovery program. The whole Twelve-Step meeting model approximates the sixfold reprogramming of the belief system with the help of others that constitutes an "understanding with the heart" approach to life. As the members come together, they *hear* with the heart what one sees—a group of addicts and/or codependents saying "Hi, my name's Michael and I'm a codependent." They *see* what they are doing—offering support for one another in their recovery. They *do* what they say—listening to each other's struggles to be faithful. They *say* what gets into their heart— acquiring insight by hearing other people's stories so they can better cope with their own struggles. They *receive* the stories—by getting encouragement to live one more day at a time, they can *keep* faithful to their recovery program.

Seeking God's Reign of Justice and Care

In the institutional church, being very aware of the addictive power of the "looks" that the institutional leaders can give, keeping us in their control, as well as the looks that are self-imposed, and working to be detached from the looks by becoming grounded in understanding and care, we can now move to the third step in becoming pure of heart in order to see God and live in God's reign: We can respond to our recovery or the call to conversion by seeking first God's reign of justice and care.

This stage involves two dimensions, which constitute steps eleven and twelve. In the eleventh step we seek through prayer and mediation to improve our conscious contact with God as we understand God, praying only for the knowledge of God's will for us and the power to carry it out. However the search for God's reign begins by *keeping* in regular contact with our child within, who continually invites us to be detached and poor in spirit in such a way that God's reign will be ours. Naturally to remain attuned to that reign demands prayer, meditation, and contemplation geared to improving our conscious contact with God.

I am continually impressed by the serious effort recovering addicts and codependents make to live from their true *selves*. Invariably at the meetings I attend at least one person mentions that he or she has just returned from a guided meditation weekend, or attended a consciousness-raising seminar, or sought channelling, or had something happen during prayer that morning. With many other recovering Capuchins I also can say that I often hear more about God and higher power at such meetings than I hear in many gatherings of religious. But, again, we are not talking about religious professionals; we are with spirituality seekers.

Trying to improve one's conscious contact with God automatically flows into our relationships with others. Here a contemplative, centered, child-based approach brings recovery into those situations that previously supported our disease. Here is where nonviolent, nonmanipulative, and noncontrolling dynamics begin to become evident. Grounded in the effort to be in conscious contact with God, we can have fruitful contacts with God's people. We can now work the twelfth step, using the previous steps to help us try "to carry these messages to addicts and codependents, and to practice these principles in all our affairs."

The best way I have discovered to do this is by paying attention to my *self*, my center, where my child and God's reign can be found. I know I am not relating to others in this way when I sense that I am operating in my head, leaving everything below abandoned. My body getting tight also reveals my need for centering. Just relaxing my arms often is enough to lead me back to a more centered stance.

The further away we get from our original experience of the reign of God within us—which helps us to remain centered in our heart and bowels—the more easily we can return to our heads, going back to former cerebral ways of thinking, feeling, and relating. Thus, maintaining conscious contact with God in contemplation and a contemplative approach to life and to others keeps the original experience fresh. Living from that center can make us more aware when we might "stop" thinking, feeling, and acting that will return us to our diseased way of being. Living in that reign of God will make us more concerned also to bring it and its justice into our world in a non-controlling way. This demand of Matthew's Jesus that we seek first God's reign and God's *way of justice* (6:33) is critical for disciples of Jesus in their recovery from addictions and/or codependency. Concern for others through the promotion of justice is a sign that one has begun to love neighbor as self (22:39).

In early 1990 *The New York Times Book Review* section featured a piece quite cynical and critical of the whole addiction/codependency movement and literature.[8] This followed by just three months another scathing indictment of Twelve-Step programs by Alison Humes in a now defunct New York-based weekly treating contemporary movements and issues. Both articles point to an alleged lack of concern for social justice manifest in recovery groups. Humes writes:

> At its worst, the codependency movement makes a sickness out of everyday life. It offers a bitter, militant ideology, in which life is a struggle between the lure of destructive dependencies and the clear brilliant light of autonomy. It also makes a sickness out of women's most endearing qualities. By labeling the traits of caretaking a disease, it leaves no room for a positive view of women's abilities to take care of others. By denigrating caretaking, the theory puts women down very covertly, undermining women's faith in their abilities to take care of their children, their aged parents. It makes loving people an addiction.
>
> At its most insidious, codependency is creating a class of sick people for codependency therapists to treat. It is capitalizing on Americans' desire to have a name for what ails them and books to cure them of it. It does not recognize the

political, social, or economic realities that people live with. It does not recognize that some dependencies are good, or that some are unavoidable, or that some are politically imposed. The problem with the popularization of codependency is that it makes the political entirely personal.[9]

When the political becomes purely personal, personal recovery is *all* that is needed to make the system better. Meanwhile the addictiveness in the system—which has nurtured, if not created, the individual addiction—goes on unchecked. In her critique, Wendy Kaminer also pointed to the lack of political concern:

Codependency authors are not nearly so materialistic or oblivious to social injustice as Dr. Peale, who believes most problems are caused by bad attitudes; nor do they claim recovery will be easy. But they owe him much—the reliance on simple, universal techniques to facilitate individual change and the belief that we need never be victims of circumstances, that the wounds of childhood need not be fatal. Codependency experts share with Dr. Peale the conviction that each of us carries within the power to heal ourselves, that happiness, health and wisdom are acts of will, grounded in faith.[10]

Both Humes and Kaminer seem to be saying that because there is no overt discussion of the political and economic circumstances that contribute to the addictive process in individuals, and because Twelve-Step meetings don't urge people to address these circumstances as they deal with their own issues, the narcissism of a Twelve-Step program leaves the weightier things—like justice and mercy toward others—undone.

Their argument has some merit. To those not working on their own wounded past, listening to others share their struggle to be liberated can seem quite egocentric. Maybe the programs they visited were the way they described; maybe they did represent a kind of orgy of people getting pleasure from sharing their pain. Quite possibly they didn't take time to discover where these people worked and with whom they worked. If they did, they would find citizens sharing their concerns as well as many people quite concerned about helping others abused by families and systems, volunteering their talents for good causes, and promoting justice in their own unique ways.

One cannot seek God's reign and come under the authority of a higher power and not seek the reign of God's justice—on earth as it is in heaven. One cannot authentically live in that reign of God and God's justice without working to challenge addictions in persons as well as in institutions and infrastructures that undermine the revelation of that reign. Perhaps it might be just the opposite case that represents the motivation of many participants in Twelve-Step meetings: the healers helping others come to be helped to heal their own wounds and to keep recovering from them so that they might be better ministers to others.

Remaining in God's Care

The sixth Beatitude promises: "Blessed are the pure in heart, for they will see God" (5:8). This chapter has suggested a way to develop purity of heart that finds us considering the power of the "looks" on our addictions and codependency, detaching ourselves from those looks by becoming grounded in God's care, and by responding to God's care by seeking first God's reign and God's caring way of justice. Seeking these things as part of our recovery and ongoing conversion, we should attain some degree of purity in our heart; our treasure will have begun to be reordered toward God and God's reign.

However, the fact that we have climbed a mountain, that we have clean hands and pure hearts, does not necessarily mean that we will see the face of the living God (Ps 24:3–6). Seeing God, or contemplation, is a gift of grace; it cannot be achieved by our own efforts. Seeing God is totally dependent on our experience of being heard by God, seen by God, created by God, spoken by God, received by God, and kept by God. In this experience one experiences self as free from any control by God. On the contrary, there is only the experience of God's unconditional positive care.

Unconditional positive care, despite the images conjured by therapists and the dreams bandied about at Twelve-Step meetings, is virtually impossible; humans are never totally free from some self-interest. However, grace represents unconditional positive care. It is this care which constitutes the way we understand in our hearts that God sees us. Care becomes the basis of our contemplative experience. Experiencing this care grounds us in our effort to be free of the cares induced by the addictive process. Expressing this care in our compassion toward ever-widening circles of people, including the least of our brothers and sisters (25:31–46), becomes a sign of the authenticity of any contemplative experience we might have.

One sign, one fruit, manifesting that we are growing in care appears as we move into ways of thinking and feeling that God's care for us is unconditional. The more we recover in love, the less conditional and the more caring our own love for others will become. Conditional love is controlling love. Where there are conditions, there is control; where there is control, there is no genuine care.

We might wonder if we are truly contemplating when we make our regular attempt to be in conscious contact with our God. Rather than wondering if we are climbing the mountain correctly, we need to ask what is happening when we leave the mountain and relate to others. Here we will find whether the previous experience has been authentic. It is authentic if we are becoming free of attachments and/or addictions connected with the looks and are serving the needs of others. Gerald May writes:

> True freedom from attachment is characterized by great unbounded love, endless creative energy, and deep pervasive joy. Nor need I worry about freedom from addiction taking suffering or caring out of life, for compassion takes the place of attachment. Where there was the agony of clinging to and grasping one's own attachments, freedom brings a feeling of unity with the pain of the world.[11]

By his stress on grace, May clarifies what people in Twelve-Step programs have been saying for years. Only a higher power can deliver us from our addictions. If the addictive process is the undermining of our thinking, the seduction of our desires, and the sign of the mammon-forms to which we are given over, then the process of wholeness involves thoughts grounded in faith, the consecration of our desires, and the evidence of a whole new way of being. That way of being—grounded in the experience of God's gracious and unconditional care—is evident in the way we express that gracious care in our dealings with others, especially those who depend on our compassion.

The Third Step makes clear that, in order to be free of the power of addiction, we need to commit ourselves to come under the care of God "as we understand God." In my mind, for us codependent Catholics and for the institutional leaders of Catholicism, this is the critical step into recovery (i.e., "conversion").

Behind institutional Catholicism's self-understanding stands the system of patriarchal clericalism with its monarchical God who reinforces addictive discrimination rather than a trinitarian God who announces liberation. This trinitarian God—as I now understand God—reveals a community based on equity among persons and the fullest possible sharing in the blessedness of God's compassionate justice. The result of this non-discrimination in the Godhead is that all these blessed persons have equity in resources available in the community.

In the trinitarian reign of God all persons are equally blessed insofar as all share equally in everything possessed by the other. If we are to seek on earth the reflection of the heavenly reign of God—which is God's justice (see 6:33)—we need a new criteria by which we judge whether our lives and wills are turned over to the care of that God. This criteria is the reign of God's trinitarian care expressed in justice. If the Catholic church is to more fully reveal the reign of God, it will further be able to do so to the degree it turns over its present patriarchal clericalism and becomes transformed into that trinitarian justice which reveals the care of God.

CHAPTER ELEVEN

Prophetic Proclamation
vs.
Clerical Consciousness

Because they challenged the prevailing interpretation of reality, the prophets offered a different way of ordering the community's life. Because Matthew's Jesus lived in a religious environment in which he understood God's reign as an alternative to the addictive patterns around him, he prophetically challenged the prevailing ways of thinking, feeling, and acting. Because Matthew's Jesus said the leaders had eyes to see, ears to hear, and hearts to understand—but would not—he promised that his disciples, who followed the prophets and lived in a different way, would be blessed. Finally, because the demand for justice involves judging all realities in light of the trinitarian reign of God, Matthew's Jesus promises that, if such a way of justice is promoted, those advancing the cause of justice can expect persecution— but this very persecution stands as a sign that the reign of God *is* theirs (5:10–12).

A simplified analysis of the social structures around us is necessary if we are to read the signs of our times and then bring the gospel to bear upon our contemporary reality. I see all reality composed of four levels: the individual; the interpersonal; the infrastructural, which contains institutions, "isms," and ideology; and the environmental. The infrastructure is "culturally addictive." And denial at the level of the individual addict becomes institutional ideology at the infrastructural level.

Denial insures survival for the addictive process. Facing survival in the midst of dissolution and carnage, the survivors of Hiroshima and Nagasaki rapidly developed a unique coping mechanism. In studying

217

their patterns of thinking, feeling, and behaving, Robert Jay Lifton discovered evidence of what he called "psychic numbing."[1] In other words, because basic survival was at stake, the living victims soon developed ways of not seeing the carnage around them, not hearing the cries of the dying, lest they allow their hearts to become involved in helping them.

Psychic numbing not only refers to these "identified victims"; it also characterizes the perpetrators of the violence. It identifies those who call saturation bombing "protective reactionary strikes." It insulates those who push the buttons from the wholesale carnage. In all cases psychic numbing is the coping mechanism invoked to keep eyes from seeing and ears from hearing so that the present situation can continue.

Psychic numbing is to survival what clerical ideology has become to the male, celibate, clerical way of thinking, feeling, and acting in institutional Catholicism. Whether related to the culture's story or the church's story, *the story* in the first gospel clearly speaks of this "hardness of heart."

> The reason I speak to them in parables is that in "seeing they do not perceive, and hearing they do not listen, nor do they understand." With them indeed is fulfilled the prophecy of Isaiah that says:
> "You will indeed listen but never understand, and you will indeed look but never perceive. For this people's heart has grown dull, and their ears are hard of hearing, and they have shut their eyes so that they might not look with their eyes, and listen with their ears, and understand with their heart, and turn—and I would heal them."
> But blessed are your eyes, for they see, and your ears, for they hear. Truly I tell you, many prophets and righteous people longed to see what you see, but did not see it, and to hear what you hear, but did not hear it (13:13–17).

Matthew's Jesus makes it quite clear that the prophets and just ones saw and heard, thought and felt, in contrast with the leaders who would not open their eyes and ears lest they understand and turn to a power higher than themselves for healing. Fidelity as disciples with prophetic perception and a vision of justice demands that we examine scripture in forming our response to contemporary clerical consciousness, which serves as the ideological justification for the continuation of clerical patriarchy.

Walter Brueggemann's book dealing with the First Testament's insights on this subject is a contemporary classic: *The Prophetic Imagination.*[2] In the face of the psychic numbing and hardness of heart among today's hierarchical leaders in Catholicism, his insights are provocative. I will develop them at length in this section, aware of one significant difference: Brueggemann limits his application of prophetic thinking, feeling, and ministry in response to the dominant culture's story in a way that might not be recognized as applicable to the church's story as such. The latter is challenged only insofar as it feeds into and from the addictive patterns in the wider culture. In this case religion gets co-opted by society's mammon-addiction with the result that the gospel's message and authentic church teaching loses its hold on church members. Noting this eroding influence on faith, Brueggemann writes:

> The contemporary American church is so largely enculturated to the American ethos of consumerism that it has little power to believe or to act. This enculturation is in some way true across the spectrum of church life, both liberal and conservative. It may not be a new situation, but it is one that seems especially urgent and pressing at the present time. That enculturation is true not only of the institution of the church but also of us as persons. Our consciousness has been claimed by false fields of perception and idolatrous systems for language and rhetoric.[3]

At the time of Solomon around 962 B.C.E. a radical shift took place in the foundations of Israel's life and faith. Solomon was able to counter completely the counter-culture of Moses in three ways: 1) he challenged Moses' economics of equality with the economics of affluence; 2) he challenged Moses' politics of justice with the politics of oppression; and 3) he challenged Moses' religion of God's freedom with a religion wherein God could be managed.[4] The dominant culture of that Solomonic period tells a story of incredible well-being and affluence, which had been realized, in part, by a way of thinking and acting that survived on power for some and oppression for others. Both the affluence and the oppression were reinforced by "the establishment of a controlled, static religion in which God and his temple have become part of the royal landscape, in which the sovereignty of God is fully subordinated to the purpose of the king."[5]

As a resistant response to this royal consciousness, the prophets exercised their ministry. Their ministry nurtured, nourished, and evoked a consciousness and perception opposed to the consciousness and perception of the dominant culture in two ways: it *criticized* the dominant consciousness, and it *energized* persons and communities toward an alternative way of thinking and living. In response to the destructive consequences of the royal consciousness, the prophets' ministry challenged the psychic numbing that the royal power achieved in its members and among its people. As such, it functioned as a critique of the existing order, which, like all addictive processes, was headed toward death.[6] In response to the feeling of powerlessness in face of the addictive behavior around it, the prophets' ministry also offered an alternative way of thinking and acting, offering new options to the old order: "The royal consciousness leads people to despair about the power to new life. It is the task of prophetic imagination and ministry to bring people to engage the promise of newness that is at work in our history with God."[7]

Building on Brueggemann's model, the next section concentrates on organizational Catholicism today and suggests a way contemporary prophecy can challenge its institutional clericalism.

Challenging Addictive Catholicism

If it is true that institutional Catholicism is addictive, its leaders will move to recovery only by "bottoming-out" or by intervention. However, I am not aware of any "bottoming-out" within the *universal* expression of institutional Catholicism. With church leaders buoyed by increasing numbers of seminarians and ordinations worldwide,[8] the papacy and Curia, taking a longer, global view, can ride out the losses in some parts of the family in Western Europe and North America, believing the future of the church is in the Third World, especially in Africa, which seems more subservient to Roman power and more ready to reinforce that power with its own patriarchal and hierarchical forms.

The leaders of the socialistic institutions in the U.S.S.R. and Eastern Europe began moving from their addiction to power because they realized that economic realities—like starvation—had made them powerless; they could no longer manage their political economies or their people. In 1989, as millions of East Germans poured through the Berlin Wall, Soviet President Mikhail S. Gorbachev told an emergency congress of East Germany's Communist Party: "We Soviet Communists know from our own experience that life cannot be put into the chains of dogmas. Lack of faith in the people and in the creative energy of the masses leads to a fall in confidence in the party and thus to the erosion of its role of a political vanguard."[9]

What the Soviets and Eastern-bloc nations learned of governing paralleled what corporate executives have learned about industry. If you do not change, you will die; the threat of death (loss of market share) represents a kind of "bottoming-out" that results in conversion. Whether it's an IBM undergoing "the most radical cultural change in IBM's history,"[10] or an automotive company like Milwaukee-based A.O. Smith, which reorganized itself collegially after years of management-labor warfare, the fear of "bottoming-out" constitutes the incentive for recovery from addictive and self-destructive forms of behavior. As one management/labor consultant said of such conversions on the part of both management and labor: "You need a cultural change that can't be legislated by contract or law; the people have to want to make the transformation, and it must evolve from their own experience."[11]

Catholicism's institutional leaders reject the notion that the church is "bottoming out." Controlled by their sexist dogmas, they refuse to read the signs of the times as they are presented by the death of the church in many parts of Western Europe and the increasing disillusionment of its intellectuals and activists elsewhere, looking instead to the Third World. Among many ministers and conscientious laity who remain in the church from the First World—who are aware of what is happening but are too paralyzed to act—increasing codependency is the only response.

We need an alternative to our codependent fixation on changing what will not change. I envision one possibility grounded in the twofold approach of the prophets and their disciples: a continual, loving critique of the dominant clerical consciousness, and the creation and energizing of communities based on alternative ways of thinking, feeling, and being church.

The communities must be free of the addictive need to control. They must be aware of the enslaving power of the addictions and the empowerment that comes from the higher authority. Ongoing

conversion and recovery can then become a way of life. This alternative way will manifest a process of wholeness in contrast to
a process of addiction, a prophetic praxis to clerical consciousness.
These communities, based on Twelve-Step programs addressing clerical addiction and clerical codependency will have two main functions:
first, they will be communities of resistance to clerical consciousness and clerical control; and second, they will be support systems
that mirror alternative ways of "being church" that more closely reflect the collegial community of disciples experienced in the primitive
church.

First of all, these prophetic communities will resist the dominant
consciousness that reinforces patriarchal clericalism. In rejecting the
opinion of the United States Supreme Court that allowed the termi-
nation of life in unborn infants, the Administrative Committee of the
National Conference of Catholic Bishops concluded: "We reject this
decision of the Court because, as John XXIII says, 'if any government
does not acknowledge the rights of man or violates them . . . its orders
completely lack juridical force.'"[12] Building on this notion, I wrote
in 1977: "Such a stance of resistance must be applicable to *whatever*
situation is sustained by the denial of access to the resources needed
for life and the right to live as an image of God."[13]

At the time I wrote the above, I envisioned abuses in the Catholic
church that denied people the right to the eucharist and other basic
rights. The primary right of people to the sacraments, particularly the
eucharist and reconciliation, takes precedence over the secondary right
of whether male or female, married or unmarried priests will preside
over the church's celebration of these sacraments. When the latter
happens, one's conscience takes priority over "orders [that] completely
lack juridical force." The argument can no longer be sculpted about
the right of women or men to the priesthood, but the right of God's
people to the bread of life and the forgiveness of sins.

What the Congregation for the Doctrine of the Faith declared in
the mid–1970s about the denial of the primary right to life (re: abortion) can be applied equally to the primary right of male and female to
participate fully in church resources: "It must in any case be clearly understood that a Christian can never conform to a law which is in itself
immoral. . . . On the contrary it is the task of law to pursue a reform
of society and of conditions of life in all milieu."[14] Nonconformity
to immoral laws, especially when the lawgivers or law-interpreters

have defined them as moral, demands an understanding and commitment to the higher law of justice and a willingness to accept the risks
of obeying the reign of God over that of humans. The Congregation
continues:

> Following one's conscience in obedience to the law of God
> is not always the easy way. One must not fail to recognize
> the weight of the sacrifices and the burdens which it can
> impose. Heroism is sometimes called for in order to remain
> faithful to the requirements of the divine law. Therefore, we
> must emphasize that the path of true progress of the human
> person passes through this constant fidelity to a conscience
> maintained in justice and truth.[15]

In the face of *any* order that denies people their right to image
God and to have access to needed resources, conscience demands
resistance.

Developing Communities of Resistance

Resistance is the addict's way to cease further involvement in
the addictive process. Resistance is the addict's way of stopping his
or her obsessive "running after" what will be eaten, drunk, or worn,
or whatever else the object of addiction might be. Resistance is the
addict's way of beginning the process of recovery from death into life.

The recovery process begins with "stopping," moves to "seeking," and then starts a new approach to living alternative ways of
thinking, feeling, and acting. Ideally, in creating alternative communities of resistance, these same processes should be guided by a kind
of heart-based "law of understanding," which supplants the heartless
nonunderstanding of the former addictive process. Besides trying to
stop their own codependent behaviors, members of these communities will develop noncontrolling ways aimed at stopping the addictive
behavior of the institutional church. Trying to stop the obsessive thinking, anxiety, and addictive behaviors around the preservation of the
male, celibate, clerical model of the church will be guided by two nonviolent forces that will continually challenge, in noncontrolling ways,
the addictive organization: just anger and religious disobedience.

Several years ago I gave a retreat to a large group of religious
from various congregations in New York. After it was over, a sister
working in the area of justice and peace for her congregation said to

me, "Mike, that was a very good retreat and I benefitted greatly from it. However, I'm going to pray for you for one thing."

"What's that?" I asked.

"I'm going to pray that you will be able to love the Curia."

"Oh, I love the Curia," I responded immediately. And as she gave me the look of one who knows better, I left for my room. Once there I realized I was in denial. I was trying to control the Curia. And one of the themes I had stressed on that retreat was that correction without care is control!

I was obsessed with trying to correct, to challenge, to confront, to convert the Curia. And the Curia is obsessed with doing the same to me and others like me. This sister's minor intervention that day forced me to admit that neither of us really cared about each other; we were obsessed with controlling each other. The Curia's controlling hooked into my codependency; my codependency fed into the Curia's addictive way of insuring the clericalization of the church. Both of our ways of thinking and behaving contributed to the continuation of dysfunctionality in the church.

The sister picked up the anger in me that results from trying to correct without care. Since that day in New York, I have made it part of my recovery to try to express an anger that does not feed into or from the addictive process but one that is justified and free from the need to control what will happen.

How can we tell whether our anger is justified or not? For me, the answer revolves around the issue of control. There is nothing wrong with being very clear to others about our convictions, but when these others do not act on our insights, the question returns to us: What do we do? Do we become obsessive about the situation, or do we turn it over to our higher power, to that God-revealed-in-Jesus Christ, who has all authority over his church?

God is a God of freedom, not obsessed with control, yet the scriptures reveal God as getting angry. Justifiable anger, then, can reveal our participation in trinitarian revelation. Jesus could get angry—especially at the hardheartedness of the religious leaders and the failure of the religious institutions to convert. According to William Sloane Coffin, Jr., "Jesus was angry over 50% of the time, and it's very dangerous theology to try to improve on Jesus. The anger needs to be focused, but anger is what maintains your sanity. Anger keeps you from tolerating the intolerable."[16] The model of Jesus' anger serves well clerical critics and recovering codependents in the church.

Anger is neutral; my choice makes it negative or positive. Its negative dimensions are connected to the addictive process; its positive force is part of the process of perfection or wholeness. Far from being an overt expression of hostility, of contempt, of the need to control, healthy anger—as exemplified in the way Matthew's Jesus criticized the institutions and leaders around him—shows a readiness to defend one's vital interests. I have not discovered many examples of Jesus' getting angry except in response to the unwillingness of his institution and its leaders to enter into recovery (11:21; 18:7; 23:13–29). It would seem from his example that anger directed toward clerical consciousness and control is a sign of fidelity to *the story*. This kind of anger should be honored as our God-given capacity to ensure that God's reign of justice will be realized despite institutional obstacles.

Anger is elicited when we think or feel that some basic need is being violated. We seek to name the need being denied and to recognize the barriers that keep that need from being met. Once a barrier is named, we can examine what must be done to get rid of it or to be free of its power. According to this explanation, anger becomes a trigger-mechanism that mobilizes us to confront the obstacles that get in the way of our needs and those of others. It can become a graced emotion, inviting us to challenge injustice and indifference. For instance, when the eucharist and reconciliation are denied to people, and when women and marriage are rejected by the leaders of the institutional church for priestly ministry, unnecessary barriers are established in the church's familial system. The underlying barrier needs to be named for what it is: an addiction to the preservation of male, celibate clericalism. Anger is the appropriate response to this abusive manifestation of authority, which denies people their need to the sacraments; *not* to be angry makes us silent reinforcements at the barrier. Expressing anger in the name of care is grace; repressing anger in the name of control creates and sustains obsessions and perpetuates codependency in the face of addiction.

Fran Ferder shows that, among the personalities that generate the most levels of anger in us are antisocial types of people. Many times these people are the very ones who control social organizations. Once called sociopathic personalities, these leaders can exude charm, be evasive (or lying), appear impervious to guilt regarding their position, and exert control under the guise of care. According to Ferder:

> Antisocial personalities have a strong need to control people and maintain power. They are the types who will issue statements that stress characteristics such as obedience, orthodoxy, and faithfulness.... Another critical trait is a high tolerance for pain. They can stand tension and interpersonal pressure. It just does not get under their skin. Most of the time they can outlast us. Finally, it is critical to be aware of what occurs when these people feel betrayed. Their primary tactic is retaliation. They will get back at you sooner or later. They might sit down and, eyeball to eyeball, nose to nose, lip to lip, earlobe to earlobe, tell you how grateful they are that you confronted them. Six months later you will be searching through the Help Wanted section of the newspaper.[17]

But, as always, the addiction of the leaders is only one side of the coin; we also need to be aware of our own codependency—and our anger. If we are sensitive to the working of the Spirit in our lives—the One who produces the fruit of peace—we need not look to others to point out our anger. We should be able to tell quite easily to what degree negative anger in the form of our obsession with controlling the addictive processes in the church still dominates us and to what degree caring anger motivates us to turn our life and will (and our church) over to the care of God. The difference revolves around the obsessive need to control as opposed to turning the church over to the Lord rather than its lords.

As indicated earlier, another sign indicating whether our anger is positive can be found in the way it evolves. The more that pattern of Jesus' anger becomes our own, the more our anger over the addictiveness of the institutional church and its leaders' unwillingness to enter recovery will move from rage to grief. Moving in that direction is an indication that we are moving from a codependent addictive process of anger to a freed and holistic process of spirituality of grieving; it may show whether we are still hooked by clerical consciousness and control or healed by prophetic proclamation and practice. The latter echoes what Brueggemann notes as a key element in developing a prophetic stance in the church and society:

Prophetic ministry seeks to penetrate the numbness to face the body of death in which we are caught. Clearly, the numbness sometimes evokes from us rage and anger, but the numbness is more likely to be penetrated by grief and lament. Death, and that is our state, does not require indignation as much as it requires anguish and the sharing in the pain. The public sharing of pain is one way to let the reality sink in and let the death go.[18]

Only when we resist the addictive process of clericalism, moving from rage and anger to lament and grief, can we hope to recover ourselves. In the process we will also be able to begin to forgive those who have created so much pain for so many in the family. This forgiveness will be based on that kind of understanding that makes us aware of the disease that touches *all* of us in the family. We merely have been its victims in different ways.

The second way communities of resistance can show their fidelity to the process of recovery from the institutional church's addictive processes is by nonparticipation in forms of thinking, feeling, and acting that perpetuate the addictive and codependent cycles in the church. This takes two forms: loving criticism and religious obedience to the higher power. Conscientious critics will be called disloyal; those who are more faithful to the Lord than their "lords" will be called disobedient.

Loving criticism of institutional addiction is called disloyalty by those controlled by a clerical consciousness. The prophets' critique of the oppressive ways of the kings generated name-calling around the issue of loyalty. The same can be expected today. Pushing the shame button called loyalty—to the church, the pope, the magisterium, the bishops, the teachings of the church, the guardians of the faith, etc., etc.—immobilizes the codependent. This shame button is the last defense of hypocrisy. A claim to authority and power that justifies the denial of fundamental equality in the church based on spurious arguments and faulty premises belies the truth and ensures the title of hypocrite by Matthew's Jesus. The response to such misrepresentation and distortion is either codependent subservience to this authority and power or prophetic proclamation of the truth to those same authorities and powers.

According to Hans Morgenthau, there are four ways people respond to abusive forms of power in society. These can be applied to the situation of power in the institutional church and the ways ministers and others in the church choose to react to that power. The first response finds us retreating into our ivory towers with an intellectual, noninvolved attitude. We just go our way, unconcerned about the pain around us. This makes us irrelevant in the system, merely codependent survivors. The second response finds us offering expert advice in such a way that we become servants of the system's self-interests. One of the clearest manifestations of this approach occurs when experts are used to help church leaders uncover the psychological authority problems they believe must underlie criticism of positions taken by the papacy, the Curia, and the hierarchy. The third response reflects an absorption into the institutional machinery, taking on its ways of thinking and behaving. We actually believe and repeat statements such as "the church is not a democracy," unmindful that, in its primitive setting, it *was* a form of democracy wherein all members *chose* their hierarchical leaders. People of the third option don't realize that if the church isn't a democracy, it does not canonize autocracy either. This absorption-approach makes us agents of the system. The fourth response is to challenge the system by what Morgenthau calls "prophetic confrontation" in the way we "preach truth to power." Such was the way of Jesus before the powers of his day; his justice and truth before their injustice and hypocrisy. According to Morgenthau, when the fourth option is followed, the prophet "must be 'the enemy of the people' who tells the world things it either does not want to hear or cannot understand."[19] In the case of the church, the prophet tells the leaders and the people things they do not want to hear or cannot understand, even though they have ears to hear and hearts to understand. Matthew's Jesus expects such a prophetic stance within the system from his disciples.

Discipleship and Dissent

Speaking truth to power implies submission to truth represented in a higher power and nonsubmission to non-truth as represented in statements from other powers. However, when this truth to power is preached and acted out in noncooperation, this prophetic approach to clerical consciousness is fraught with risks. On the one hand there is the risk of becoming deluded—when one becomes one's own magisterium, one's own highest authority, impervious to other positions. To be free of such delusions demands ongoing peer-criticism and good spiritual direction. Another risk involves personal rejection from other well-meaning people. To be rejected and to suffer persecution from those one loves on earth because of taking a stand on truth and justice is never easy, even if the long-term rewards might be great in heaven.

Not questioning the teachings of popes and bishops represents conformity; challenges fall under the general rubric of dissent. In a special way dissent refers to papal teaching that is criticized by believers. While there may be many others, in my own quite extensive ministry I can count on both hands the clerics in the church who intellectually assent to and actively work to encourage others to support the papal teachings in the church today dealing with both sexual morality and social justice. Some agree with the papal positions on sexual morality but pay little or no heed—if not outright reject—the issues of justice found in papal critiques of capitalism, militarism, and lack of concern for the poor and neglected. Others in the church liberally quote from papal social encyclicals and episcopal statements on race, armaments, and economics but overlook—if not reject totally—church positions on sexual reproduction, homosexual activity, divorce and remarriage, and the place of women in the church.

Despite an impressive number of papal statements oriented to the former kinds of social issues, it seems issues related to sex and the role of laypeople, and especially women, are the real obsessions of the present pope. The signatories of "The Cologne Declaration" commented on the contrast between the norms contained in *Humanae Vitae* and "the responsibility of the faithful to their own conscience" and concluded, "A pope who refers so often to the responsibility of Christian women and men in secular activities should not systematically disregard it in this critical area. Moreover, we regret the intense fixation of the papal teaching office on this single problem area."[20]

From the viewpoint of clerically controlled consciousness and codependent submission to its manifestations, dissent such as that displayed in "The Cologne Declaration" is diametrically opposed to the current curial translation of the church's story. Those criticizing such dissent find support in Pope John Paul II: "It is sometimes claimed that dissent from the magisterium is totally compatible with being a 'good Catholic' and poses no obstacle to the reception of the sacraments. This is a grave error that challenges the teaching office of the bishops of the United States and elsewhere."[21] To codependents in the church who fit one of the first three kinds of response to power noted above, the statement goes unchallenged. The first kind of respondent accepts the statement at face value. The "servants of the system" justify the statement with a kind of "diplomatic theology," which tries to show that the pope *really meant* the opposite of what he said. The third kind of respondents to this misinterpretation of the meaning of the magisterium—the agents of the system—uncritically accept it along with its implication that those dissenting are in grave danger of losing salvation by their actions. The fourth response, which preaches truth to power, examines not just the words of the statement but what thinking, feeling, and behavior lie behind the statement.

The papal statement above was addressed to the United States bishops. It stated as its concern challenges to "the teaching office of the bishops of the United States." At the same time, the Vatican, under Cardinal Ratzinger, was intent on undermining the power and influence of national bodies of bishops. Juxtaposing the papal statement with curial actions creates some form of cognitive dissonance to those aware of clerical politics. Challenges to the teaching authority of national hierarchies—when these *differ* from papal or curial positions—are actually supported in Rome. Thus one must go further in the statement to find the real concern. The real issue is not challenges to the teaching office of the bishops of the United States but challenges to the teaching office elsewhere, namely, Rome. When there exists a real attempt to identify and isolate the magisterium of the church with the papacy and not admit to its extension among the bishops—much less to the faithful as it took place until the last century—a grave error does indeed exist, as well as an abuse of power.

The official reference to the "ordinary magisterium" of the church did not come from the church of Matthew 18, but from that which I have called the church of Matthew 16. In an 1863 reaction to the independent tendencies of various intellectual Catholics whose views differed from his own, Pius IX published *Tuas libenter*, in which he proffered the notion of ordinary magisterium as church teaching. During and after Vatican I, the idea entered mainstream thinking and came to be limited to *solemn* conciliar and papal definitions. A broader interpretation of ordinary magisterium developed under Pius XII, who stated in *Humani generis* that Catholics must give their assent not only to solemn papal definitions made *ex cathedra* but also to encyclical letters where doctrine is "taught with the ordinary teaching authority [magisterium]."[22] Pope John Paul II gives the impression that the notion goes beyond encyclicals to the whole corpus of his thought and statements. However, his thoughts and statements as pope might be better balanced with those he articulated shortly before becoming pope.

In 1979 Karol Cardinal Wojtyla wrote that those who voice their opposition to the general or particular rules or regulations of the community do not thereby reject their membership. Rather, their actions reflect a certain attitude of solidarity that is needed to maintain an effective healthy community. He insisted that, in order for such opposition to be truly constructive,

> the structure, and beyond it the system of communities of a given society, must be such as to allow opposition that emerges from the soil of solidarity not only to express itself within the framework of the given community but also to *operate* for its benefit. The structure of a human community is correct only if it admits not just the presence of a justified opposition but also the practical effectiveness of opposition required by the common good and the right of participation.[23]

Within families, deviation from the control of the addict is considered disruptive and disloyal. In such ways the minds of family members can become controlled to reinforce the addictive thinking and acting of the active addict, who has control in the family. Such addicts are in their addiction to the point that they block alternative input; they honestly believe dissent manifests infidelity, disrupts the family, and counters unofficially sanctioned codependency. However, a brief examination of church history reveals that some of its greatest saints actively resisted male clerical control in very creative ways.

Rudolph Bell has suggested that extreme fasting, similar to what we call anorexia today, was used by Catherine of Siena and Clare of Assisi—among many others—as their only way of escaping male clerical control and establishing some degree of personal autonomy.[24] The way the prophetic church of Matthew 18 challenged the absolutizing tendencies of the church of Matthew 16 makes it clear that, unless the questionable teachings of the latter are not accepted as normative the people today will be victimized in the same way as they were during the period when it was said: "Where there is no prophecy, the people cast off restraint" (Prv 29:18; see Amos 8:11).

The prophetic dimension is absolutely necessary if the teaching authority of the church—one, holy, catholic, and apostolic—is to be enlivened, ensured, and kept credible.

While the prophetic challenges of Catherine of Siena to papal practices are well-known, I want to recall here the issues and attitudes surrounding the conflict between the papacy and Clare of Assisi. I prefer this approach because Clare, with Francis of Assisi, constitutes the heart of my own tradition. She is the one I invoke for support when I begin to regress into my disease and think I might be disloyal for challenging papal interpretations and demands for certain practices.

Clare of Assisi (1194–1253) founded a community of women called the Poor Ladies, known today as the Poor Clares or Clares. She believed she had been inspired by God to write her Rule for the sisters. Following Francis's example, she declared in her Testament unswerving loyalty and fidelity to the Holy See. She wrote: "On bended knees and with all possible respect, I commend all my sisters, both those present and those to come to our holy Mother the Church of Rome, to the supreme Pontiff, and especially to the Lord Cardinal who has been appointed [Protector] for the Order of Friars Minor and for us."[25]

Clare penned these words in utter sincerity. In her mind, the fact that the majority of her years found her violently dissenting from papal efforts to impose a way of life on her and her sisters did not contradict in the least her respect for papal authority properly expressed and executed. When it was not expressed or executed in such a way she not only challenged it, she refused to comply with its decisions and actively supported her sisters in their refusal to obey as well.

In 1217 the Cardinal Protector of the Poor Ladies, Cardinal Hugolino of Ostia, gave the Rule of Saint Benedict to the community to be followed. Later he became Pope Gregory IX. We know from outside sources that Clare had serious differences with him as cardinal and pope when it came to issues of governance of the community. A detailed examination of the various manifestations of her dissent, which included different kinds of noncooperation, a hunger strike, and even a refusal to obey papal authority, shows that she justified her dissent by her desire to obey her higher power, Christ. Speaking of her conflicts with Hugolino, later Gregory IX, Sigismund Verheij writes:

She was not going to be led off her course even by his supreme authority. When a papal decree made it practically impossible for the Friars Minor to preach the word of God to the sisters, she was so distraught that she dismissed the friars-almoners. She refused to accept food for the body when the pope deprived her of the dispensers of spiritual food. Her sharp reaction led the pope to change his decree. Early on, she had "fearlessly withstood him and refused to yield an inch" and accept his well-meant offer of material support. When he pressed further and offered to dispense her from her vow, her answer was clear and unequivocal: "Holy Father, in no way will I ever be freed from following Christ."[26]

Clare's conflicts with the papacy were not limited to Gregory IX. In 1247 Pope Innocent IV wrote a second Rule for the Poor Ladies. It modified the former rule of Hugolino. Since neither Rule supported the practice of intense poverty that she considered to be the heart of her way of life as revealed to her by God, she rejected the new Rule and began writing her own. Despite papal protests she continued following her Rule. She refused to conform to papal attempts to impose its vision of religious life on her until the very end of her life, insisting that she must follow her conscience and the Rule, which she understood to be from God. This action, remember, took place even though in the same Rule she had promised "obedience and reverence to the Lord Pope Innocent and to his canonically elected successors, and to the Roman Church."[27] Unrelenting in her convictions, she was prepared to stand before God. Two days before her death the pope relented. She received final papal approval for her Rule.

At that time in the church, such forms of dissent, disobedience, and debate were not considered forms of disloyalty. Rather they manifested fidelity to the spirit working in one's life, despite institutional differences. In fact, some of the above expressions of her dissent with the papacy and her unyielding resistance in the face of papal efforts to control her Order were cited as concrete evidence of Clare's sanctity in the Bull of Alexander IV that officially approved her canonization.[28]

Given this tradition, what responses are open to the Capuchin Franciscans in reaction to Rome's effort to impose on the Order (with appropriate emotional assent and behavior) a clerical status? We could follow one of the first three options outlined by Morgenthau and remain codependently under the control of this interpretation by 1) uncritically accepting the decision as God's will; or 2) attempting to convince ourselves that it is because of our own clericalism that we have been defined as such; or 3) becoming "agents" by making sure that clericalism continues to define the Order. Or we could choose the fourth option—preaching truth to power in the mode of Clare of Assisi. Our leaders could act on their previously quoted statement that an inclusion of the clerical statement in the Constitutions is against their conscience and refuse to obey, as the Rule suggests. In this they also could appeal to the Testament of Francis, in which he noted that his Rule—which assumed equality among all members in the community and leadership open to all members—was inspired not by human authority but the highest power in heaven and on earth: "No one showed me what I should do, but the Most High Himself revealed to me that I should live according to the form of the Holy Gospel. And I had this written down simply and in a few words and the Lord Pope confirmed it for me."[29]

Recovery: The Role of the Twelve Steps

Recovery from the addictive processes noted by Matthew's Jesus begins when we stop running after what we will eat, drink, or wear, or addiction's other objects, relations, and processes. This is followed by seeking an alternative way of life. This alternative way of living can be realized in communities of conscientization and conversion, whose members function in a way that reinforces the process of wholeness and perfection. Such communities include ongoing efforts to reinforce their members' decision to stop their own codependent behavior in the church family and to work nonviolently and in a noncontrolling way to influence the "identified patient" and to stop his power addiction as well. Secondly, in these groups Recovering Catholics will find support in their seeking role. Whereas the "stopping" relates to their own codependent thinking, feeling, and acting and involves resisting the institution's addictions, or criticizing its dominant clerical consciousness, or making denunciations, the "seeking" will involve supporting a holistic way of being church, energizing themselves and others to alternative ways of thinking, feeling, and acting as church, and the annunciation, by their ongoing conversion and recovery, that the reign of God is at hand (4:17).

In the early 1980s I noted the value of Twelve-Step programs to aid our recovery from addictions in our culture. In the late 1980s I called for a "recovery program" that would do the same in our churches:

Within Matthew's social world the house-churches provided an alternative way of life. Today there is an equal
need, within the institutional churches of the First World,
to create alternative communities, contemporary "house-
churches," so that like-minded disciples can experience hos-
pitality in places of meaning, mutuality, and empowerment.
Some of the deepest forms of religious experience and the
most profound alleviation from the suffering caused by various addictions can be found in the regular meeting. Regularly coming together to share in the struggle to be free of
addictions, to stop running after society's enticements and
clerical power struggles, and to share in a faith-struggle and
vision in offering an alternative—that will be at the heart
of future discipleship in the First World.[30]

At such meetings for Recovering Catholics the specific agenda
should not be limited to the participants' efforts to be free from memories and hurts created from past abuse or present addictions and/or
codependency in the church. Since the majority of these participants
will be from the First World, especially North American countries of
the First World, they also will need to share their struggle to be free
of the addictive processes that have become the way of life in our
culture's story. In a social world that has become secular with the god
of mammon as its lord and in a church-world that has become driven
by the god of power, the members of these new Twelve-Step groups
will share their efforts to be free of all these gods. They will be supported in their search to keep turning their lives and wills over to the
trinitarian God and God's reign of caring justice. Above all, they will
be helped to keep conscious contact with God through contemplation
and meditation and to witness to that turning of their lives over to God
through their faith, their courage, and their commitment to love God
with their whole hearts, their whole souls, and their whole minds, and
their neighbors as themselves.

Fidelity to the Twelve-Step model will keep the members of these
communities from the fate of the primitive house-churches—the institution of hierarchical forms that assumed the dominating role (and the
destruction of the group). Remaining part of the institutional church,
but not part of its addictive processes, they will follow the ninth tradition about never becoming organized and the eighth tradition about
remaining forever nonprofessional.[31] Wherever they will be, from
Newfoundland to San Diego and from Dublin to Rome, they will

"keep coming back" to be with other Recovering Catholics. There, in addition to the mutual support they will give and receive in the telling and hearing of their own stories, they will continually find support and challenge by recalling *the story*. In a special way they will try to remember the stories that Matthew's Jesus said must be remembered. They will recall "what she did"—the woman who anointed Jesus—by being in solidarity with other victims and, from her story, share their effort to bring good news to the poor and other addicts and codependents around them. They will celebrate *the story* by developing ways to help one another experience forgiveness of their sins and struggle to unbind each other from their painful memories and addictive processes. Above all, these Recovering Catholics will celebrate in his memory the breaking of the bread and the sharing of the cup—even if they may have to do so without an ordained cleric.

At the meetings they will find new significance for being collegial and courageous in their recovery as they share the Lord's Prayer as well as in the prayer that has come to symbolize hope for millions of other recovering addicts and codependents: "Lord grant me the serenity to accept the things I cannot change, the courage to change the things I can, and the wisdom to know the difference." Finally at these meetings they will be encouraged continually by the words of Matthew's Jesus, which I have translated and which have served as the foundation of this book (6:33–34):

> Seek first God's reign and God's way of justice
> and all these things will be given you as well.
> Therefore do not be anxious about tomorrow;
> for tomorrow will bring worries of its own.
> Today's trouble is enough for today.

ENDNOTES

CHAPTER ONE   Introduction

1. I have used the New Revised Standard Version of the scriptures for my text. (New York/Oxford: Oxford, 1989). Quotations from Matthew will not have the traditional "Mt" in front of the chapter and verse citation.

2. In writing this book I have tried to be mindful of two audiences. The first is the hierarchy and theologians; informed Catholics are the second. I have chosen to write this book for informed Catholics in a way that I hope will not be offensive to scholars. For a more technical discussion of the intent of Matthew's gospel and the way it evolved see my *House of Disciples: Church, Economics, and Justice in Matthew* (Maryknoll, New York: Orbis Books, 1988). It has an extensive table of contents and index. Thus specific technical questions related to exegesis of Matthew might be found therein.

3. Ibid., p. 16.

4. Bruce J. Malina, *The New Testament World: Insights from Cultural Anthropology* (Atlanta: John Knox, 1981), p. 25.

5. Richard Sennet, *Authority* (New York: Alfred A. Knopf, 1980), p. 47.

6. Ibid., p. 48.

7. Malina, p. 27.

8. John Bradshaw, *Healing the Shame that Binds You* (Deerfield Beach, Florida: Health Communications, 1988), p. 8.

9. Pope Paul VI, *Ecclesiam Suam*, nos. 58–115, passim, in *The Pope Speaks* 10 (1965), pp. 275–291.

CHAPTER TWO   The Dynamics of Addiction and Discovering Them in Matthew

1. Sigmund Freud, *Civilization and Its Discontents*, trans. James Strachey (New York: W. W. Norton, 1961), p. 91.

2. Michael H. Crosby, O.F.M.Cap., *Spirituality of the Beatitudes: Matthew's Challenge to First World Christians* (Maryknoll, New York: Orbis Books, 1991), pp. 64–73.

3. For various definitions proposed by WHO for addiction, see *Bulletin of the World Health Organization* 59 (1981), pp. 225–242; WHO Technical

Report Series, no. 273 (1964); M. Gossop and M. Grant, eds., *Preventing and Controlling Drug Abuse* (Geneva: World Health Organization, 1990), p. 20.

4. Dr. Robert Lefever, *How to Identify Addictive Behavior* (London: Promis, 1988), p. ix.

5. Anne Wilson Schaef, *When Society Becomes an Addict* (San Francisco: Harper and Row, 1987), p. 18.

6. Gerald G. May, M.D., *Addiction and Grace* (San Francisco: Harper and Row, 1988), p. 78.

7. Ibid., p. 11.

8. Stanton Peele, with Archie Brodsky, *Love and Addiction* (New York: New American Library, 1975), inside front page.

9. Stanton Peele, *Diseasing of America: Addiction Treatment Out of Control* (Lexington, Massachusetts, and Toronto: Lexington Books, 1989). Peele's book scores the "addiction treatment industry" and strongly argues against considering any addiction as a disease.

10. For a critique of how codependency may have a limited foundation in empirical data, see Tadeusz Gierymski and Terence Williams, "Codependency," *Journal of Psychoactive Drugs* 18 (1986), pp. 7–13.

11. Melody Beattie, *Codependent No More: How to Stop Controlling Others and Start Caring for Yourself* (New York: Harper/Hazelden, 1987), p. 31.

12. Timmen L. Cermak, M.D., "Children of Alcoholics and the Case for a New Diagnostic Category of Codependency," *Alcohol Health and Research World* 8 (1984), pp. 38–42. See also his "Diagnostic Criteria for Codependency," *Journal of Psychoactive Drugs* 18 (1986), pp. 15–20.

13. Pia Mellody, with Andrea Wells Miller and J. Keith Miller, *Facing Codependence* (San Francisco: Harper & Row, 1989), p. 4.

14. Robert Subby, M.A., and John Friel, Ph D., *Co-dependency and Family Rules: A Paradoxical Dependency* (Deerfield Beach, Florida: Health Communications, 1988), p. 3.

15. George A. Mann, M.D., *The Dynamics of Addiction* (Minneapolis: The Johnson Institute, 1983), p. 6.

16. May, p. 78.

17. Ibid., p. 83.

18. By "genetic" I do not necessarily follow the theory that says some people are genetically prone to addiction. While that has some merit, "genetic" here refers to what happens in the addictive cycle.

19. William White, interviewed by John Du Cane, "Sick Systems in Treatment: The Impact on Staff and Clients," *C.D. Professional* (October/November/December, 1989), p. 6. See also William L. White, *Incest in the Organizational Family: The Ecology of Burnout in Closed Systems* (Bloomington, Illinois: Lighthouse Training Institute, 1988).

20. Ibid.

21. "Conclusions and Recommendations," *The Report of the Archdiocesan Commission of Enquiry into the Sexual Abuse of Children by Members of the Clergy* (St. John's, Newfoundland: Archdiocese of St. John's, 1990), p. 2 and passim.

22. Schaef, p. 13.

23. Ibid., p. 37.

24. Anne Wilson Schaef and Diane Fassel, *The Addictive Organization* (San Francisco: Harper and Row, 1988), p. 54.

25. John P. Hewitt, *Self and Society: A Symbolic Interactionist Social Psychology*, 3rd ed. (Boston: Allyn and Bacon, 1984), p. 5.

26. Ibid., p. 49.

27. Edwin H. Friedman, *Generation to Generation: Family Process in Church and Synagogue* (New York and London: Guilford, 1987), p. 13.

28. My definition is grounded in that of Anne Wilson Schaef, *Co-Dependence: Misunderstood-Mistreated* (San Francisco: Harper and Row, 1986), p. 21. Again, I am aware that institutions and infrastructures do not think or feel; neither do they behave as such. Only individuals and groups exhibit these functions. However, since symbolic interactionism shows the social dynamic of interaction, I believe individual demeanor can be projected analogously beyond individuals, to interpersonal groups, to institutions, and infrastructures. This projection of personal dynamics to groups is evident in notions of the "corporate culture" or "corporate personality" found in Matthew when he writes about all Jerusalem being "troubled" (2:3), or when Jesus "began to upbraid the cities where most of his mighty works had been done, because they did not repent" (11:20), and grieved over Jerusalem for rejecting him and his message (23:37).

29. It has been suggested that Matthew has structured the dynamics around God and mammon chiastically in 6:25–34. For background on the meaning and significance of "chiasmus," see Nils Wilhelm Lund, *Chiasms in the New Testament: A Study in Formgeschichte* (Chapel Hill: University of North Carolina, 1942).

30. Malina, p. 99.

31. For the economic background of Matthew's community, see Crosby, *House of Disciples*, pp. 40–43.

32. Chapter 10 will further elaborate on 6:22–23.

33. Karl Ludwig Schmidt, *"Basileia,"* in *Theological Dictionary of the New Testament* I, ed. Gerhard Kittel, (Grand Rapids: Wm. B. Eerdmans, 1981), p. 579.

34. My reflections on mammon have been helped by those of Friedrich Hauck, *"Mamonas,"* in Kittel IV, 1983, pp. 388–90.

35. Ibid., pp. 389–90.

36. Karl Heinrich Rengstorf, *"Doulos, etc.,"* in Kittel II, 1982, pp. 267–71.

37. May, p. 14.

38. Sebastian Moore, *Let This Mind Be in You: The Quest for Identity Through Oedipus to Christ* (New York: Harper and Row, 1986), p. 5.

39. I have used the terms "First" and "Second" Testaments of the main scriptural sources for the Jewish and Christian scriptures. In the past these were called the "Old" and "New" Testaments. Then some called them the "Jewish" and "Christian" scriptures. However, for Catholics, not all Jewish scriptures are in their "Old" Testament. The Greek-speaking Jews gave rise to the Deuterocanonical books. Thus, along with a growing number of people writing about both testaments, I prefer the use of the terms "First" and "Second."

40. James W. Fowler, "Faith and the Structure of Meaning," *Faith Development and Fowler*, ed. Craig Dykstra and Sharon Parks (Birmingham: Religious Education Press, 1986), p. 18.

41. Wilhelm Michaelis, *"Proton,"* in Kittel and Friedrich, VI, III, 1982, p. 870.

42. For the connection between good deeds, bearing fruit, a rich harvest, God's will, and justice, see Crosby, *House of Disciples*, p. 57 and passim.

43. Friedrich Hauck, *"Thesauros, Thesaurizo,"* in Kittel, III, 1982, p. 137.

CHAPTER THREE *The Story*: Does the First Gospel Address the Addiction to Authority?

1. Barrington Moore, Jr., *Injustice: The Social Bases of Obedience and Revolt* (White Plains: M. E. Sharpe, 1978), p. 9.

2. Moore, p. 14.

3. Since the leaders represent for Matthew a united front against Jesus, they, despite the exceptions, are treated as a body either because of their critical mass or because of the secretiveness or silence of those who differed from the main leadership body. The same basis will be used when I discuss the addiction to authority among the contemporary body of leaders in Catholicism.

4. Thomas W. Manson, *The Sayings of Jesus as Recorded in the Gospels According to Saint Matthew and Saint Luke* (London: SCM, 1964), pp. 164–66.

5. Moore, p. 19.

6. Jack Dean Kingsbury notes that while "the Matthean picture of these several groups does not always square with what is known of them historically, the rhetorical effect of the way they are presented is to make of them a monolithic front opposed to Jesus. See Jack Dean Kingsbury, *Matthew as Story* (Philadelphia: Fortress Press, 1986), p. 17.

7. For more background on Jesus as a charismatic figure, see Martin Hengel, *The Charismatic Leader and His Followers*, trans. James Greig (New York: Crossroad, 1981).

8. For more on this see Crosby, *House of Disciples*, pp. 198–203.

9. Kingsbury, p. 85.

10. An extended interpretation of chapter 23 will be found in Chapter 7.

11. Bruce J. Malina and Jerome H. Neyrey, *Calling Jesus Names: The Social Value of Labels in Matthew* (Sonoma, California: Polebridge, 1988), p. ix. Jack Dean Kingsbury has stated: "The element of conflict is central to the plot of Matthew. As the royal Son of God in whom God's end-time Rule is a present, albeit hidden, reality, Jesus is the supreme agent of God who 'thinks the things of God' (3:17; 12:28; 16:23). The conflicts in which he becomes embroiled are with Satan (4:1–11), demons (12:28), the forces of nature and of illness (cf. 4:23–24; 8:9; 11:5; 12:9–14, 15, 22; 14:14, 15–21, 22–23; 15:21–28, 29–31, 32–38; 17:14–21; 19:2; 20:29–34; 21:14–16, 18–22), civil authorities (such as Herod and Pilate [cf. 2a; 27; also 14:1–12]), gentiles

(including Roman soldiers [cf. 8:28–34; 27:27–31, 32–37]), and Israel (cf. 11:16–19, 20–24, 25; 13:10–13), above all its leaders" (Kingsbury, p. 3).

12. John Pilch, "The Health Care System in Matthew: A Social Analysis," *Biblical Theology Bulletin* 16 (1986), pp. 102–06.

13. I follow the theory that between the infancy narrative (1:1–2:23) and the passion-death-resurrection narrative (26:3–28:20), Matthew sculpted his story around five books, each with a narrative and discourse.

14. My statistics came from "Catholics 'True' Despite Beliefs," Religious News Service, *The Arizona Republic*, November 30, 1985. See also Andrew Greeley, *The Catholic Myth* (New York: Scribner, 1990).

CHAPTER FOUR The Culture's Story: Examining Mammon Addiction in the United States

1. Ad for Gaviidae Common, *Minneapolis Star Tribune*, August 18, 1989.

2. Jim Henderson, "Ethics Hits New Low in America," fourth in a series, "The Mean Decade, 1980–1989," *Dallas Times Herald*, December 27, 1989.

3. "The Casino Society," *Business Week*, September 16, 1985.

4. Russell Baker, "Slaves to Oil," *The New York Times*, August 22, 1990.

5. William J. Eaton, "Company Accused of Exploiting 'Just Say No' Campaign," *Los Angeles Times*, August 13, 1988.

6. Elizabeth Greene, "Shifts in Students' Attitudes Seen As Threat to Liberal Arts," *Chronicle of Higher Education*, November 5, 1986.

7. Norman Lear, "The Culture of Capitalism," *Media & Values*, (Summer 1989), p. 3.

8. Alan Riding, "Church Stifled by Good Life's Roar," *The New York Times*, August 4, 1989.

9. Lewis H. Lapham, *Money and Class in America: Notes and Observations on Our Civil Religion* (New York: Weidenfeld & Nicolson, 1987), p. 131. Interestingly, reviews of Lapham's book one week apart, in *Fortune* and *Business Week*, did not fault his analysis. See Stephen Birmingham, "What's Wrong with the Rich," *Fortune* (February 29, 1988), pp. 121–22; and Daniel Moskowitz, "Would America Be Happier If It Loved Money Less?" *Business Week* (February 22, 1988).

10. Felix G. Rohatyn, Speech to the Urban League of Greater New York, December 2, 1986, quoted in *The Wall Street Journal*, December 5, 1986.

11. Harry Schwartz, "System, Not Ethics, Is Congress' Problem," *USA Today* (December 27, 1989).

12. Karen Pennar, "Commentary: The Free Market Has Triumphed, But What About the Losers?" *Business Week* (September 25, 1989).

13. Carolyn Hymowitz and Timothy D. Shellhardt, "The Glass Ceiling; A Special Report on the Corporate Woman," *The Wall Street Journal*, March 24, 1986.

14. Center on Budget and Policy Priorities press release, p. 6.

15. Anne Wilson Schaef, *When Society Becomes an Addict* (San Francisco: Harper and Row, 1987), pp. 5, 7.

16. Richard Barnet, "The Tyranny of the Bomb," *Desert Voice* 6 (1989), p. 1.

17. Anne Wilson Schaef and Diane Fassel, *The Addictive Organization* (San Francisco: Harper and Row, 1988), p. 136.

18. Ibid.

19. The Bishops' Committee on Priestly Life and Ministry, "Reflections on the Morale of Priests," Washington, D.C., 1988, pp. 5–6.

20. Larry Wright, cartoon in *The Detroit News*, March 12, 1989.

21. National Conference of Catholic Bishops, *Pastoral Letter on Catholic Social Teachings and the U. S. Economy*, first draft, no. 63, in *Origins* 13 (1984), p. 348.

22. Pope John Paul II, "Peace with All Creation," no. 13, December 8, 1989, in *Origins* 19 (1989), p. 467.

CHAPTER FIVE The Church's Story 1: Examining Addiction in the Institutional Church

1. Hippolytus, *The Apostolic Tradition of Hippolytus*, trans. and ed. Burton Scott Easton (Hamden, Connecticut: Archon Books, 1962), p. 33.

2. Cyprian of Carthage, *Letter* 67:3–4, in *Saint Cyprian Letters* (1–81), trans. Sister Rose Bernard Donna, C.S.J. (Washington, D.C.: Catholic University of America, 1964), pp. 233–35.

3. John C. Dwyer, *Church History: Twenty Centuries of Catholic Christianity* (New York and Mahwah, New Jersey: Paulist Press, 1985), pp. 157, 158.

4. John Gilchrist, ed. and trans., *The Collection in Seventy-four Titles: A Canon Law Manual of the Gregorian Reform* (Toronto: Pontifical Institute of

Medieval Studies, 1980), esp. pp. 72–85. Title I of the "Seventy-four Titles" was termed: "On the Primacy of the Roman Church." It featured various texts taken from popes and councils which not only appealed to the Matthean text as the rationale for papal claims (Capitula 2, p. 72), but went so far as to declare that "the Roman Church is the foundation and form of all churches" and that "all churches receive their origins from this church" (Capitula 7, p. 77).

5. Alexander Murray, *Reason and Society in the Middle Ages* (Oxford: Clarendon, 1986), p. 60.

6. Gratian's *Decrees, Distinctio*, no. 63, *Decretum Gratiani* (Venetiis: Apud Iuntas, 1595), p. 299.

7. P. Delhaye, "History of Celibacy," *New Catholic Encyclopedia*, III (New York: McGraw-Hill, 1967), p. 371.

8. Robert L. Benson, *Bishop-elect: A Study in Medieval Ecclesiastical Office* (Princeton: Princeton University Press, 1968), p. 379.

9. Ibid., p. 138.

10. *Codex Iuris Canonici*, Canon 329, 2 and 3 (Romae: Typis Polyglottis Vaticanis, 1917), pp. 86–87.

11. R. I. Moore, *The Formation of a Persecuting Society: Power and Deviance in Western Europe, 950–1250* (Oxford and New York: Basil Blackwell, 1987), p. 5.

12. Ibid., p. 71.

13. Ibid., p. 152.

14. Ibid., p. 116.

15. Pope John Paul II, Address to the National Conference of Catholic Bishops, II, no. 6, September 16, 1987, in *Origins* 17 (1987), p. 261.

16. Pope John Paul II, Address to Brazilian Bishops, quoted in Catholic News Service Release, *Prairie Messenger*, Muenster, Saskatchewan, February 26, 1990.

17. Gregory Baum, *Theology and Society* (Mahwah, New Jersey: Paulist Press, 1987), p. 240.

18. Guenter Lewy, *The Catholic Church and Nazi Germany* (New York and Toronto: McGraw-Hill, 1964), p. 326.

19. Sidney Hook, "Integral Humanism," *Reason, Social Myths and Democracy* (New York: Humanities Press, 1950, p. 91.

20. F. X. Kaufmann, "The Church as a Religious Organization," in Gregory Baum and Andrew Greeley, eds., *The Church as Institution* (New York: Herder and Herder, 1974), p. 77.

21. John Coleman has noted eight "distinct organizational problems of the church to which theology often remains blind." See his *"Raison d'èglise*: Organizational Imperatives of the Church in the Political Order," in Jeffrey K. Hadden and Anson Shupe, eds., *Secularization and Fundamentalism Reconsidered*, Religion and the Political Order III (New York: Paragon House, 1989), p. 253.

22. Ibid., p. 255.

23. *In Solidarity and Service: Reflections on the Problem of Clericalism in the Church* (Washington, D.C.: Conference of Major Superiors of Men, 1983), p. 2.

24. Leonardo Boff, *Church: Charism and Power: Liberation Theology and the Institutional Church*, trans. John W. Diercksmeier (New York: Crossroad, 1985), p. 72.

25. I am indebted to my Capuchin confrere, John Celichowski, for making this connection for me. The application is my own.

26. Edwin H. Friedman, *Generation to Generation: Family Process in Church and Synagogue* (New York and London: Guilford, 1987), p. 197.

27. David C. McClelland, William N. Davis, Rudolph Kalin, Eric Wanner, *The Drinking Man* (New York: Free Press, 1972).

28. Andrew A. Sorenson, *Alcoholic Priests: A Sociological Study* (New York: Crossroad/Seabury, 1976), p. 137. I am indebted to Sorenson for the insights from Adler, Sullivan, and McClelland.

29. Frederick W. Faber, *Devotion to the Pope* (Baltimore: John Murphy, 1860), p. 23.

30. Pope Pius X, *Il Fermo Proposito*, in *Acta Pontificia* III (1905), p. 81.

31. Ana Maria Bidegain, *From Catholic Action to Liberation Theology: The Historical Process of the Laity in Latin America in the Twentieth Century*, Working Paper 48 (Notre Dame, Indiana: Kellogg Institute, 1985), p. 6.

32. Bertram F. Griffin, J.C.D., "Response to Address of the Most Reverend James W. Malone, Bishop of Youngstown, to the Canon Law Society Convention, Baltimore, October 12, 1988," unpublished text, p. 2. I am thankful to Father Griffin for sharing this speech with me.

33. Ibid., p. 3.

34. For an application of some of these role models to people in ministry in the Catholic church, see Sean Sammon, "Understanding the Children of Alcoholic Parents," *Human Development* 8 (1987), p. 33–34.

35. Adolph Guggenbühl-Craig, *Power in the Helping Professions*, trans. Myron Gubitz (Dallas: Spring Publications, 1986), p. 18.

36. Judith A. Rinek, "Co-Dependency as a Subversive Element in Teamwork," *The Journal for the Catholic Campus Ministry Association* 1 (1988), pp. 15, 46–47.

CHAPTER SIX   The Church's Story 2: Power, Roles, and Religion in the Institutional Church

1. David Lonsdale, "Authority: The Sources of Abuse," *The Way* 29 (1989), p. 330. This entire issue is devoted to authority and leadership and contains a wide range of excellently crafted articles.

2. Edwin H. Friedman, *Generation to Generation: Family Process in Church and Synagogue* (New York and London: Guilford, 1987), p. 195. See also Peggy Friedl-Yee, *Church as Family: Family Systems Theory as Applied to the Church* (Berkeley: Franciscan School of Theology, 1989).

3. Friedman, p. 221.

4. Ibid., p. 202.

5. Ibid., p. 27.

6. C. Margaret Hall, *The Bowen Family Theory and Its Uses* (New York: Jason Arankson, 1983), p. 177.

7. Anne Wilson Schaef and Diane Fassel, *The Addictive Organization* (San Francisco: Harper and Row, 1987), p. 167.

8. Ibid.

9. Second Vatican Council, "Perfectae Caritatis," no. 2, in Austin Flannery, O.P., ed., *Vatican Council II: The Conciliar and Post Conciliar Documents* (Collegeville, Minnesota: Liturgical Press, 1975), p. 612.

10. Jacques Belanger, O.F.M.Cap., "An Order of Brothers," in *Proceedings from the Joint Meeting of the Five Families Dealing with the Clerical Status Given to Our Fraternity* (Ames, Iowa: Acme Printing, 1989), p. 6.

11. Schaef and Fassel, p. 61.

12. Sharon Wegscheider-Cruse, *Choice-Making for Co-dependents, Adult*

Children and Spirituality Seekers (Pompano Beach, Florida: Health Communications, 1985), p. 16.

13. Rembert Weakland, quoted in Marie Rohde, "Weakland Expects Truce With Vatican," *The Milwaukee Journal*, December 7, 1990, p. B2.

14. Bishop Kenneth Untener, quoted in Knight-Ridder news reports. See Alissa Rubin, "Bishops Revise Views on Sex," *The [Akron] Beacon Journal*, November 15, 1990.

15. Joseph Cardinal Ratzinger, quoted in Walbert Bühlmann, *Dreaming About the Church: Acts of the Apostles of the 20th Century*, trans. Peter Heinegg (Kansas City: Sheed and Ward, 1987), p. 153. The same use of the Generalate of the Dominicans to monitor (and subsequently silence) Matthew Fox was at work in his imposed sabbatical year, which "officially" came from the Dominicans but was orchestrated by the Roman Curia.

16. Pope Pius X, *Motu proprio: Fin dalla prima*, December 18, 1903, *Acta Sanctae Sedis* 36 (1903–4), p. 341.

17. Philip S. Kaufman, *Why You Can Disagree and Remain a Faithful Catholic* (Bloomington, Indiana: Meyer Stone, 1989), p. 70.

18. Bernard Häring, quoted in Kaufman.

19. Richard P. McBrien, "Academic Freedom in Catholic Universities: The Emergence of a Party Line," *America* 159 (1988), p. 457. While McBrien's point about an emerging party line is ominous, it is not yet the norm. The United States' Catholic bishops have been quite supportive, as a group, of the unique role of theologians in developing the intellectual basis of our faith. See also Thomas J. Reese, S.J., "Bishops and Theologians," *America* 161 (1989), pp. 4–6.

20. I will not footnote the source, the diocese, or the seminary involved. The no-talk rule binds me as well!

21. *The Report of the Commission of Enquiry into the Sexual Abuse of Children by Members of the Clergy* (Winter Commission Report) (St. John's, Newfoundland: Archdiocese of St. John's, 1990), pp. 35–36. See also, James G. Wolf, *Gay Priests* (San Francisco: Harper & Row, 1989).

22. The Winter Commission, p. 1.

23. Ibid., p. 13.

24. Ibid., p. 2.

25. Ibid.

26. Ibid.

27. "Georgia Priest Apologizes for His Critique of Celibacy," *National Catholic Reporter*, April 29, 1989.

28. Pope John Paul II, "Sundays in Priestless Parishes," *Origins* 17 (1989), pp. 127–28.

29. *Dogmatic Constitution on the Church*, no. 37, in Austin Flannery, O.P., ed., *Vatican Council II: The Conciliar and Post Conciliar Documents* (Northpoint, New York: Costello, 1981), p. 394.

30. Codex Iuris Canonici (Romae: Typis Polyglottis Vaticanis, 1917), p. 32.

31. Code of Canon Law, no. 208 (Washington, D.C.: Canon Law Society, 1983). This code repeats the sense of the *Conciliar Document on the Church*, no. 32.

32. Antonio Cardinal Innocenti, quoted in Don Lattin, " 'Candor, Kindness' as Papal Talks End," *San Francisco Chronicle*, March 13, 1989.

33. The phrase "tyranny of logic" has been used by Patricia Mary Walsh to describe the mental processes of the addicted, especially of clerics and religious. See Patricia Mary Walsh, *The Tyranny of Logic* (Elberon, New Jersey: Emmaus House Publications, 1989).

34. Richard P. McBrien, referred to in James Winters, "In Critical Condition," *Notre Dame Magazine* (1989), p. 22. This theme can be found in many of Kennedy's writings. See especially his *Cardinal Bernardin: Easing Conflicts and Battling for the Soul of American Catholicism* (Chicago: Bonus, 1989).

35. George Kocan, "A Church of the Absurd?" *Homiletic and Pastoral Review* (1987), pp. 27, 28.

36. Karl Rahner, "Perspectives on Pastoral Ministry in the Future," in Walbert Bühlmann, *Worldchurch: New Dimensions—A Model for the Year 2001*, (Maryknoll, New York: Orbis Books, 1986), p. 188.

37. Pontifical Commission for Justice and Peace, "The Church and Racism: Toward a More Fraternal Society," no. 5, *Origins* 18 (1989), p. 616.

38. John Cardinal O'Connor, excerpt from speech to the national convention of the National Office for Black Catholics, *Origins* 19 (1989), p. 194.

39. "The Church and Racism," nos. 14, 28, pp. 619, 623.

40. Eric Brazil, "S.F. Study Finds Why Hispanics Leave Catholicism," *San Francisco Examiner*, March 21, 1990.

41. Penny Lernoux, *People of God: The Struggle for the World Church* (New York: Viking, 1989), p. 155.

42. Anne Wilson Schaef, *When Society Becomes an Addict* (San Francisco: Harper and Row, 1987), p. 135.

43. Congregation for the Doctrine of the Faith, no. 28, October 15, 1989, in *Origins* 19 (1989), p. 496.

CHAPTER SEVEN The Church's Story 3: The Challenge to Religious Leaders in Matthew 23

1. David E. Garland, *The Intention of Matthew 23* (Leiden: E. J. Brill, 1979), pp. 2–3.

2. Ibid., p. 62.

3. Ibid., p. 38.

4. Pope John Paul II, "Address to the Bishops, part 1," September 16, 1987, in *Origins* 17 (1987), p. 257.

5. See Pope Pius XII, *Humani Generis*, August 12, 1950, no. 21 (Washington, D.C.: United States Catholic Conference), p. 10.

6. Canadian Conference of Catholic Bishops, "Replies to the Consultation on the Lineamenta," October 5, 1989 (Ottawa: Canadian Conference of Catholic Bishops), addendum no. 7, p. 1.

7. Ibid., p. 2.

8. Wolfgang Trilling, *The Gospel According to Matthew*, vol. 2, ed. John L. McKenzie (New York: Crossroad, 1981), p. 171.

9. Ibid., p. 137.

10. See Michael Crosby, *House of Disciples: Church, Economics, and Justice in Matthew* (Maryknoll, New York: Orbis Books, 1988), p. 104–124, passim.

11. *Webster's Ninth New Collegiate Dictionary* (Springfield, Massachusetts: Merriam-Webster, 1986), p. 593.

12. Crosby, pp. 57–59, passim.

13. Rudolph Meyer and Hans-Friedrich Weiss, "Pharisaios," *Theological Dictionary of the New Testament*, IX, ed. by Gerhard Friedrich, trans. Geoffrey W. Bromiley (Grand Rapids: Wm. B. Eerdmanns, 1974), pp. 11–48.

14. Garland, p. 111.

15. Donald Senior, *Invitation to Matthew* (Garden City, New York: Doubleday Image Books, 1977), p. 223.

16. Richard P. McBrien, "A Papal Attack on Vatican II," *The New York Times*, March 12, 1990.

17. Ibid. At this press conference Bishop Dailey reportedly said he would bar Mario Cuomo, the Catholic governor of New York, from speaking about abortion in Brooklyn's 220 churches because of Cuomo's support for abortion rights.

18. Leo Karrer, "At Loggerheads in Chur," *The Tablet* 244, August 11, 1990, pp. 1005–1006.

19. "The Cologne Declaration: Authority Out of Bounds," reprinted in *Commonweal* 116 (1989), p. 101.

20. For the committee's response to the catechism, see press reports. See also Peter Steinfels, "U.S. Bishops Fault Guide on Teaching," *The New York Times*, April 19, 1990.

21. Wolfgang Trilling, *Das Wahre Israel* (Leipzig: St. Benno-Verlag, 1959), p. 200.

22. Garland, pp. 149–50.

23. National Conference of Catholic Bishops, "Economic Justice for All: Catholic Social Teaching and the U.S. Economy," no. 354, *Origins* 16 (1986), p. 446.

24. Laura Colby, "Vatican Bank Played a Central Role in Fall of Banco Ambrosiano," *The Wall Street Journal*, April 27, 1987.

25. Penny Lernoux, *People of God* (New York: Viking, 1989), p. 50.

26. Michael Crosby, *Spirituality of the Beatitudes: Matthew's Challenge for First World Christians* (Maryknoll, New York: Orbis Books, 1989), pp. 127–29.

27. Anonymous curial official quoted in John Thavis, CNS, "Line Between Priesthood and Politics Zigzags," *National Catholic Reporter*, October 27, 1989.

28. Garland, p. 157.

29. 1971 Synod of Bishops, "Justice in the World," no. 40, in Joseph Gremillion, *The Gospel of Peace and Justice* (Maryknoll, New York: Orbis Books, 1976), p. 522.

30. Anne Wilson Schaef and Diane Fassel, *The Addictive Organization* (San Francisco: Harper & Row, 1988), p. 54.

31. Garland, p. 172.

32. See Crosby, *House of Disciples*, pp. 116, 263.

CHAPTER EIGHT   Biography: Story and My Story

1. I am indebted to Mary Ann Zollmann for introducing me to the notion of person as story. For more on this see Mary Ann Zollmann, "The Person as Story in the Formation Theory of Adrian van Kaam and the Personality Theory of Rollo May," *Studies in Formative Spirituality* 10 (1989), pp. 341–61.

2. Wendy Kaminer, "Chances Are You're Codependent Too," *The New York Times Book Review*, February 11, 1990, p. 27.

3. Rollo May sees meaninglessness as the core struggle that leads people into suicide or the choice for life.

4. Viktor E. Frankl, *The Unheard Cry for Meaning: Psychotherapy and Humanism* (New York: Simon and Schuster Touchstone Books, 1978), p. 20.

5. Fortunately I wrote these books under the name I received when I joined the Capuchins and they are no longer in print.

6. Michael H. Crosby, O.F.M.Cap., "Responsibility in the Marketplace: The Church and Responsible Investing." Excerpt from "Catholic Church Investments for Corporate Social Responsibility," in *Origins* 3 (1974), pp. 457, 459–461.

7. John Bradshaw, *Healing the Shame That Binds You* (Deerfield Beach, Florida: Health Communications, 1988), p. 13.

8. Ibid., p. 14.

9. Anne Wilson Schaef, *Co-Dependence Misunderstood-Mistreated* (San Francisco: Harper & Row, 1986), p. 68.

10. The first sign is when a key person in the organization is an addict; the second is when people take their addictive disease into the organization; and the fourth is when the organization itself functions as an addict.

11. Anne Wilson Schaef and Diane Fassel, "The Organization as the Addictive Substance," in *The Addictive Organization* (San Francisco: Harper & Row, 1988), pp. 118–36.

12. Anne Wilson Schaef, "Is the Church an Addictive Organization?" *The Christian Century* 107 (1990), p. 20.

13. Schaef and Fassel, p. 123.

14. Jeremiah Crosby, O.F.M.Cap., *Bearing Witness: The Place of the Franciscan Family in the Church* (Chicago: Franciscan Herald Press, 1965), p. 12.

CHAPTER NINE   The Spirituality of Becoming Wholehearted (Mt 6:19–34)

1. United States Bishops' Pastoral Message and Letter, "Economic Justice for All: Catholic Social Teaching and the U. S. Economy," no. 328 (quoting the 1971 Synod of Bishops) in *Origins* 16 (1986), p. 444.

2. Eugene Kennedy, *Tomorrow's Catholics/Yesterday's Church: The Two Cultures of American Catholicism* (San Francisco: Harper & Row, 1988).

3. Ibid., p. 8.

4. Ibid., p. 10.

5. Ibid., p. 24.

6. David Berenson, "Alcoholics Anonymous: From Surrender to Transformation," *Networker* (1987), p. 29.

7. Anne Wilson Schaef, *When Society Becomes an Addict* (San Francisco: Harper & Row, 1987), p. 50.

8. Certified letter from Philip Morris to Michael H. Crosby, February 13, 1990.

9. Schaef, p. 51.

10. W. H. Auden, quoted in Rollo May, *Power and Innocence* (New York: W. W. Norton, 1972), p. 65.

11. Alexander Solzhenitsyn, "Live Not by Lies," *Washington Post*, February 18, 1974.

12. Pope John Paul II, *Redemptor Hominis*, 13, *Origins* 8 (1979), p. 633.

13. Solzhenitsyn.

14. Jonas Ellis, "Why Alcoholics Anonymous Is Probably Doing Itself More Harm than Good by Its Insistence on a Higher Power," *Employee Assistance Quarterly* 1 (1985), pp. 95–97.

15. Gerald May, *Addiction and Grace* (San Francisco: Harper & Row, 1988), p. 1.

16. For a good background on fear, see "Fear: The Basic Emotion," in Michael Cavanaugh, *Make Your Tomorrows Better* (New York / Mahwah, New Jersey: Paulist Press, 1980), pp. 66–85.

17. Peter C. Orlando, Ph.D., "The Pastoral Minister and Anxiety," *Human Development* 6 (1985), p. 46.

18. Cavanaugh, p. 79.

19. Brendan Callaghan, "Courage and Cowardice," *The Way* 21 (1981), p. 192.

20. Rosemary Radford Ruether, "Courage as a Christian Virtue," *Cross Currents* 33 (1983), p. 12.

21. The Eightfold Path involves 1) right views; 2) right resolve; 3) right speech; 4) right conduct; 5) right livelihood; 6) right effort; 7) right mindfulness; and 8) right concentration.

22. For an application of this process of detachment see Yvonne McKenny Vowels, "A Feminist Appropriation of Tibetan Buddhism and the Twelve-step Program," paper for the Western Regional Conference, American Academy of Religion, Spring, 1989.

23. This quotation is the subtitle of a classic—though controversial—contemporary study of the habits of the heart of the people of the United States. See Robert N. Bellah, Richard Madsen, William M. Sullivan, Ann Swidler, and Steven M. Tipton, *Habits of the Heart: Individualism and Commitment in American Life* (Berkeley, Los Angeles, London: University of California Press, 1985).

24. Margaret A. Farley, *Personal Commitments: Beginning, Keeping, Changing* (San Francisco: Harper & Row, 1990), pp. 12–13.

25. In Matthew, Peter did not seek Jesus as such; Jesus found him (4:18). Jesus always does the calling to discipleship. I am using the notion of Peter's seeking Jesus in the sense that something was going on in his heart that enabled him to "sell" what he had to follow in discipleship. In John's gospel (Jn 1:42), Jesus is sought and found by Peter.

CHAPTER TEN   Seeking Purity of Heart in Order to See God (Mt 6:22–23)

1. Richard Byrne, O.C.S.O., *Living the Contemplative Dimension of Everyday Life*, unpublished dissertation (Pittsburgh: Duquesne University, 1973). I am indebted to Byrne for his approach to contemplation, which is the basis for the first part of this chapter.

2. Martin Heidegger, *Being and Time*, trans. John Macquarrie and Edward Robinson (New York: Harper & Row, 1962), pp. 216–17.

3. Anne Wilson Schaef, *When Society Becomes an Addict* (San Francisco: Harper & Row, 1987), p. 69.

4. Ibid., p. 70.

5. Dominic Savino, O.Carm., Ph.D., "The Shame of the Co-dependent Religious," *Human Development* 10 (1989), p. 8. Besides perfectionism, the other ways adults try to mask shame is by denial, rage, blaming, toughness, and compulsive behavior.

6. Anne Wilson Schaef, *Co-Dependence Misunderstood-Mistreated* (San Francisco: Harper & Row, 1986), p. 75.

7. I have based my model on the "Law of Hearing" developed by Chuck Brissette. He has not written about his model in any publication; my notes are from a class I attended April 9, 1990. His model was inspired by the "Law of Hearing" found in the Letter of James, so-called by Kenneth Hannigan in an evangelical teaching.

8. Wendy Kaminer, "Chances Are You're Codependent Too," *The New York Times Book Review*, February 11, 1990.

9. Alison Humes, "The Culting of Codependency," *7 Days*, November 1, 1989, p. 26.

10. Kaminer.

11. Gerald May, *Addiction and Grace* (San Francisco: Harper & Row, 1988), pp. 144–45.

CHAPTER ELEVEN Prophetic Proclamation *vs.* Clerical Consciousness

1. Robert Jay Lifton and Richard Falk, *Indefensible Weapons: The Political and Psychological Case Against Nuclearism* (New York: Basic Books, 1982), p. 101.

2. Walter Brueggemann, *The Prophetic Imagination* (Philadelphia: Fortress Press, 1985).

3. Ibid., p. 11.

4. Ibid., pp. 36–37. I have changed the third part of the Solomonic triad from Brueggemann's "religion of accessibility" to my own "religion of God's manageability" because it fits my approach and is, I believe, true to his meaning.

5. Ibid., p. 34.

6. Ibid., p. 46.

7. Ibid., pp. 62–63.

8. The latest Vatican statistics indicate that the number of seminarians increased nearly two percent in 1988, to about 92,000, while the number of priests ordained worldwide in 1988 jumped about ten percent, the biggest increase in at least two decades. However, despite the rise in vocations and ordinations, the total number of priests worldwide continued to decline due to deaths and departures from the ministry. "Global Priest Numbers Increase, Vatican Says," Catholic News Service, *Western Catholic Reporter* (Edmonton, Alberta), February 26, 1990.

9. Mikhail S. Gorbachev, quoted in "Gorbachev: Europe's Upheaval Inevitable," Los Angeles Times New Services, *The Cincinnati Enquirer*, December 17, 1989.

10. Bob Djurdjevic, quoted in Joel Dreyfuss, "Reinventing IBM," *Fortune*, August 14, 1989, p. 31.

11. "The Cultural Revolution at A. O. Smith," *Business Week*, May 29, 1966, p. 66.

12. "Pastoral Message of the Administrative Committee," quoting Pope John XXIII, *Pacem in Terris*, no. 16, National Conference of Catholic Bishops, February 13, 1973 (Washington, D.C.: United States Catholic Conference, 1973), pp. 1–2.

13. Michael H. Crosby, O.F.M.Cap., *Thy Will Be Done: Praying the Our Father as Subversive Activity* (Maryknoll, New York: Orbis Books, 1983), p. 108.

14. Sacred Congregation for the Doctrine of the Faith, "Declaration on Procured Abortion," nos. 22, 23, *The Pope Speaks* 19 (1975), p. 260.

15. Ibid., no. 24, p. 261.

16. Rev. William Sloane Coffin, Jr., "Be Angry, But Do Not Sin: A Spirituality for the Long Haul," *Pax Christi* 14 (1989), p. 31.

17. Fran Ferder, "Zeal for Your House Consumes Me: Dealing With Anger as a Woman in the Church," *Miriam's Song* (Washington, D.C.: Quixote Center, 1989), p. 15.

18. Brueggemann, p. 111.

19. Hans Morgenthau, quoted in Arthur Schlessinger, Jr., "Intellectual's Role: Truth to Power?" *The Wall Street Journal*, October 12, 1983.

20. "The Cologne Declaration," reprinted in *Commonweal* 116 (1989), pp. 103, 104.

21. Pope John Paul II, Address to the Bishops of the United States, II, *Origins* 17 (1987), p. 261.

22. Pope Pius XII, *Humani generis*, no. 20 (August 12, 1950), in Claudia Carlen, IHM (McGrath, 1981), p. 178.

23. Karol Cardinal Wojtyla, *The Acting Person* (London: Reidel, 1979), pp. 286–87.

24. Rudolph Bell, *Holy Anorexia* (Chicago: University of Chicago, 1985).

25. Clare of Assisi, "The Testament of Saint Clare," no. 13, in Regis J. Armstrong, O.F.M. Cap., and Ignatius C. Brady, O.F.M., eds., *Francis and Clare: Their Complete Works* (New York/Ramsey/Toronto: Paulist Press, 1982), p. 230.

26. Sigismund Verheij, "Personal Awareness of Vocation and Ecclesiastical Authority as Exemplified in St. Clare of Assisi," trans. Ignatius McCormick, O.F.M.Cap., *Greyfriars Review* 3 (1989), p. 38.

27. Clare of Assisi, "The Rule of Saint Clare," no. 3, in Armstrong and Brady, p. 211.

28. Verheij, p. 38.

29. Francis of Assisi, "The Testament," no. 14, in Armstrong and Brady, pp. 154–55.

30. Michael H. Crosby, O.F.M.Cap., *House of Disciples: Church, Economics, and Justice in Matthew* (Maryknoll, New York: Orbis Books, 1988), p. 260.

31. The "Twelve Steps" are supported by parallel traditions which are related to the dynamics of AA meetings. The traditions serve as guidelines for the steps.